International
human resource
management

International human resource management

Think globally, act locally

DEREK TORRINGTON

Prentice Hall

NEW YORK LONDON TORONTO SYDNEY TOKYO SINGAPORE

First published 1994 by
Prentice Hall International (UK) Limited
Campus 400, Maylands Avenue
Hemel Hempstead
Hertfordshire, HP2 7EZ
A division of
Simon & Schuster International Group

Typeset in 10/12pt Sabon
by Hands Fotoset, Leicester

Printed and bound in Great Britain by
Redwood Books, Trowbridge, Wiltshire

Library of Congress Cataloging-in-Publication Data

Torrington, Derek, 1931–
    International human resource management : think globally, act
locally / Derek Torrington.
        p.   cm.
    Includes bibliographical references and index.
    ISBN 0-13-009978-3
    1. International business enterprises–Personnel management.
I. Title.
HF5549.5.E45T593   1994
658.3–dc20   93–26164
                                                                CIP

British Library Cataloguing in Publication Data

A catalogue record for this book is available from
the British Library

ISBN 0-13-009978-3 (pbk)

---

1 2 3 4 5   98 97 96 95 94

Contents

Preface

This book has a simple purpose: to describe management action in connection with employing people in an international company. That simple purpose is difficult to achieve because so much of human resource management works strictly within cultural and geographical boundaries. The conventions on recruitment and selection and the legislation on dismissal, for instance, change from country to country. One approach to international human resource management is therefore to have dozens of different versions, according to the country in which management action has to be carried out. However useful, that is insufficient, as human resource management takes on different features that affect the whole business when the company is working internationally. To use the phrase that is the title for the first chapter, people have to think globally in order to act locally.

There is something more to international human resource management practice than infinitely variable practice within geographical boundaries. I was only able to find one text that seemed adequately to address this issue, by Peter Dowling and Randall Schuler, an admirable Australian/American collaboration that relied entirely on published work and the studies of the two authors.

The approach of this book is to attempt a combination of the academic and the practical. I have written the first eight chapters and the last as a result of my own international experience and reading everything I could get my hands on. It is inevitably eclectic and partial, but may at least help to clarify the thinking of those who find fault with it!

Part II is the practical element with accounts of practice in companies of varying size, but with the common feature of being international: Anglo/Dutch, British, French, Franco/American, Franco/British (or should that one be Anglo/French?), Japanese and Singaporean. The list is again eclectic and partial. Five of the seven are in manufacturing, there is no bank, retailer, media company or hotel chain. There is no company with a head office in North America, Germany or Hong Kong. They were chosen because they vary from the mighty to the modest, each has a distinctive and important story to tell, a success story to tell, and each has a variety of experience to report.

I wish to record my great appreciation to all those who have written the chapters in Part II. They were willing to take on a task which most of them found to be rather more difficult than they expected, they have produced fascinating material of great diversity, they nearly all managed to keep to the timetable for producing their chapters, and they have been very patient through the protracted publishing process.

Derek Torrington
Manchester, March 1993

Reference
Dowling, P. J. and Schuler, R. S. (1990), *International Dimensions of Human Resource Management*, PWS-Kent, Boston, Mass.

About the authors

Chapters 1 to 8 and Chapter 16 are written by Derek Torrington, Professor of Human Resource Management in the School of Management at UMIST, UK. The authors of the other seven chapters are as follows:

Chapter 9 – *Ferranti-Thomson Sonar Systems: An Anglo-French venture in high tech collaboration* – Ann Moran, Manufacturing Planning Manager, UK.

Chapter 10 – *NEC: International HRM with vision* – Dr Nigel Holden, Lecturer in International Marketing, School of Management, UMIST, UK.

Chapter 11 – *Singapore Airlines: Strategic human resource initiatives* – Dr Ling Sing Chee, Lecturer in Organisational Behaviour, National University of Singapore.

Chapter 12 – *Rhône Poulenc Agrochemicals: A Franco-American takeover* – Evalde Mutabazi, Lecturer in Management, Ecole Supérieure de Commerce, Lyons, France.

Chapter 13 – *The development of a global human resource management approach in ZENECA Pharmaceuticals* – Reg Carr, Personnel Manager International, ZENECA Pharmaceuticals, UK.

Chapter 14 – *How Shell's organisation and HR practices help it to be both global and local* – Cynthia Haddock, Head of Organisational Effectiveness and Basil South, Head of Organisation Division, Shell International, London, UK.

Chapter 15 – *Generale de Service Informatique (GSI)* – Heather Lussey, Independent Consultant, High Wycombe, UK.

CHAPTER I

Think globally, act locally

> Successful international managers, whether mobile or non-mobile, must be able
> to act locally, but to plan and think strategically and globally.
> *Barham and Rassam*, 1989, p. 149.

This book is designed to provoke both discussion about and action on the international
dimension of human resource management (HRM). It is intended to assist personnel
specialists in particular to pick up on the demands and opportunities of their role, no
matter what that role may be. We are not only addressing the high-flying, multilingual
elites, and we are not only dealing with strategic matters. The quotation at the head
of this chapter is used because it seems to express so succinctly the universal nature
of international questions for personnel specialists. Like all managers, they act in a
local situation, but the greatest management challenge at the close of the millennium
is for them to place their local actions in a framework of global thought and strategy.

Human resource management:
the international dimension

As an organisation increases its international activities, it inevitably steps up the
degree of decentralisation, but it would be an oversimplification to suggest that
internationalism is simply a form of decentralisation. It is the most complex form of
decentralising operations and involves types of difference – language, culture,
economic and political systems, legislative frameworks, management styles and
conventions – that are not found in the organisational growth and diversification that
stay within national boundaries.

In these circumstances human resource management logically follows, as well as
helping to shape, the strategic direction set by the financial, marketing and operational
decisions. In practice there may be a different pattern, as Hendry (1990, p. 93) makes
the interesting point, that in the process of decentralisation personnel often remains
one of the last centralising forces because of its instinctive belief in the importance of
such features of management as equity, order, consistency and control. Although the
personnel function will relinquish these aspects of human resource management

reluctantly, they are likely to have other contributions to make in operating the corporate internal labour market:

> The loss of some central tasks through decentralisation – especially the orchestration of central bargaining, and the management of pay structures and job evaluation – and gaining new ones . . . represent a significant shift in the corporate personnel role. (*op. cit.*, p. 102)

The extensive discussion about the growth of the European Community, 1992, and other aspects of our managerial future, has produced a great deal of comment on the threats and opportunities of internationalisation or globalisation. These have been mainly directed at social, economic and legal differences between the various countries of the world – particularly Europe. Some of the important contextual features of human resource management are brought out by this discussion. One of the key points is the persisting variations in practice:

> Systems which in most countries have evolved incrementally over the course of many decades – even centuries – have each acquired a distinctive coloration, adapted to the idiosyncrasies of national socio-economic structure, national political regimes, and perhaps also national temperaments. (Ferner and Hyman, 1992, p. xvii)

At the same time there is the ever-increasing significance of the multinational company as the means whereby individual economies are integrated into a global economy, with a small number of very large companies accounting for a disproportionately large number of the people in employment. However important these issues may be, they mainly lie outside the scope of this particular book, which is focused on content and process more than on context.

There have also been a number of publications about practice in particular countries that may not be familiar to the reader. These include comparative studies across two or more countries (for example, Beamish, 1988; Bournois, 1991; Springer, 1991; Tayeb, 1991), as well as those with a single-country focus (for example, Dunphy, 1987; Jones, 1988; Warner, 1990; Wriston, 1990; Papalexandris, 1991). These all contribute greatly to our international understanding by broadening our management perspective, but their practical value is limited to those managers with an interest, or potential interest, in the particular country concerned.

A further emphasis in most of the emerging literature on international HRM (IHRM) is the concentration on strategy, for example: 'I have sought to emphasise throughout this book that the main contribution a Personnel Manager can make to a business will be at the strategic rather than operational level' (Pinder, 1990, p. 117).

This, of course, has become a managerial obsession through the 1980s and has run through all the HRM thinking that has been current, whether international or not. That which is strategic is important (and well rewarded, involving a comfortable managerial lifestyle), while that which is operational is for others to do. This general emphasis on strategy has probably been encouraged by academics, many of whom are always happier when dealing with broad issues rather than the muck and nettles.

It would be foolish to deny the overwhelming importance of strategy in all aspects of international HRM, but management is much more than just strategy, and the implementation of strategy is quite as important as its conception. It is of passing interest that the favourite British management guru of the 1980s was John Harvey-Jones, and he hardly ever used the term. Having retired from the chairmanship of ICI during one of the most successful periods in the history of that great company, he wrote a book that was soon a best seller (1988). The word strategy does not appear once in the index, nor does it appear in the chapter entitled 'Setting the direction'.

Strategy has had great importance in the late 1980s because of its emphasis on creating the future rather than waiting for it to happen to you in an unpleasant way; or waiting for a future that never does happen. Strategic thinking provides a clear sense of direction and focus on where the business is going. Although obvious, this can have a profound effect. If, for instance, you are running an airport, what business are you in – providing parking space for aeroplanes, providing a service for airlines, providing an agreeable, efficient service for passengers, or something else? Specific business and management objectives can best be derived from a clear sense of purpose.

Concern with strategy can go wrong: it is not the sure-fire route to business success and can present the following problems. First, strategy can simply be wrong but very difficult to change because it has been hammered out and agreed over a long period and with the involvement of many people who have become committed to it. It can become the dominant activity of managers rather than a means whereby they run the business. Thought is no substitute for action, plans are not an alternative to operations and analysis can aid but never replace judgement. There is the risk of management decision-making becoming so rational and clear-headed that only safe courses of action are pursued while opportunities are lost or elementary errors made. The infamous Charge of the Light Brigade in the 1854 Battle of Balaclava is sometimes cited as a classic case of poor communication because the British commander's message 'You will be supported by infantry which have been ordered to advance on two fronts' was accidentally distorted to 'You will be supported by infantry which have been ordered. Advance on two fronts.' Whereupon the valiant 600 rode into the valley of death. It is also, however, a case history of a chosen strategy being pursued because it had been agreed, despite evidence that it was not working.

A further frequent problem with strategy is the rush to find strategic initiatives, without actually having a strategy at all. The most telling recent example of this in Britain has been the moves during the late 1980s to introduce performance-related pay. This was seen, quite rightly, as a major strategic initiative that would change employee attitude and behaviour (Murlis, 1992). But what was the change being made for? Was the initiative suitable for the organisational context into which it was introduced? Was it suitable for the business context in which the organisation was operating? Strategic initiatives designed to introduce significant change are at best valueless and at worst dangerous if they are not part of a total strategy within which each initiative has a logical place. Apparently even Shell UK has had to rethink a strategic initiative because the initiative of decentralising decision-making diluted the traditional corporate culture that had been so successful in the past: 'while we had adopted new ideas with the best of intentions, it was working against some of the fundamental principles on which our business success is based' (Wybrew, 1992). Keeping up to date is perilously close to being fashionable, and being fashionable emphasises the ephemeral and transient at the expense of substance.

Internationalisation presents a real risk of 'strategic seduction'. There are so many issues and aspects that it becomes something that can scarcely be grasped managerially in any other way than by talk and analysis, with strategic importance replacing management action as a criterion. There is an apocryphal story of the male management consultant explaining his liberated views something like this:

> I make all the major decisions in the family, like our attitude towards the United Nations, our position on the Third World debt, and the date we will convert our cars to use unleaded petrol. My wife makes all the operational decisions, like where we will live, the house we will live in, where the children will go to school, and how we balance the household budget.

Part of the mission of this book – its strategy – is to occupy the middle ground of international human resource management. Not only the grand issues of global strategy, nor the limitless examples of minutiae, such as memorising the different meaning of all 10 Neapolitan gestures, but what there is to get done and how it is made to happen.

What, then, is international HRM?

In suggesting what international HRM is, we need first to consider two things that it is not.

First, international HRM is not simply copying practices from the Americans, the Germans, the Taiwanese, the Koreans or the Japanese. Technically, operationally and financially that may be appropriate, but not in HRM. The British have long followed American practices without too much success, because American practice suits the American national culture and institutions, without necessarily transferring effectively to Edinburgh or London. More recently the Americans started following Japanese practices because they were selling more motor cars and producing them more cheaply, but the Japanese culture operates differently from the American, despite the massive impact of American ideas and ideals since the end of the Pacific War in 1945.

People management methods do not necessarily transfer from one culture to another.

Secondly, international HRM is not a process of all managers learning the cultures of every country in which they have to deal and suitably modifying their behaviour when dealing with those nationals. This is implicit in much of what is being written currently, but is a misconception because it is simply too difficult. Cultures are robust and subtle and we have great difficulty in achieving more than a modest level of behaviour adaptation. The idea, implied by some writers, that international HRM

Topics covered in five books on International Human Resource Management.

	Hodgetts & Luthans	Pinder	Barham & Oates	Evans, Doz & Laurent	Dowling & Schuler	
Training	●	●	●	●	●	5
Recruitment	●	●	●		●	4
Organisation	●		●	●	●	4
Expatriates	●		●	●	●	4
Culture	●			●	●	3
Industrial relations	●	●			●	3
Leadership	●		●	●		3
Communication	●	●				2
Pay		●			●	2
Motivation	●					1
Planning					●	1
Performance appraisal					●	1

Figure 1.1   Topics in IHRM literature

requires all managers to move confidently between Argentina, Indonesia, Norway and Alaska with effortless adaptation is unrealistic.

One of the few recent books (see Figure 1.1) that concentrates on the content rather than the context of IHRM has the following chapter headings (Dowling and Schuler, 1990, pp. xiv–xvi):

• Introduction and overview
• Strategic corporate planning and international HRM planning
• Recruitment and selection of international employees
• Performance appraisal
• Training and development
• Compensation
• International labor relations.

That suggests that international HRM has the same main dimensions as HRM in a national context, but with some additional features. The approach of this book is different in ruling out some of the conventional chapter headings on the grounds that the *practice* is essentially national rather than international. There is no chapter on recruitment and selection, nor is there a chapter on industrial relations. The reason for this is that employees are selected in one country or another, and wherever the selection is undertaken there are a range of conventions and legal requirements that have to be met. The person appointed will usually have a contract of employment that will fit within the legal framework of one country but probably not another. Recruitment and selection is therefore a national activity, not an international activity. Similarly, negotiation with trade unions and the nature of agreements vary markedly between countries, so industrial relations is a national rather than international activity.

In many ways international HRM is simply HRM on a larger scale; the strategic considerations are more complex and the operational units more varied, needing co-ordination across more barriers. It is possible, however, to identify some activities that are different in nature when a business is international: they form the structure of the first part of this book.

The seven Cs of international HRM

There are seven different areas of international HRM work, each of which happens to begin with the letter 'C' as follows:

1 *Cosmopolitans* HRM in international companies involves the employment of people who spend part of their time in another country. In Chapter 2 there is examination of the employment practices in relation to five broad categories of such employees.

First, there are the true *cosmopolitans*, the high-flying, multilingual elite referred to at the beginning of this chapter. Constantly on the move, they are the most significant integrators of a dispersed operation. Then there are *expatriates*, who relocate for several years to a different country, usually taking family with them, and often having significant problems on repatriation. *Occasional parachutists* are those who drop in for short periods to an overseas subsidiary or partner to deal with a specific technical matter. The term *engineer* is used very widely indeed to cover those who spend a period of weeks or months at an overseas location, usually to install new equipment or to set up a production operation. They do not usually 'live' in the country in the same way as the expatriates, but they become more a part of the local operation than the occasional parachutist. Finally, there is brief reference to the *mobile worker*, the person who is seeking employment in a foreign country as opposed to being sent out as an existing employee. This category is the briefest because there seems to be little management initiative to make special arrangements for such personnel.

2 *Culture* Chapter 3 reviews the differences in cultural background across the globe and the problems of adapting management and employment initiatives to avoid misunderstanding and inefficiency.

3 *Compensation* People expect to be paid and to have their expenses reimbursed. Once their employment takes them away from their national home base, and out of their home income tax situation, a whole range of issues have to be

addressed, from the level of incentive needed to persuade someone to move for three years to Alaska or Afghanistan to the knotty problems of who travels business class in the aircraft and who travels economy.

4 *Communication* Writers on management can seldom resist including a chapter on communication and personnel specialists in international companies have to arrange methods that will overcome the problems of culture, geography and rivalry.

5 *Consultancy* A more unpredictable chapter is on the use of consultancy, both as a bought-in service and as a personal managerial role. In international HRM, the use of this facility is quite different from that within national boundaries. There is a greater need to buy in expertise, often in a foreign country, to deal with the myriad of issues which require local expertise that the parent company does not possess, and may not understand. There is also a greater need to work with subsidiary or partner organisations overseas in a consultancy mode on a wide range of HRM issues.

6 *Competence* Any business needs continually to develop the competence of its people: the international business has to develop the competence of a wider variety of people and to include the skills that only become necessary when the organisation is working across cultural, political and geographical boundaries.

7 *Co-ordination* The first part of the book closes with a short chapter on co-ordination, not different types of divisional structure, but the formal and informal methods whereby the different parts of the business work together to create synergy.

A possible eighth C is for chain. Although this is often a symbol of bondage, it is also a series of links, and all of the seven Cs connect with each other and have to be combined to produce effectiveness.

It was only after developing this concept and testing it out with a number of international groups, that I discovered that Yoshinori Yokoyama of McKinsey in Tokyo had for some time been talking of 'the six Cs'. The letter 'C' obviously has a powerful significance for international management!

The 7C framework creaks slightly in application, but it is a useful way of teasing out those features of HRM which are essential in international companies and where the international dimension makes the activity fundamentally different. The idea is based on a careful reading of accounts of how various companies are preparing and some succeeding (for example, Barham and Rassam, 1989; Evans, Doz and Laurent, 1989; Bournois, 1991; Hodgetts and Luthans, 1991). It is based on a consideration of what has been done so far in a number of companies in which I have had searching and illuminating discussions, and on a consideration of the opportunities that face us.

The model stems from a belief that there is a need to develop a technology for international HRM work that goes beyond simply being aware of differences in the context within which organisations operate, in order to describe what to do and how to do it. This is very hard to find in any contemporary writing and the 7C model is proposed in the hope that someone will produce a better one.

In the intriguing closing chapter of a short book of readings, Brewster and Tyson (1991, p. 258) warn us against the risk of attributing all variations in international HRM to cultural differences and ignoring organisational differences. The second half of the book contains case studies of international HRM in organisations. This is partly because of the risk that Brewster and Tyson identify. The differences in practice between Singapore Airlines and NEC or Rhône Poulenc are largely because of the type of industries they are in. It is also for the special benefit that case studies always provide: real people facing real problems and finding answers.

International HRM and change

When a business becomes international, there are real and deep challenges of change for all managers, but especially for personnel managers. The finance manager has a professional speciality that changes only in a specific way: your Swiss franc is worth exactly the same as my Swiss franc on any given day. Operations managers are dealing with products and processes that vary only slightly: a Volvo HGV is a Volvo HGV, whether you are using it in Sweden or in Indonesia. HRM is the management speciality where the move from London to Brussels or from Pittsburgh to Jakarta means that your managerial world has turned upside down.

Personnel managers develop their competence by mastering the subtleties of behaviour, relationships, values and traditions in one national culture or even regional culture, so that operating outside that particular framework is a sharp challenge, made more difficult by the current obsession with change. We hear so often that successful managers are those who can introduce change that it becomes at the same time an axiom – a truth that is so obvious that it needs no justification – and a mantra – a word that is assumed to hold some mystical spiritual power.

Just as all organisations need to change to survive (the axiom), international organisations may have to change more rapidly and more frequently. This involves changing certainty into uncertainty (the mantra), which is one of the hardest things that any human being has to undertake, but we should remember: 'organisations have a much greater capacity for change than smaller organisms like the individuals who populate them, or larger entities like the societies and cultures that constitute their environment' (Evans et al., 1989, p. 85).

Relationships between structural entities are more amenable to change than the entities themselves. The individual and society are both stable structural entities. An introvert does not readily become extrovert, an autocracy does not readily become a democracy (although it can revert), an agrarian society does not readily become an industrial economy and the deep-seated values of a nation do not quickly change.

There is a strong tendency for an organisation's members to import into the organisation the values and certainties from the structural entities of their individual personae and the national culture from which they come. An employing organisation is, however, a temporary system of relationship between entities of individual and society, a field of transactions, stemming from both choice and initiative exercised by the people who make up the organisation. They have chosen to be there, they have taken an initiative to be there and they are anxious to remain, so in that temporary system of relationships there is considerable potential for change.

Iain Mangham describes organisations as theatre (Mangham and Overington, 1987), and this is a particularly useful analogy for international organisations. We need to emphasise the role-playing aspect of the actors, so that we move away from embedding the personal and societal reality into organisational life, but play a part in a different, temporary reality.

It is suggested by those who have studied organisation turn-round that change is achieved either by crisis or by evolution, but with a preference for crisis as the trigger. There seems to be an inescapable need for destruction of the old to be replaced with the new. It has been likened to a dentist enlarging a cavity before filling it. To some extent the past culture has to be discredited, otherwise there will not be sufficient commitment to the risk of the new. If the members of the organisation see themselves as playing a part, they can more readily cope with organisational destruction and renewal, providing that they are skilled performers, who can work with more than one script. It is often said that the American film star John Wayne always played John Wayne: for the international manager Dustin Hoffman or Meryl Streep would be more appropriate role models.

The need to operate internationally presents the greatest current change challenge. Doing things differently is obviously necessary, but the general uncertainty about what exactly needs to be done differently can easily lead to changes that are not properly thought through. The fundamental starting point is that citizens of different countries from your own are conditioned by the culture in which they have matured and from which they have acquired their values and attitudes. This produces differing notions of change itself, just as other facets of the tasks and responsibilites of management vary. For the Japanese, for instance, there is a saying that 'change is just part of the job of the manager'. For British and French managers, change is taken much less for granted in managerial life.

References

Barham, K. and Oates, D. (1991), *The International Manager*, Business Books, London.

Barham, K. and Rassam, C. (1989), *Shaping the Corporate Future*, Unwin Hyman, London.

Beamish, P. W. (1988), *Multinational Joint Ventures in Developing Countries*, Routledge, London.

Bournois, F. (1991), 'Pratiques de gestion des resources humaines dans cinq pays européens', *Revue Française de Gestion*, April.

Brewster, C. and Tyson, S. (eds) (1991), *International Comparisons in Human Resource Management*, Pitman, London.

Crozier, M. and Friedberg, E. (1977), *L'Acteur et le Systeme*, Editions du Seuil, Paris.

d'Iribarne, P. (1985), 'La gestion française', *Revue Française de Gestion*, January–February pp. 5–13.

Dowling, P. J. and Schuler, R. S. (1990), *International Dimensions of Human Resource Management*, PWS-Kent, Mass.

Dunphy, D. (1987), 'Convergence/divergence: a temporal review of the Japanese enterprise and its management', *Academy of Management Review*, July, pp. 445–59.

Evans, P., Doz, Y. and Laurent, A. (1989), *Human Resource Management in International Firms*, Macmillan, London.

Ferner, A. and Hyman, R. (1992), *Industrial Relations and the New Europe*, Blackwell, Oxford.

Harvey-Jones, J. (1988), *Making it Happen: Reflections on leadership*, Collins, London.

Hendry, C. (1990), 'Corporate management of human resources under conditions of decentralisation', *British Journal of Management*, vol. 1, pp. 91–103.

Hodgetts, R. M. and Luthans, F. (1991), *International Management*, McGraw-Hill, New York.

Jones, M. (1988), 'Managerial thinking: an African perspective', *Journal of Management Studies*, September, pp. 481–90.

Lalanne, H. (1990), 'The roles of accounting and management information systems in different management styles and different national contexts', paper presented to the European Accounting Association Congress, Budapest, April 1990.

Lawrence, P. (1991), *Management in the Netherlands*, Clarendon Press, Oxford.

Mangham, I. L. and Overington, M. A. (1987), *Organizations as Theatre*, John Wiley, Chichester.

Mead, R. (1990), *Cross-Cultural Management Communication*, John Wiley, Chichester.

Mole, J. (1990), *Mind Your Manners: Culture and class in the single European market*, The Industrial Society, London.

Murlis, H. (1992), 'Performance pay will not go away', *Personnel Management*, February, p. 7.

Olins, W. (1989), *Corporate Identity*, Thames and Hudson, London.

Papalexandris, N. (1991), 'A comparative study of human resource management in selected Greek and foreign-owned subsidiaries in Greece', in Brewster, C. and Tyson, S. (eds), *International Comparisons in International Human Resource Management*, op. cit.

Pinder, M. (1990), *Personnel Management for the Single European Market*, Pitman, London.

Poirson, P. (1989), 'Personnel policies and the management of men' (translated by Thierry Devisse), Ecole Supérieure de Commerce de Lyon, France.

Schein, E. H. (1985), *Organizational Culture and Leadership*, Jossey-Bass, San Francisco.

Springer, B. (1991), 'Changing patterns of employment for women in banks: case studies in the UK, France and the USA', in Brewster and Tyson (eds), *op. cit.*

Standish, P. and Scheid, J-C. (1986), 'Accounting standardisation in France and international accounting exchanges', paper presented at the DHS-ICAEW Accounting Research Symposium, London Business School.

Tayeb, M. (1991), 'Socio-political environment and management – employee relationships: an empirical study of England and India', in Brewster and Tyson (eds), *op. cit.*

Warner, M. (1990), 'Developing key human resources in China: an assessment of the university management schools in Beijing, Shanghai and Tianjin in the decade 1979–1989', *The International Journal of Human Resource Management*, vol. 1, no. 1, June, pp. 87–106.

van Wolferen, K. V. (1989), *The Enigma of Japanese Power*, Macmillan, London.

Wriston, W. (1990), 'The state of American management', *Harvard Business Review*, January–February, pp. 78–83.

Wybrew, J. (1992), reported in *Personnel Management Plus*, vol. 3, no. 4, April, p. 10.

PART I

A chain of Cs

CHAPTER 2

Managing the cosmopolitans

The three men and one woman who got into conversation in the executive lounge of Frankfurt airport represented the four types of international employee most often found in contemporary companies. Elsewhere in the airport a fifth traveller waited in slightly less comfortable surroundings.

Willem is the genuine *international manager*. He speaks fluent English and German as well as his native Dutch and moves regularly throughout Europe and the United States, making deals and opening up opportunities for his company. His mind travels easily across the barriers of culture and language. Although constantly on the move, he is seldom away from his base for more than a week at a time and he only deals with the representatives of companies and agencies he visits; there is little involvement with their internal structures and management arrangements. It is quite stimulating and he often meets the same people who seem to operate a similar circuit in the high-powered, esoteric world of international business. His marriage has not survived, but he is still young enough – at 34 – to try again when he eventually gets off this crazy merry-go-round of 747s and identical five-star hotels.

Charles is the *expatriate*. He had two years in the Middle East a little while ago and is now on the way to a three-year assignment in South East Asia. This time he is accompanied by his wife, Caroline, who has had to leave behind her burgeoning career in journalism, and by their 2-year-old son. He picked up a smattering of Arabic in the Middle East, but his key expertise is in the product line and communicating and articulating the business philosophy of his company. After this tour he is assured that his next move will be to a key position in head office and that his globe-trotting days will be over; Caroline would not have agreed otherwise.

Chow Hou is the *engineer*. He will be away for three months installing the equipment and training the local staff. He has moderate technical English, as no one seems to speak his native Mandarin, but he can usually carry out the training by showing and doing, or by using figures. He is not always away for as long as three months and he usually spends at least half the year back at headquarters, bringing himself up to date and being asked by all sorts of people for advice and assistance.

Inge is the *occasional parachutist*. She has never been to Italy, but usually makes two or three short overseas trips a year for the company, because of her highly specialised expertise. The last one was when she had three days in England on a systems query that they could not sort out. It is the same type of thing this time: a quick trip to sort a problem that ought not to take more than a few days. Inge finds that it keeps her on her toes to have the occasional trip completely alone without any back-up.

In a different lounge of the same airport Benedicte, the *mobile worker*, is waiting for a plane to London. She spent some time there as a student on an ERASMUS exchange and got on really well, although the weather was not quite the same as in her native Lyons, and the food . . .! Her English mother had warned her that it would not be quite the same. After graduating she worked for a while as a computer specialist and has just finished six months in a Frankfurt job, but now it is back to England, where she has managed to land a contract with a company in Swindon, who want to use her French and German in developing their new line in software.

Although there are variants on these themes, and there is no particular significance in the nationalities, these are the main types of overseas worker for whom management arrangements have to be made. The demands of working overseas can be considerable, requiring a degree of commitment to the organisation that is greater than that of the executive who agrees to a move from Birmingham to Glasgow, or vice versa.

In many organisations a job in management used to be regarded as a job for life, or as long as you wanted to hold on to it, but the security of the corporate management career has lessened, so that fewer managers are willing to entrust their futures to a benign employer to the extent of willing compliance with relocation that is domestically or socially unattractive because 'they will look after you'. Relocation has to be considered very carefully, weighing the undoubted attractions with associated risks, that were less noticeable before the 1980s.

> Personal achievement and life satisfaction are probably less likely to be solely equated with promotion within organizational structures; instead, career advancement is seen as a means of enhancing personal lifestyles which are separated from, rather than subordinated to, work roles . . . in the context of increased competition for a diminishing number of opportunities at senior managerial levels, they are less prepared to sacrifice their 'selves' or make the kind of open-ended commitments that might harm their domestic lifestyles. (Scase and Goffee, 1989, pp. 82–3)

We need, however, to be cautious with the weight we put on this type of reported opinion, which the French sometimes call 'blah blah'. Although people frequently say this sort of thing, it is less often reflected in their executive lifestyles. It is easy to be sucked into a way of life and then to feel better for saying how intolerable it is.

The remainder of this chapter considers the management of these five categories of employees.

The international manager

There is a small, elite group of genuinely international managers in the world of global business, people who are not only familiar with different countries and regions but who operate internationally with other managers occupying similar roles in other companies. This is similar to the diplomatic corps in the world's embassies, who have their own conventions and who develop their own culture and ways of working together. By becoming international in their thinking and working, these managers and deal-makers acquire the ability to work and negotiate with each other in a separate cultural world, inhabiting identical international hotels instead of embassies.

For a German to 'think Arab' one day and 'think Korean' the next is simply too demanding except at the most superficial level. What is necessary is a mode of working where everyone 'thinks international' all the time, so that they move out of national culture-boundedness in order to operate in an international culture. There is evidence that this common international culture is already developing among this elite group (Everett *et al.*, 1982).

Pinder (1990) quotes from a survey by an executive search agency on the Euro-executive. The profile certainly sounds as if only the Holy Ghost on a good day need apply:

> Fluent in at least one other Community language, of greater importance is exposure to a diversity of cultures stemming both from family background – he or she is likely to have a mixed education, multi-cultural marriage and parents of different nationalities – and working experience . . . graduating from an internationally-oriented business school . . . line management experience in a foreign culture company . . . experience through various career moves of different skills, roles and environments. (Pinder, 1990, p. 78)

This, however, is only for a few, who think globally and act globally. Most people will have to think globally, but act locally. This is the reality of IHRM for most managers: international awareness for national action.

International managers will be mobile and experienced in a number of overseas locations. George van Houten describes the Philips job-rotation approach:

> The job rotation practice leads to a rich exchange of perspectives. When you send a Norwegian to Brazil, a Pakistani to Singapore, or an American to the Netherlands, the cultural influences that are traded are bound to result in an international point of view in the company as a whole. (van Houten, 1989, p. 110)

It is one thing to draw up the specification of what the international manager should be, but how do you get there? Is there a means whereby potential members of this elite group can be trained? One possibility is to acquire an MBA or similar qualification, such as the French Descaf, from a business school with genuine international credentials. Business schools can claim to be international at various levels.

First, is the *student body*. A mixture of nationalities and cultures produces a genuinely cosmopolitan discussion of cases and similar material. If the students also have business experience in different countries, that is a further significant advance. The full-time MBA programmes at London and Manchester Business Schools both have half their students from outside Britain and London has 39 different nationalities represented so that students there learn cultural sensitivity 'almost by osmosis' (Arkin, 1991, p. 29).

The next level of development is the internationalisation of the *teaching staff*. Most academics spend one or more of their early years of academic training in another country, usually the United States, although there is a growing amount of European interchange which gives them a broader perspective than that of working in a single country. A business school will enrich the internationalism of its faculty much more if it is able to recruit foreign nationals on temporary or long-term contracts. British and American schools have the considerable advantage of their native tongue being either already mastered by many overseas academics, or of the opportunity to achieve such mastery being much wanted. Most have at least 10 per cent of their faculty who are foreign nationals. It is harder for schools in other countries that do not teach in English, but the leading European schools all have a significant foreign faculty. In the Faculty of Business Administration at the National University of Singapore 89 of the faculty are Singaporean, but a further 51 are distributed across a number of nationalities:

Malaysia	13
United States	8
Canada	6
Hong Kong	5
Australia, India, Philippines, Taiwan	3
Sri Lanka, United Kingdom	2
Bangladesh, Ghana, Indonesia	1

The third level of development is in the nature of the *learning experiences* that the students undergo. Increasingly, MBA students carry out group projects. The multinational nature of the student groups means that companies are often very interested in them carrying out international assignments, which provide invaluable experience and learning. In some schools there is also the opportunity for exchanges with MBA students in other countries as part of the course.

The MBA experience in an international business school is valuable for all managers, but a carefully selected programme can be an invaluable part of the international manager's preparation.

Apart from academic preparation, there is the value of language proficiency, which is the Achilles heel of those for whom English is their native tongue. It is not simply the ability to communicate in a second or third language that is important, it is the confidence and ease in dealing with people of different nationalities that accompanies language proficiency. The Scandinavians and the Dutch have long enjoyed the benefit of multilingualism because of the inaccessibility of their own languages. For most

Malaysians, Singaporeans and Hong Kong Chinese there is a similar benefit as a result of having been British colonies.

International managers must have fluent English, whether it be their native tongue or not, but their competence will be greatly extended by some degree of proficiency in one or two other languages with wide currency, such as Arabic, Cantonese, French, German, Japanese or Russian.

The international management lifestyle is specialised and demanding. In a material sense there are likely to be substantial benefits, but the physical and emotional demands of constant relocation are considerable. Business Class travel is comfortable enough, but the time between the airport and the hotel, the delays in the departure lounge, the change of climate, time zone, medical facilities and culture can tax even the most robust physique and the most resilient nervous system.

From a social and emotional point of view international managers probably have to sacrifice some or all of the humdrum pleasures of life that many people value. Being constantly on the move and constantly away from home is a way of working that is more attractive to, and feasible for, the independent individual without significant domestic responsibilities or on-going social commitments. International managers need to have ready access to information and they need to be quick and perceptive in their dealings with people, where much of the contact is superficial and potentially confrontational. The independence, referred to above, can make them vulnerable if they lack the normal forms of social support that come from work, as well as those that come from the domestic situation of home and family.

Managing the international manager therefore requires careful selection, so that those who move into these demanding roles are emotionally and physically equipped for the challenges involved. It requires extensive and specialised preparation – probably through a well-chosen MBA – to acquire international competence and expertise. It requires people with language proficiency and the intercultural self-confidence that such proficiency develops.

The final point about the international manager is to indicate what a small number of people come in this category:

> The number of executives falling into this category is extremely small, with each firm counting them in tens rather than hundreds, and even in the largest firm in our study, this group was said to number about 200. It is therefore as numerically insignificant as it is qualitatively vital. (Atkinson, 1992, p. 74)

The expatriates

International managers pass through foreign countries; expatriates go and live in them. This requires thorough management of the process – before they go, while they are away and, crucially, when they come back:

> UK multinationals are becoming increasingly conscious of the importance of a successful repatriation process . . . preparing for expatriation and developing an

adequate support system for expatriates while overseas . . . are now well established and are generally well done. Attention must increasingly turn to repatriation as the third element in the process. (Johnston, 1991, p. 108)

Many Western countries have long experience of expatriates, but mainly in the colonial mode. After administrators in India, tea-planters in Sri Lanka, rubber-planters in Malaysia, mining engineers in Africa, Scots doctors in Russia and Italian architects everywhere, there has been a continuing tradition of organisations despatching young managers to manage local workforces. That tradition is now in decline and expatriation is no longer one-way. Cynthia Haddock and Basil South in Chapter 14 indicate the growing proportion of Shell's expatriates are of nationalities other than British or Dutch.

Of the five examples at the beginning of the chapter, the stereotype of the expatriate is the one that is altering. There are fewer people who spend their whole career overseas and more who include one or two spells of up to three years on overseas assignment as part of the process of acquiring the necessary breadth of experience and vision to operate at senior level in an international organisation.

Expatriation usually enhances career prospects, but that cannot be guaranteed, and the impact on the expatriate personally and on the expatriate's family is likely to be considerable. The great majority of expatriates are men, usually married men, leading to the 'army wife' syndrome. Whether male or female, the expatriate's spouse is nearly always placed in a position of total or partial dependency by corporate expatriation: one career is subordinated to another. This dependency is not only economic. Charles will have all the preoccupations and social networks of his job to absorb him, as well as a position and social status that are likely to be attractive. Caroline may well have a pleasant house and plenty of money, and may be lucky enough to enjoy an agreeable climate, but her social position will be that of wife and mother and the social activities may well be limited to coffee mornings with other expatriate wives. For the increasing proportion of expatriate wives with a professional career in suspension, adapting to this can require considerable ingenuity.

Susan Harris was an expatriate wife and mother in Malaysia, who had readily suspended a career in management consultancy so that her husband could take the career opportunity that three years in Kuala Lumpur offered. Provided with a house and servants there, she dealt with the problem of enforced idleness by working voluntarily as a tutor with students taking management qualifications.

Because of the demands that expatriation makes, it has to be managed carefully and thoroughly.

Selection for expatriation

In some organisations, like the armed forces, the preparedness to work as an expatriate is determined on initial recruitment, as virtually a condition of employment. In others the possibility of an extended overseas assignment can come as a shock, which may or may not be welcome, presenting all the problems of considering the potential career handicap of turning down the opportunity and the potential domestic problems of accepting it. Employers seldom have the luxury of a large number of appropriately qualified people readily available to fill any vacancy, so that situations in which one person 'really has to go' cannot always be avoided, but the most satisfactory general approach to selection for expatriation is through the combination of annual appraisal and career planning.

A feature of annual appraisal can be a discussion of whether people are interested in working overseas at all, the degree of technical expertise and managerial experience they possess and the domestic/social constraints that would affect the timing of such a move. That can then be developed by identifying timings that would be appropriate for such a move, preferred locations and even some language training. As with all career management initiatives, this sets up expectations of the future that the management may not be able to deliver because of changes in business activity, but it provides a cadre of people who would welcome an overseas move.

The question of expatriation or not is the major question in selection, but the particular location is the next most important determinant in matching the person to the job. Among the most important issues are the following:

Culture How different from home is the culture of the country – religion, the social position of women, the degree of political stability/instability, personal security and petty crime, local press and television, cable television, availability of foreign newspapers, health hazards?

Economic development How well developed is the economy of the country – standard/cost of living, availability of familiar foods and domestic equipment, transport, post and telephone, local poverty, health and education facilities, availability of international schools?

Geographical location How far away is it and where is it – climate, in a cosmopolitan city or more remote, the importance/unimportance of language proficiency, the size of the local expatriate community, employment prospects of spouse?

The job What has to be done and what is the situation – nature of the organisation, proportion of expatriates, technical, commercial and managerial demands of the job, staffing and support, the extent of role in managing local nationals?

Determining whether the person is right for the post is a process that does not differ from determining the suitability for any demanding assignment, and the most important feature is making sure that the potential appointee and members of the family have a full understanding of what will be involved.

It is essential, however, that those proceeding on an overseas posting should be selected for it. If there is not an appropriate person in the organisation, then recruitment from outside is preferable to assigning someone about whose suitability there are doubts. There is no profile of the ideal expatriate, but here are some selection issues arranged under the four headings used already:

CULTURE

How well prepared is the expatriate family for an unfamiliar culture? In many ways the developed countries of Western Europe present fewer problems than those further afield, but English is spoken more widely in Singapore than, for instance, in France. Malaysia is a multi-ethnic society, but with a Muslim majority in the population. The Muslim dominance of life in most Middle East countries has profound implications for expatriates, requiring a degree of puritanism that will be unfamiliar and a social role for women that is quite unlike that which Western women experience. In the developing countries of the East there may be superb hotels, but little else to do in the evening. Manila and Bangkok have plenty of after-dark facilities for men on their own, but little for couples and even less for women on their own. Whatever the culture is, open-mindedness and tolerance are essential qualities for the expatriates to develop.

ECONOMIC DEVELOPMENT

Some Eastern countries now enjoy a standard of living and material convenience that match or surpass those of the West, so that the expatriate will find excellent systems of transportation, postal and telephone services that will be similar to those of the home country. Elsewhere the situation will be very different and everyday life will require a great deal more adjustment once one is outside the air-conditioned cocoon of the multinational company's offices. Medical and dental facilities may be sparse and few expatriate families can avoid being affected by the conditions of those among whom they live. Not only may they be distressed by the living conditions they see in most parts of the Indian sub-continent and South America, for instance, they will also have to contend with very high urban crime rates in some places. The employment prospects of the spouse – especially of a wife – may be very poor.

GEOGRAPHICAL LOCATION

This is a further twist to the economic development question. The heat and humidity of tropical climates are supportable when moving from air-conditioned home, via air-conditioned car to air-conditioned office or shopping mall. Those moving to more remote areas have greater problems in coping with the climate and the relative isolation, so they need to be emotionally self-sufficient and not too dependent on outside stimulation. The distance from home is another determinant of personal suitability to the posting. The Parisian working in Brussels could easily contemplate weekly commuting: the Bruxellois working in Madagascar could not. There will be a smaller expatriate community in most Italian cities than in Hong Kong, so that the expatriate family may have to work harder at establishing social contacts, and will therefore require considerable social skill and self-confidence. The geographical location will also determine the importance of local language proficiency for all members of the expatriate family.

THE JOB

In worldwide companies, like most of those in Part II of this book, questions about the job may initially seem unproblematic. Many expatriates are simply moving to exercise their well-developed company expertise in a different location. The situation will, however, always be different, no matter how similar the conventions and procedures. The various demands of the job need to be thoroughly considered, especially what may be involved in managing local nationals, where the subtleties of response to leadership and expectations of authority will probably still baffle the expatriate when he or she is finally on the way home from the tour of duty.

Preparing for expatriation

> Ideally, preparation for an international assignment should begin a year or more in advance so that global awareness and thinking internationally about the business become part of a continuous process . . . All too often everything is condensed into a flurry of international briefings just before departure. (Rothwell, 1992, p. 35)

If there is the relative luxury of a 12-month period of preparation, language training can make real progress. This comes to life most effectively when there is a strong flavour of cultural orientation and familiarisation as well, so that two of the basic requirements of preparation are dealt with simultaneously. The nature of the language training provided is usually slightly different for the expatriate employee and for the expatriate spouse. Training for the employee will concentrate on technical and business terms, while that for the spouse concentrates on those aspects of the language that will be useful in everyday matters like shopping and trying to get the washing machine repaired, or in local social contacts. An example of an interesting combination of linguistic expertise is the expatriate couple in Japan, where he speaks Japanese and she reads it, so he deals with waiters and taxi drivers, while she navigates and copes with restaurant menus.

More general aspects of cultural familiarisation can be achieved by various means, often depending on the individual. Some will read avariciously, both travel books and the range of novels that have been written about most parts of the world. Others prefer film and video. Can there be any better preparation for Australian suburban life than watching several episodes of 'Neighbours'?

Nigel Holden's case study of NEC, in Chapter 10, describes how the company uses returned expatriates to write and present case histories about the country. This has the obvious advantage of being able to discuss with someone face-to-face their experiences in a situation which you are about to meet. It should also be automatic for the potential expatriate to meet socially any nationals from the country of expatriation who may be visiting the host company during the pre-departure stage.

It should not be assumed that a similar cultural heritage obviates the need for cultural familiarisation. The British and the Americans share a common language and considerable common feeling, and most Britons believe that their televiewing and cinema-going have provided them with a detailed knowledge of downtown Los Angeles and middle-American family life, but there are, in fact, a host of differences and the common language can actually make things difficult, as one makes fewer allowances when dealing with someone who speaks your language fluently.

Physical proximity makes the British believe they know how to handle the French, but the detailed account of adjustment over 12 months by Peter Mayle (1989) shows just how different everyday domestic and business arrangements are. The remarkable popularity of the book shows how fascinated the British are by the 'strangeness' of the French.

The success of an overseas assignment will be enhanced by some previous experience overseas and some experience of the location, but brief business trips scarcely qualify as previous experience. A holiday could be better, as people on holiday usually go at least partly to see the country and the people. Much better is a visit before the move, which is made to prepare for the move. By this method it is possible to deal with such crucial issues as housing. Nothing reassures more about impending relocation as knowing where one is going to live. If there are children, arrangements for their schooling can also be made.

The prospective expatriate will need support and advice during this preliminary visit. If no local organisation already exists, it may be possible to arrange support through a relocation agency or the local embassy. If there is a local branch of the company, it is helpful if a member of staff can be assigned at least on a part-time basis to make preliminary arrangements and then to act as guide and helpmate in dealings with property agencies, schools, legal bodies and any other organisations. Social contacts can also be made, so that the prospective expatriates can get to know the social and economic ambience as well as doing business.

Continuing back-home arrangements while abroad can be expensive. There may be children remaining in boarding schools, or elderly relatives to be catered for and pets to worry about, as well as renting the family home and many more. There may be a need for some company help, especially with financial and similar arrangements.

Travel arrangements themselves are relatively straightforward, but still have to be organised. There may be a need for family visas and one or more work permits, removal of household effects as well as personal baggage, health checks and whatever range of 'jabs' and medication are required.

Repatriation

Coming back from an overseas assignment seldom receives the attention it needs. It is not expected to be problematic and therefore receives little attention: all the problems are expected to be connected with going out and getting settled. Why should there be problems about coming home?

The first potential problem is the nature of the overseas experience. If it has been thoroughly satisfactory for all members of the family, with an enhanced lifestyle, plenty of career development and scope for the employee, plenty of money and exciting experience for the family in an agreeable climate, then there may not be much initial enthusiasm for returning. It will be like coming back from an extended holiday, with all the reluctance about leaving good friends and stimulating experiences to return to dreary old Basildon, or Bremen or Baton Rouge.

On the other hand the overseas experience may have been difficult, with a loss of social life, disagreeable climate, frustrations and disappointment at work and all sorts of petty inconveniences. Then the prospect of returning home can become an obsession, with the days ticked off on a calendar and a great build-up of anticipation. Home is surrounded by a warm, nostalgic glow as the nice things are remembered and the nasty things are forgotten. When the day of return to hearth and home at last comes, Basildon (or Bremen or Baton Rouge) may soon seem just a little ordinary compared with the wonderful picture that had been built up in expectation.

The second major problem is the career situation of the returning expatriate. Johnston (1991) found that virtually all repatriated personnel experienced some personal difficulty in reintegrating on return to a UK organisation. The main complaints were loss of status, loss of autonomy, lack of career direction and lack of recognition of the value of overseas experience (p. 103). These findings reflect very closely those of American studies a decade earlier (e.g. Harvey, 1982), perhaps suggesting that both nations have a degree of cultural insularity that makes 'abroad' a strange place and therefore tends to undervalue experience gained there. Furthermore, even the most sophisticated companies did not always recognise the difficulty:

> little appears to be done at a personal level for the returning managers who are expected in the main to work things out for themselves. No companies within the Chemicals, Manufacturing and Services sectors sample had a formal company reorientation for repatriates to aid their social and professional integration into what will inevitably be a substantially different organisation from that which they left. (Johnston, 1991, p. 106)

It may be considered not a management responsibility to fuss over a manager's personal readjustment, but an American study (Adler, 1991, p. 238) showed that the effectiveness of expatriates took between 6 and 12 months to return to an acceptable level on repatriation, so there are some hard-headed reasons for taking it seriously.

The engineer

The term 'engineer' is used here broadly to cover all those technical specialists who spend spells of a few weeks or months at a time in an overseas location to carry out a particular job. Most often it is commissioning new plant and training local personnel in its use. The period overseas is not as long and the role is much more specific than that of the expatriate, so that the level of preparation is less. It is similar to seafarers, airline crew, travel couriers and the increasing number of Western academics who spend a few weeks or months abroad. They are not living abroad: simply away from home for a spell, but with all the frustrations of air travel.

The selection criteria must be strict, as the engineer needs complete technical expertise and the ability to cope with unforeseen technical problems without recourse to colleagues or specialised equipment, both of which are probably lacking. There will also be a need for personal resourcefulness and the ability to handle a wide variety of social situations. For this reason some level of cultural awareness training will probably be needed.

Compared with international managers and expatriates, engineers are more likely to be assigned to remote locations, with all the social isolation and possible climatic problems that go with such areas, even though they are usually accommodated in an international hotel. It can be a monotonous life, with little scope for social activity apart from the hotel bar and pool. Some extrovert and gregarious engineers cope successfully with people in different countries, striking up friendships and taking a keen interest in their surroundings, but most simply settle down to getting the job done through long working days followed by a couple of drinks in the bar after a shower and a relaxed meal.

Regular health checks are essential as are efficient administrative arrangements for travel, accommodation and contact with base during assignment. Some engineers find it very difficult to settle back into the more routine tasks that often await them when the days of travelling are over.

The occasional parachutist

Occasional parachutists also need efficient administrative arrangements for travel and accommodation. Like the engineer, they are representatives of the company and will be able to act as an invaluable communication link in both a formal and informal way during and after the visit. Large numbers of employees move between countries only in this mode and the exchanges can be very important in developing mutual understanding between the nationalities and compatibility of the systems and procedures of the two organisations.

The potential for doing harm should not be underestimated. Someone visiting for only a few days has little incentive for taking the trouble to learn about the country and the people, and may therefore carry stereotyped assumptions that could be very damaging to the relationships within the company. It can be helpful if novices travel together with an experienced person and talk before travelling with an expatriate or someone else familiar with the culture.

The mobile worker

The four types of overseas worker we have considered so far have all been company employees and there has been the assumption of considerable support and facilitation by the company. It has also been indicated, particularly in the section about expatriates, that the level of support may be considerable. The example of Benedicte is of that growing band of people who move themselves, with very little support from anyone else. Even the most xenophobic Briton will consider moving to another country. Results of a survey of 26,800 readers of *The Guardian* in October 1988 demonstrated this.

> Over one in five stated that they would actually prefer to work in other EEC countries and nearly half would consider working in France or in Australasia . . . Interest is even stronger among the young, among Londoners and among those at director level in their companies. (Beaumont, 1989, p. 43)

In the opposite direction Britain remains a work destination of enormous appeal to almost all other nationalities. European universities have considerably increased their programmes for student exchanges, as the number of courses that require or permit a period overseas has grown rapidly. The EC has introduced the ERASMUS programme to enable students in higher education to carry out part of their study in countries of the EC other than their own for between 3 and 12 months. Over one-fifth of the annual exchanges involve the British, with 2500 or more students spending time abroad each year.

COMETT is a programme that provides experienced managers and professionals, as well as students, with the opportunity to undertake technological training in another member state of the Community. The objective is to develop joint ventures between the companies and universities. The development of a common pattern of national vocational qualifications will aid still further the movement of people between Community countries.

There remains, however, uncertainty about the degree to which people will actually seek employment in a different country, despite the professed interest and the apparent opportunities. Atkinson (1992) demonstrates that there is some increase in the number of foreign nationals working in the United Kingdom, exceeding 1 million by 1988. However, half of these are what he calls corporate transferees (or expatriates in the language of this chapter) mainly as a result of companies expanding through acquisition of foreign subsidiaries:

> entry by acquisition, followed by expansion through organic growth seemed to be the preferred mode . . . intensifying the internationalisation of the internal labour market (as key staff are placed in senior positions in the acquired company) while reducing or postponing it externally, as the acquired company continues to recruit locally as before. (Atkinson, 1992, p. 73)

Managing the mobile workers is a process that companies do not yet seem to have worked out, presumably because it is not yet generally regarded as worth encouraging. If a foreign national wants to come and work for the organisation, they are seldom short-listed unless there is a clear need, such as domestic shortage. This was the situation that brought large numbers of temporary foreign workers, or Gastarbeiter, to Denmark, Germany and Switzerland. More recently it brought significant numbers of Dutch and German teachers into London schools during the 1980s. Rarely, however, does a company have the need for such a cohort of people, which will justify investment in a specific initiative of dedicated recruitment staff, advertising and arrangements for assistance with transport, housing and resettlement. In the London case the recruitment was thorough and successful. When people are recruited singly, there is rarely the same degree of assistance.

An interesting, but unusual, case was the staffing of Euro Disney in 1992. This is a massive international enterprise, with the assumption of a polyglot clientele, so that there had to be widespread international recruitment.

Recruiting across national boundaries requires detailed specialist knowledge of the local employment law and labour market conventions. For this reason it is usual to use consultants to assist with the process, but an excellent introduction to varying practices within the EC is to be found in the IDS/IPM European Management Guide to Recruitment (1990).

IHRM and the cosmopolitans

As with so many aspects of international human resource management, managing the cosmopolitans operates at two distinct levels: the European and the global. For all EC countries the creation of the single market is a significant step in internationalisation with the bringing together of so many different languages, cultures and conventions, but Europe also enjoys a common heritage and the coming together of Europe is perhaps no more dramatic than the forging of international communities among the Commonwealth of Independent States or the United States of America.

Although it broke up so cataclysmically in 1991, the USSR had been a single economic and political entity for 70 years despite ethnic, linguistic, religious and cultural differences quite as great as those in Western Europe. The United States has been made up largely of European emigrants, some of whom retain strong affiliations with the lands from which their grandparents or great-grandparents came. However, the proximity to South America now threatens the dominance of English as the universal language of the country.

To all EC nationals, but especially to the British, the development of the European Community presents a huge challenge and opportunity, and there is the tendency to think that international management means managing in a European context. That, however, is only a beginning to the more complex processes of global thinking for local action.

The genuine international managers will increase in number as a result of programmes like ERASMUS and international MBAs, although more of them will operate Europe-wide than globally. The elaborate support facilities for expatriates will probably reduce when applied to relocation within Europe, but will remain important for relocation outside Europe.

Managing the mobile worker remains on the managerial back burner. There are examples of considerable efforts being made (for example, Neale and Mindel, 1992), but the attention that was being devoted to the issue in the late 1980s has waned as skill shortages and demographic decline have not presented the problems that were anticipated, due to a rise in levels of unemployment in most countries of the EC as well as most other countries of the world.

Although not referred to specifically in this chapter, Brewster's book on managing expatriates (1988) is an excellent source of guidance. Organisations providing specialist assistance include:

> The Centre for International Briefing,
> Farnham,
> Surrey GU9 0AG.
>
> Employment Conditions Abroad,
> Anchor House,
> 15 Britten Street,
> London SW3 3TY.

References

Adler, N. J. (1991), *International Dimensions of Organizational Behaviour*, PWS-Kent, Boston, Mass.

Arkin, A. (1991), 'How international are Britain's business schools?', *Personnel Management*, vol. 23, no. 11, November, pp. 28–31.

Atkinson, J. (1992), 'Corporate employment policies, women and 1992' in Lindley, R. M. (ed.) *Women's Employment: Britain in the single European market*, HMSO, London.

Beaumont, R. (1989), 'Would you work abroad?', *The Guardian*, 12 April, 1989.

Brewster, C. J. (1988), *The Management of Expatriates*, Cranfield School of Management Monograph.

Everett, J. E., Stening, B. W. and Longton, P. A. (1982), 'Some evidence for an international managerial culture', *Journal of Management Studies*, vol. 19, no. 2, pp. 153–62.

Harvey, M. (1982), 'The other side of foreign assignments: dealing with the repatriation dilemma', *Columbia Journal of World Business*, vol. 17, Spring, pp. 53–9.

IDS (1990), *Recruitment*, European Management Guides, Institute of Personnel Management, London.

Johnston, J. (1991), 'An empirical study of the repatriation of managers in UK multinationals', *Human Resource Management Journal*, vol. 4, no. 1, Summer 1991, pp. 102–9.

Mayle, P. (1989), *A Year in Provence*, Hamish Hamilton, London.

Neale, R. and Mindel, R. (1992), 'Rigging up multicultural teamworking', *Personnel Management*, vol. 24, no. 1, January.

Pinder, M. (1990), *Personnel Management for the Single European Market*, Pitman, London.

Rothwell, S. (1992), 'The development of the international manager', *Personnel Management*, vol. 24, no. 1, January.

Scase, R. and Goffee, R. (1989), *Reluctant Managers: Their work and lifestyles*, Unwin Hyman, London.

van Houten, G. (1989), 'The implications of globalism: new management realities at Philips', in Evans, P., Doz, Y. and Laurent, A. (eds), *Human Resource Management in International Firms*, Macmillan, London.

CHAPTER 3

Culture

The culture of an organisation is the characteristic spirit and belief demonstrated within it, for example, in the norms and values that are generally held about how people should behave and treat each other, the nature of working relationships that should be developed, and the attitudes to customers and to change that are conventionally held. Although essentially a 'soft' concept, it is an important way of understanding what is going on and how things could be improved.

Through the 1980s in particular, there was great interest in organisational culture as the key to improved organisational effectiveness. This was largely directed to comparisons within national boundaries (for example, Deal and Kennedy, 1982; Handy, 1985) and has complemented the earlier preoccupation with organisational structure. Organisation charts may be useful in clarifying reporting relations and subtleties of seniority, but the culture or ethos of the business is believed to be an equally important determinant of effectiveness.

Although it sounds strange to attribute human qualities to organisations, they do appear to have distinctive identities. Wally Olins (1989) cites the example of the world's great chemical companies, which superficially seem similar and produce virtually identical products selling at the same price. Yet they each have strong identities and in culture are as different as individual human beings. Managers have to understand the extent to which culture can be changed and how the changes can be made, even if the changes may be much harder and slower to make than most managers believe and most circumstances allow. They also have to understand the influence that the culture may have on their personal style and success. This can be very difficult for senior managers moving to a new organisation. They are used to doing things 'their' way, but do not always realise how much they were successful as a result of reflecting accurately the values that obtained in their previous organisation.

Managers who deliberately or unwittingly work counter-culturally will constantly be frustrated by failing to get a response from colleagues, by being misunderstood or by being bypassed. Managers who try to work out the nature of the culture in which they are operating can at least begin the process of change and influence the direction of the cultural evolution, because culture has qualities that structure can never enjoy. It is dynamic and human in the sense that it is the creation of all those who participate, both past and present. It will strengthen and support the efforts of those who adapt to it, as surely as it will frustrate the efforts of those who ignore or contradict it.

No organisation is isolated and insulated from its surroundings, so attempts to develop its culture must take account not only of the intentions of those in charge and the expectations of those employed, but also of developments in the surrounding society, both nationally and internationally. The international dimension is the thrust of this chapter and the treatment is tentative because international cultural issues are such a puzzle that none but the most exceptional managers will be able to unravel them – but it is only the foolish who ignore them. The history of the European Community in attempting to establish a supranational institution is one of constant, but reluctant recognition of the stubbornness of national differences and the accentuation of regional differences among, for instance, the Basques, the Flemish and the Scottish. The cultural diversity and intensity of feeling on national issues in a close-knit and economically developed region like Western Europe indicate the significance of cultural difference on a global scale. Nationality is important in human resource management because of its effect on human behaviour and the consequent constraints on management action.

Some things that initially appear specific to a particular national culture turn out to be understood and welcomed in almost all cultures. How strange that Italian pizza should have been adopted in most countries of the world, and that the expansion should have been largely brought about by Pizza Hut, which is owned by Pepsi-Cola, an American company known for a drink that has also gone to every corner of the globe. Who would have expected that Muscovites would daily queue up outside the largest McDonald's in the world? Newspapers and magazines in social democracies and socialist republics frequently devote more space in twelve months to the British Royal Family than to any other topic, despite the fact that the institution is utterly British and theoretically alien to their political system. Countless millions every day follow the fortunes of some very ordinary people in the Australian suburb of Ramsey Street, and even more watch football.

The wide international acceptability of these things could suggest that we are all members of the global village with converging tastes and values. Yet certain facets of national culture remain deeply rooted and have a way of undermining that argument.

It is difficult to prove that any given language determines management behaviour in specific ways. Nevertheless, it seems incontestable that the French have developed their language as a precision tool for analysis and conceptualisation; that the Japanese use their language as an emollient for creating an atmosphere conducive to harmonious interaction; and that the Americans use their version of English as a store of snappy neologisms to excite, distract and motivate (Holden, 1992).

Managers need to understand what the underlying culture of their organisation is, why it is like that and how they can be effective within it. They need a capacity to pick up signals about culture and to perceive values: they need cultural sensitivity. Managers in organisations with an international dimension, and personnel professionals in particular, have a job that is forcing them to be more internationally minded almost daily, yet seldom are they aware of the impacts of different national cultures on management practices. The following sections illustrate how culture-specific features give management a distinctive national quality.

Management in different cultures

Britain

British culture remains obstinately anti-business and somewhat xenophobic. Managers do not enjoy the professional status accorded to their American counterparts and their relatively high earnings are often resented by those in other walks of life.

> As a rule, leaders of commerce and industry in England over the last century have accommodated themselves to an elite culture blended of preindustrial aristocratic and religious values, and more recent professional and bureaucratic values that inhibited their quest for expansion, productivity and profits. (Wiener, 1985, p. 127)

Foreigners are typically seen as people who speak strange languages in far-off places, seldom treating the British with the respect they deserve and all too often winning in truly British sporting activities like cricket and football. This hangover from an imperial past is exacerbated by one of the huge advantages of that past and from the position of the United States since World War II: the worldwide use of English as the contemporary lingua franca.

The statistics on the use of English are staggering. It is the mother tongue of 350 million people and the population of countries in which it is an official language is 1400 million, which is way ahead of other major languages such as Russian (270 million), French (220 million), Arabic (170 million) and Japanese (120 million).

> English is used as an official language in over 60 countries and has a prominent place in another 20. It is the main language of books, newspapers, airports and air-traffic control, international business and academic conferences, science, technology, medicine, diplomacy, sports, international competitions, pop music, and advertising. Over two-thirds of the world's scientists write in English. Three quarters of the world's mail is written in English. Of all the information stored in the world's electronic retrieval systems, 80% is stored in English. (Crystal, 1987, p. 358)

The worldwide use of the language is a problem as well as an advantage to native English speakers. There is insufficient incentive to learn other languages and it is difficult to appreciate that someone who speaks your language with apparent ease may not necessarily share the same cultural assumptions that you do. The French have reluctantly come to terms with a changed geo-political situation to a greater extent because their language is not so widely used. French business schools teach some of their courses in English.

Management education exhibits the same characteristics. Although there has long been an element of international business teaching in management schools, it is only recently that this has moved beyond an interest in international trade towards an interest in how business is done and how businesses are managed in different cultures:

> European (business) schools . . . spurred on by 1992, have taken the internationalisation of business in their stride . . . a reasonable guess is that European schools use twice as much teaching material (such as non-domestic case studies) as their American rivals. (*The Economist*, 2 March 1991, p. 11)

A distinctively British aspect of business management is what some European commentators (for example, d'Iribarne, 1985) describe as consensualism. Open conflict is avoided at all costs and British managers seek to convince everyone that they are pleasant, sociable and wishing to please everybody. Individual convictions tend to adjust themselves and to converge:

> Although each individual remains responsible for his own decisions, he has to consult everybody before making the decision. Listening to the others, explaining, convincing, good faith and good reasons become crucial to such a society. Acceptance must be created by arguing: facts, data are prevalent to create a pragmatic agreement. (Lalanne, 1990)

Lalanne offers the intriguing explanation of British economic decline as being caused by the convention of the 'shared secret', combined with a lack of action attributed to a lack of expression. Whereas a standard sociological explanation of secrecy is as a means to gain and reinforce power (Crozier and Friedberg, 1977), in British organisations it is used as a means of group cohesion. The secret is shared by insiders but not outsiders, creating a complicity between members of a group, rather like finding one's way into the Brownie Ring. In organisational terms this leads to complacency, as a common secret among members of a management team is that all is well, despite the worrying signs. In the end the managers convince themselves that it is actually the case – simply because it is the shared secret. Allied to this is the traditional British reserve and a distaste for expressing anything other than carefully considered opinions.

A different version of this in the 1990s has been an increase in mutual appraisal and evaluation in management circles. Considerable management time has been devoted to the management process itself with objective-setting, negotiation of targets, assessment of progress, review of achievement, auditing of effectiveness, appraisal of performance, evaluation of programmes and similar activities until there is a danger that management will become a self-sufficient, mutual admiration society, forgetting the customer and the non-managerial members of the organisation altogether.

France

The French have had a more formal approach to management. In 1673 the

Ordonnance Colbert was intended to provide nationwide standards for business practice, so that practitioners could achieve reasonable respectability. Tradesmen had to account regularly for their business and incurred great commercial risks if they could not show proper books. This established the importance of a highly codified form of the accounts. British practice, in comparison, did not begin to formalise until 200 years later, when the emerging accounting profession set its own standards, so that the approach in Britain is to emphasise accounting principles rather than the form of the accounts (Standish and Scheid, 1986).

There is also scrupulous attention to details of hierarchy in forms of address. 'Monsieur' is ubiquitous and the niceties of 'vous' or 'tu' carefully observed. Secretaries have great power as intermediaries between anyone and their boss. You can never reach a manager without the consent of the secretary, as the role of the secretary is clearly understood. The manager who took telephone calls directly, or who delegated anything other than agreed secretarial duties, would be detracting from the role of the secretary. There is never the personal assistant type of role which British secretaries seem to cherish. People in French organisations can be very sensitive about their area of responsibility and clear-cut definitions of the boundaries are needed to avoid conflicts.

There are signs of this type of formality lessening. In Chapter 15 Heather Lussey describes aspects of working in GSI, which is a much more relaxed and informal situation.

The French use the relatively impersonal collective noun 'les cadres' to describe management. Literally, this means framework and nicely expresses the rigidity implicit in the concept of salaried middle managers passing down and administering decisions from the top. French management is intellectual and aloof, with authority concentrated around the person of the chief executive at the apex of: 'a strict hierarchy of executives organised on functional lines, with rigid lines of command' (Mole, 1990, p. 18).

The qualities of leadership and man management that feature so strongly in British management thinking are missing in France, where managers are expected to apply rationality, synthesis and logical thinking to problem-solving and administration. Management problems are defined as being intellectual problems:

> In a society which has always esteemed the intellectual, the philosopher, and the serious writer, the French manager is an exponent of culture generale . . . French managers at work display their educated strengths. They parade their powers of analysis and synthesis, they exhibit a ready mastery of the complicated, they can formulate arguments . . . (Lawrence, 1991, p. 108)

There is thus a similar tendency to that of the British for management to be separated from the rest of the people in the business, but the approach to motivation is different. The French respond positively to drama and crisis. This is nicely exemplified by the cover of a French book on management, *Gérer et dynamiser ses collaborateurs* (Bournois and Poirson, 1989). The use of the word 'dynamiser', meaning to energise, is rather more vigorous than the Anglo/American equivalent of 'motivate' and more dramatic than the more recently used 'empowerment'. But most interesting is the cover picture of a man. Not a man in thick-rimmed glasses sitting at a desk, or in earnest conversation with colleagues whilst studying a set of accounts. Instead he has both arms upraised in triumph and both feet off the ground in a leap of exultation. His jacket is undone and his hair is tousled. If it were not for the clothing you would assume he had just scored a goal in a World Cup final.

United States

The idea that Britain and America are two nations divided by a common language is nowhere more obvious than in management. Differences in connotation and usage of certain terms are most marked, the most obvious being the word 'manager'. This is one of the most potent symbols of the American way of life, representing free enterprise and the heroic materialism that made the country great. Business and management hold a central place in the American education system that bemuses the British. In the United States there is no enduring tradition of a landed aristocracy, nor of colonies to govern. The proud tradition is of the pioneers, mostly fleeing from appalling conditions in Europe who opened up a big country by their own commitment and physical endeavour.

Philippe Poirson explains the differences of cultural emphasis in management between the Americans, Japanese and French by pointing to the continuing dominance in the United States of the Protestant work ethic: 'belief in the redemptive virtue of work has built a system of values for many founders and directors of American business organizations . . . profit is legitimate, success in business evaluable, "work ethics" highly developed' (Poirson, 1989, p. 6).

The Americans, like the French, lack the dominance of financial institutions that so weakens British management. The City of London is a powerful, and socially respectable, institution that is geared to making money through financial manipulation rather than through long-term investment. The main methods are either switching investment funds between corporations that affects the gearing and frequently gets the corporation into trouble with its banks, or merger and acquisition. This is a phenomenon of all developed societies, but the United States has stronger management institutions to balance the depredations of Wall Street.

Trade union activity is at a much lower level in the United States than in Europe and organisations tend to be more open in their methods of operation than either the French or the British, emphasising the contractual relationship between managers:

> managers accept very easily – even wish – to be set precise, detailed objectives in a budget, because they feel as if they were in a 'trade relationship' with their superior, as if they had a contractual commitment. Therefore they consider that it is fair that their boss feels interested in their results – this is something normal from a client – and appraises them against the objectives set in the budget. The budget is perceived primarily as a contract by managers, not as a strategic instrument to plan the near future of the whole company. (Lalanne, 1990, p. 6)

Japan

In contrast to the Americans, the Japanese are oriented to human efficiency rather than human functioning because of their quite different heritage. There is a strong emphasis on mentoring:

> Japanese managers spend up to 30% of their time, in and outside normal office hours, educating their younger colleagues and initiating them in the lore and wisdom of the company, preparing them functionally and psychologically for operations outside the firm. (Holden, 1992, p. 31)

The idea of individual autonomy is a relatively recent development of European/ American influences. To a great extent the Japanese continue to espouse the values of an agricultural, feudal nation, living in an introverted manner by developing specific sociability: 'the group's superiority over the individual remains a fundamental particularity of Japanese sociability. However, the new role of firms seems slowly to replace the one traditionally held by the house and the village' (Poirson, 1989, p. 7).

Family conventions, religious traditions and forms of education differ markedly between countries and every adult is partly a product of these features of conditioning, with the attendant values, imperatives and beliefs that shape behaviour and expectation. American children are taught very early the values of individuality and doing your own thing; Japanese children are taught to conform, to work within a group and to develop team spirit.

Japanese culture also incorporates a strong desire for the rest of the world to admire the contribution to world culture of Japanese economic and technological achievement, at the same time as maintaining their economic power (van Wolferen, 1989, p. 415). There is no complacency, but a continuing urge to justification in international eyes, which brings with it the global thinking mentioned in the opening chapter.

Germany

The Germans are also oriented towards human efficiency, but in a different way. Here management as a concept is strongly associated with the close supervision of those with less knowledge and experience than the supervisor. There is no doubt about who is in charge and what the boundaries are between specified activities:

> The organisation and the individual's role within it are logical, methodical and compartmentalised. Functions and the relationship between them are thoroughly defined and documented. Procedures, routines, doing things by the book are important. Cutting corners, taking initiatives, skimping on the formalities are frowned upon. (Mole, 1990, p. 36)

This is associated with a strong emphasis on the product and its development. 'Vorsprung durch Technik' was used in a British advertising campaign for one product, largely because it expresses so succinctly the universal German approach:

business success requires product excellence – product excellence requires an organisation that runs like a well-oiled machine – the people of the organisation adapt their behaviour to the precision movements of the organisational machine.

Germany is renowned for its commitment to training, especially its apprenticeship scheme:

> Young people entering industry spend three days a week at school and two or three days at work for two years, receiving both technical and theoretical training and practical experience. Peter Drucker believes that the apprenticeship scheme and the skilled workers it produces are the explanation for West Germany's success in steadily increasing productivity, as it creates not only the right attitude but also the theoretical foundation. (Barham and Rassam, 1989, pp. 189–90)

A less well-known feature of German training is the *Lernstatt* or learning workshop. This is similar to the quality circle, but was introduced much earlier in Germany because of the country's heavy dependence on immigrant Gastarbeiter and has found a permanent place in German training because of its benefits in quality, motivation and problem-solving.

Arab nations

The justification for lumping together in a single categorisation a number of nations that spread across North Africa and throughout the Middle East is that they all share to a greater or lesser extent the significant influence of the Islamic faith. In practical terms this produces the direct opposite of the Protestant work ethic, behaviour is influenced by the conviction that destiny depends more on the will of a supreme being than on individual behaviour.

Another strand in the common heritage of Arab nations is their experience of insecurity. It is a region of climatic extremes and widespread shortage of natural resources, apart from abundant oil. Living conditions tend to be harsh and political regimes unstable. This can lead to wariness in developing trusting relationships. It is a region of great pride and prickly sensitivities.

Arabic fatalism also means that the status of an Arab is more dependent on family position and social contact than on personal achievement. Pezeschkupur (1978) claims that this is why Arabs frequently find satisfaction in being helpless, as the strong are resented and the weak are compensated:

> Several public administrators of equal rank took turns in meeting in each other's offices for their weekly conferences, and the host would serve as chairman. After several months, one of these men had a mild heart attack. Upon his recovery, it was decided to hold the meetings only in his office, so as not to inconvenience him. From then on, the man who had had the heart attack became the permanent chaiman of the conference. This individual appeared more helpless than the others, and his helplessness enabled him to increase his power. (p. 50)

This fatalism also inhibits Arab managers from interpersonal conflict, as shown by this comment from an American specialist in management development with extensive Middle East experience:

> on an issue favoured by the subordinates but opposed by the [Arab] executive, he is likely to let the matter drop without taking action. He values loyalty above efficiency. Many executives look upon their employees as family and will allow them to by-pass the hierarchy in order to meet them. (Barratt, 1989, p. 29)

Coming to terms with the cultural maze

In the preceding pages we have seen just a few of the cultural contrasts, with the inevitable cultural bias of the writer being apparent: Why put France ahead of the United States? Why no mention of Hong Kong, or Scandinavia, or Australasia? Why ignore Africa and South America? Cultural diversity in management practice is so extensive that anyone's brain hurts when trying to comprehend it and then trying to remember the details. For example, to the European, Israel is in the Middle East and has a government. To the Malaysian, Israel is in West Asia and has a regime.

The cultural range is so great that there is a danger of international managers operating simply at the level of caricature, folklore and trivia, such as learning how to present one's business card to a Japanese, or what it means when a German takes his jacket off. Is there any framework for fitting together the maze of cultural diversity? One classic study by Geert Hofstede was published in 1980 and then revised in 1991. It remains the most convincing analysis.

Hofstede (1980) analysed 116 000 questionnaires administered to employees of IBM in 70 different countries and concluded that national cultures could be explained by the following four key factors:

Individualism This is the extent to which people expect to look after themselves and their family only. The opposite is collectivism which has a tight social framework and in which people expect to have a wider social responsibility to discharge because others in the group will support them. Those of a collectivist persuasion believe they owe absolute loyalty to their group.

Power distance This factor measures the extent to which the less powerful members of the society accept the unequal distribution of power. In organisations this is the degree of centralisation of authority and the exercise of autocratic leadership.

Uncertainty avoidance The future is always unknown, but some societies socialise their members to accept this and take risks, while members of other societies have been socialised to be made anxious about this and seek to compensate through the security of law, religion or technology.

Masculinity The division of roles between the sexes varies from one society to another. Where men are assertive and have dominant roles these values permeate the whole of society and the organisations that make them up, so there is an emphasis on showing off, performing, making money and achieving something visible. Where there is a larger role for women, who are more service-oriented with caring roles, the values move towards concern for the environment and the quality of life, putting the quality of relationships before the making of money.

Hofstede found some clear cultural differences between nationalities. A sample of scores on the four criteria are in Table 3.1.

These findings were then compared with the large-scale British study of organisations carried out in the 1970s (Pugh and Hickson, 1976) and some unpublished analysis of MBA students' work at INSEAD, which suggested that there were clusters of national cultures that coincided with different organisational principles when Hofstede's results were plotted against two of his dimensions: uncertainty avoidance and power distance. Hofstede argues (1991, pp. 140–6) that countries emphasising large power distance and strong uncertainty avoidance were likely to produce forms of organisation that relied heavily on hierarchy and clear orders from superiors: *a pyramid of people.*

In countries where there is small power distance and strong uncertainty avoidance there would be an implicit form of organisation that relied on rules, procedures and clear structure: *a well-oiled machine.*

The implicit model of organisation in countries with small power distance and weak uncertainty avoidance was a reliance on *ad hoc* solutions to problems as they

TABLE 3.1   Cultural differences between nations

Criterion	High	Low
Individualism	Australia	Colombia
	Canada	Pakistan
	Great Britain	Peru
	United States	Venezuela
Power distance	Mexico	Austria
	Philippines	Denmark
	Venezuela	Israel
	Yugoslavia	New Zealand
Uncertainty avoidance	Belgium	Denmark
	Greece	Hong Kong
	Japan	Singapore
	Portugal	Sweden
Masculinity	Austria	Denmark
	Italy	Norway
	Japan	Sweden
	Venezuela	Yugoslavia

arose, as many of the problems could be boiled down to human relations difficulties: *a village market*.

The picture is completed by the fourth group of countries where there is large power distance and weak uncertainty avoidance, where problems are resolved by constantly referring to the boss who is like a father to an extended family, so there is concentration of authority without structuring of activities. The implicit model of organisation here is: *the family*. Table 3.2 shows which countries are in the different segments.

So now we have a classification of cultural diversity that helps us in the maze. Table 3.2 tells us that the implicit form of organisation for Britain is a village

TABLE 3.2   Types of organisation implicit in different countries

Pyramid of people	Well-oiled machine	Village market	Family
Arab-speaking	Austria	Australia	East Africa
Argentina	Costa Rica	Britain	Hong Kong
Belgium	Finland	Canada	India
Brazil	Germany	Denmark	Indonesia
Chile	Israel	Ireland	Jamaica
Colombia	Switzerland	Netherlands	Malaysia
Ecuador		New Zealand	Philippines
France		Norway	Singapore
Greece		South Africa	West Africa
Guatemala		Sweden	
Iran		United States	
Italy			
Japan			
Korea			
Mexico			
Pakistan			
Panama			
Peru			
Portugal			
Salvador			
Spain			
Taiwan			
Thailand			
Turkey			
Uruguay			
Venezuela			
Yugoslavia			

market, for France it is a pyramid of people, for Germany it is a well-oiled machine and for Hong Kong it is a family. If we can get to grips with the organisational realities and detail in those four countries, then this can provide clues about how to cope in Denmark, Ecuador, Austria or Indonesia because they each share the implicit organisational form of one of the original four.

It is not quite as easy as that, because the clusters show only relative similarities and – inevitably – other studies do not entirely agree with Hofstede (for example, Ronen and Shenkar, 1985), but there is sufficient agreement for us to regard the four-way classification as useful, if not completely reliable, although all the research material was gathered in the 1970s: there may have been radical changes since then.

In Hofstede's second book he produces a refinement of the uncertainty avoidance dimension: 'Confucian dynamism', or long-term versus short-term orientation. Management researchers are typically from Western Europe or the United States, with all the cultural bias that such an orientation involves. Working with the Canadian Michael Bond, Hofstede used a Chinese value survey technique in a fresh study and uncovered a cultural variable that none of the original – Western – questions had reached. This was long-term orientation, and the highest scoring countries on this dimension were China, Hong Kong, Taiwan, Japan and South Korea. Singapore was placed ninth. Leaving out the special case of China, we see that the other five countries are those known as the 'Five Dragons' because of their dramatic rate of economic growth. As Hofstede says: 'The correlation between certain Confucian values and economic growth is a surprising, even a sensational, finding' *op. cit.*, p. 167).

He argues that countries in the West have derived their culture largely from the three religions of Judaism, Christianity or Islam, all of which are centred on assertion of truth that is accessible to true believers, whereas none of the religions of the East are based on the assertion that there is a truth that a human community can embrace: 'They offer various ways in which a person can improve him/herself, however these do not consist in believing but in ritual, meditation, or ways of living . . . What one does is important' (p. 171).

The 'Confucian' values found attached to this long-term orientation included perseverance, clearly maintained status differentials, thrift, and having a sense of shame. In many ways these values are valuable for business growth, as they put social value on entrepreneurial initiative, support the entrepreneur by the willing compliance of others seeking a place in the system, encourage saving and investment, and put pressure on those who do not meet obligations.

This not only provides an explanation of the phenomenal economic growth on the Pacific Rim, it also suggests that international companies should consider the location of some of their strategic activities in the East. This idea was reflected in the recent comment from another expert on international human resource issues:

Philips is establishing centres of competence . . . their centre for long-range technology development was recently moved from the United States to the Far East, where the time orientation was seen as more conducive to innovation than the 'quick fix' mentality of North America. (Evans *et al.*, 1989, p. 116)

Considering the fact that Eastern cultures might have features that Western investigators could not initially see is a relatively recent development for management researchers, if not for anthropologists. It indicates the persistence of the Western assumption – well justified until very recently – that Europe and the United States dominated the world's commerce: therefore they also were the centre for understanding universal aspects of management and business.

The other major change which studies so far have not tackled is the collapse of world communism. Hofstede's work ignores (for very obvious and inescapable reasons) all the countries of Russia and Eastern Europe, as well as the Republic of China. The globalisation of management is now more real than at any time previously, but our understanding of how different cultures alter the HRM process is still slight.

IHRM and culture

Cultural diversity is so great and its implications so difficult to fathom, that it is almost too bewildering for managers to make any sense of, but so far this chapter has suggested that variations between countries and regions are significant on a wide range of attitudes and motivation. In management we always need to be aware that these variations exist. When dealing with people from a particular culture, we probably need to swot up quickly on the main behavioural features that have to be remembered to avoid making gaffes and to understand signals. We will rarely achieve mastery, but we should achieve a modicum of sensitivity.

From a strategic perspective cultural diversity has many implications for human resource management. Paul Reynolds surveyed the organisational culture literature and identified 14 cultural dimensions that were common. Hodgetts and Luthans (1991, p. 36) have selected some of these where the culture of a society can directly affect management approaches. What follows is a further development of their suggestions, but incorporating some of the Hofstede insights:

The centralisation of decision-making In some societies (especially the pyramid of people type) all important decisions are taken by a small number of managers in senior positions. In other societies (like the village markets) decision-making is more decentralised. In a joint venture between two dissimilar societies, not only will these differences of approach need to be recognised, but management systems will have to be devised to enable members of the two cultures to understand each other and work together.

Rewards and competition The level of financial rewards between countries can be a problem, when those in country A appear to receive much more money than those in country B for doing the same job, but a more subtle difference is the way in which rewards are disbursed. In some instances there is a culture favouring individual recognition, whilst elsewhere there is a convention of group rewards. Similarly some societies encourage competition rather than co-operation, and in others the reverse applies.

Risk As Hofstede demonstrated in his first study, attitudes towards taking risks are a clear discriminator between cultures, with marked variations of uncertainty avoidance.

Formality The well-oiled machine cultures place great emphasis on clear procedures and strict rules, while pyramid of people cultures emphasise clear hierarchies and observance of rank. This contrasts strongly with the village market type societies where relationships are more informal and *ad hoc* action more likely. In Part II, Ann Moran and Evalde Mutabazi describe the difficulties of French companies combining with British and American. Many of the difficulties concerned the different views of formality in working relationships.

Organisational loyalty In Japan there tends to be a strong sense of loyalty to one's employer, while in Britain and the United States there is a growing sense of identification with one's occupational group, rather than with a particular employer. The long-standing importance of professional bodies and the declining long-term reliability of corporations as wagons to which to hitch one's star have increased this sense of loyalty to occupation rather than to employer.

Short- or long-term orientation Hofstede's identification of an Eastern predilection to the long-term is beginning to influence strategic decisions on where to locate those organisational activities for which long-term thinking is particularly appropriate.

Table 3.2 gives us a rough guide to similarities between national cultures: the pyramid of people (France), the well-oiled machine (Germany), the village market (Britain) and the family (Malaysia). This classification gives us some route markings through the cultural maze. We also have the long-term orientation of Confucian dynamism, which can guide thinking on a number of strategic issues in international management.

One Australian study of the early 1980s shows signs that there is an international managerial culture that can be discerned. James Everett and his colleagues (1982) used sophisticated social psychological techniques to survey 365 managers in the Singaporean subsidiaries of 34 American, British and Japanese multinational companies; 33 of the respondents were American, 30 British, 109 Japanese and 193 Singaporean. The researchers were able to conclude that there was a shared managerial culture and:

> positive attributes are those which emphasize harmonious interpersonal relationships based on a give and take philosophy. This is in contrast to the more bombastic swash-buckling features that one might expect to be favoured by persons more entrepreneurial in outlook. (p. 161)

There are several reservations about this study. It was in multinational companies only, it involved only four different nationalities and all in one location. It also used a very specific research technique (semantic responses on 18 adjectival pairs) which might be criticised for its narrow focus. Despite the reservations, the researchers are quite clear that there was a high degree of correlation between the nationalities, which supports the idea that, for some people at least, an embryonic international managerial culture exists.

References

Barham, K. and Rassam, C. (1989), *Shaping the Corporate Future*, Unwin Hyman, London.

Barratt, A. (1989), 'Doing business in a different culture', *Journal of European Industrial Training*, vol. 13, no. 4, pp. 28–31.

Bournois, F. (1991), *La Gestion des cadres en Europe*, Eyrolles, Paris.

Bournois, F. and Poirson, P. (1989), *Gérer et dynamiser ses collaborateurs*, Eyrolles, Paris.

Crozier, M. and Friedberg, E. (1977), *L'Acteur et le systeme*, Editions du Seuil, Paris.

Crystal, D. (1987), *The Cambridge Encyclopaedia of Language*, Cambridge University Press, Cambridge.

Deal, T. E. and Kennedy, A. A. (1982), *Corporate Cultures: The rites and rituals of corporate life*, Addison-Wesley, Reading, Mass.

d'Iribarne, P. (1985), 'La gestion française', *Revue Française de gestion*, January–February, pp. 5–13.

Evans, P., Doz, Y. and Laurent, A. (eds) (1989), *Human Resource Management in International Firms*, Macmillan, London.

Everett, J. E., Stening, B. W. and Longton, P. A. (1982), 'Some evidence for an international managerial culture', *Journal of Management Studies*, vol. 19, no. 2, pp. 153–62.

Handy, C. B. (1985), *Understanding Organizations*, Penguin, Harmondsworth.

Hodgetts, R. M. and Luthans, F. (1991), *International Management*, McGraw-Hill, New York.

Hofstede, G. (1980), *Culture's Consequences: International differences in work-related values*, Sage Publications, Beverly Hills, Calif.

Hofstede, G. (1991), *Cultures and Organizations: Software of the mind*, McGraw-Hill, London.

Holden, N. J. (1992), 'Management language and Euro-communications: 1992 and beyond', in Berry, M. (ed.) *Cross-Cultural Communication in Europe*, proceedings of Conference on Cross-Cultural Communication, Helsinki, Institute for European Studies, Turku.

Lalanne, H. (1990), 'The roles of accounting and management information systems in different management styles and different national contexts', paper presented to the European Accounting Association Congress, Budapest, April.

Lawrence, P. (1991), *Management in the Netherlands*, Clarendon Press, Oxford.

Mangham, I. L. and Overington, M. A. (1987), *Organizations as Theatre*, John Wiley, Chichester.

Mole, J. (1990), *Mind Your Manners: Culture and class in the single European market*, The Industrial Society, London.

Olins, W. (1989), *Corporate Identity*, Thames and Hudson, London.

Pezeschkupur, C. (1978) 'Challenges to management in the Arab world', *Business Horizons*, August, pp. 48–52.

Poirson, P. (1989), 'Personnel policies and the management of men' (translated by Thierry Devisse), Ecole Supérieure de Lyon, France.

Pugh, D. S. and Hickson, D. J. (1976), *Organisational Structure in its Context*, Saxon House, Farnborough.

Reynolds, P. A. (1986), 'Organisational culture as related to industry, position and performance', *Journal of Management Studies*, vol. 23, no. 3, May, pp. 333–45.

Ronen, S. and Shenkar, O. (1985), 'Clustering countries on attitudinal dimensions: a review and synthesis', *Academy of Management Review*, vol. 10, no. 3, pp. 435–54.

Schein, E. H. (1985), *Organizational Culture and Leadership*, Jossey-Bass, San Francisco.

Standish, P. and Scheid, J-C. (1986), 'Accounting standardisation in France and international accounting exchanges', paper presented at the DHS-ICAEW Accounting Research Symposium, London Business School.

Wiener, M. (1985), *English Culture and the Decline of the Industrial Spirit*, Cambridge University Press, Cambridge.

van Wolferen, K. (1989), *The Enigma of Japanese Power*, Macmillan, London.

CHAPTER 4

Compensation: fixing pay and expenses

The word 'compensation' in the title of this chapter is used reluctantly and only to maintain the linking device of seven Cs. We are talking about pay and expenses, particularly for those who travel to, and perhaps reside in, countries other than their own – the cosmopolitans of Chapter 2.

Cosmopolitans are expensive. They are likely to be highly-skilled and specialised, which means that they are going to be relatively well paid anyway, but they expect a level of pay and benefits during their time abroad that transcends by a large margin what they would receive by staying put. This involves a package of special features and allowances, each of which costs money. This has to be set against a background of fluctuating currency values, problems of hyperinflation in some countries, shifting political circumstances and social conditions. If the US dollar weakens in relation to the French franc, the cost of employing US citizens in France goes up. If the cost of living and standard of living in Switzerland are persistently higher in Switzerland than in Britain, the cost of relocating a British employee to Switzerland is higher than a move in the opposite direction.

Internal relocations have an infinite number of implications that add to the complexity and the cost of compensation. Is the home-country house to be sold or rented? How will this be managed during the absence overseas? What are the tax implications of the move that might involve further compensation and assistance? What about education for school-age children, return trips on leave, removal expenses and housing costs? The most expensive aspect of all may well be the compensation of a spouse who is needing to interrupt or abandon a career, possibly without any chance of independent employment in the new relocation.

We will consider first the arrangements for the expatriate employee, moving home for a period of two years or more, and then we will turn to the other categories of cosmopolitan.

The expatriate

Salary

The expatriate will receive a basic salary while away, with various additional allowances. The first consideration is the salary to which the expatriate will return. That may seem out of sequence, but it is usually the first question asked: it provides the guarantee of the right re-entry point and maintains the expatriate's position in relation to pension provision and so forth. It may be that the home country employment contract is suspended, but there will be a clear undertaking about the mode and level of re-entry into the pay structure on return.

The level of salary to be paid will vary according to company practice and the direction of the move. If the expatriate is moving from a Western country to a developing country, the basic level may be that of the home country, as that should provide an acceptable level of material resource while away, providing that suitable allowances are paid. If the expatriate is moving to a country with a higher standard of living, it may be more acceptable for the salary to be fixed at the appropriate point in the host country pay structure. This would provide the most logical arrangement in relation to colleagues during the period of expatriation, but logic and acceptability do not always combine. Locating the expatriate in the host country pay structure may upset the pattern of differentials.

It certainly seems that the expatriate seldom earns less while away, no matter how strong the argument:

> It is easy enough to transfer a manager from a lower earnings to a higher earnings country – from the UK to West Germany, for example. The manager receives a substantial salary increase in line with the pay of local national colleagues, and everyone is happy. Problems arise in transferring a manager from West Germany to the UK however: few people, whatever their nationality and whatever the circumstances, are willing to take a drop in salary! In theory several major companies do move salaries downwards to reflect local levels but in practice various 'cushions' are often built in to compensate. (Pinder, 1990, p. 198)

Allowances

Allowances are those additional payments that bridge the gap between reasonable expenditure at home and reasonable expenditure abroad. A pragmatic approach to getting the overall income level right has been described by Reynolds (1986) as the 'balance sheet method'. This uses the earlier concept of 'keeping the expatriate whole' (Teague, 1972). Relativity with home country colleagues is maintained as the guiding principle, with the addition of an incentive to take the overseas posting and a set of compensations for the costs of international service:

the balance sheet approach to international compensation is a system designed to equalize the purchasing power of employees at comparable position levels living overseas and in the home country, and to provide incentives to offset qualitative differences between assignment locations. (Dowling and Schuler, 1990, p. 118)

The method is to assume that pay when home-based is directed in four areas: savings, goods and services, housing, tax and similar deductions. The expatriate could reasonably expect the employer to compensate for increases to the last three, to meet the costs of shipping and storage, and to provide some incentive for the move. Figure 4.1 illustrates the approach. A similar build-up of a package prepared by a British consultancy is shown in Figure 4.2.

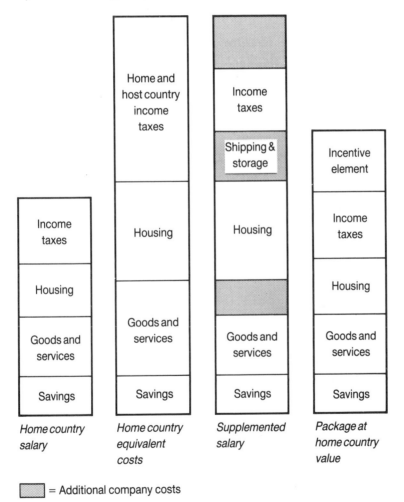

Figure 4.1   The balance sheet approach to salary setting

(Figures for a person earning £45,000, married with two children, moving from the UK to Canada)

Index for Canada: UK = 100. Canada = 1.108
Exchange rate (March 1992): UK £1.00 = C$ 2.0617

UK salary   £45,000
Net income   £32,295
Spendable income   £20,918
Housing and savings   £11,377

Local spending component = UK spendable income × Index/
                               100 × exchange rate

                            = 20,918 × 1.108 × 2,0617

               Total = **C$ 47,784**

Home component

Housing and savings	£11,377
Expatriate incentive	£ 6,750
Location allowance	£ 0
Class 1 contributions (for first year)	£ 1,336
Total	**£19,463** (C$ 40,127)

Local spending component + home component   C$ 87,911

Additional amount to cover Canadian income tax   C$ 89,929

Total gross salary   C$177,840
(Not including benefits in kind)

Additional costs to the company

Company car	C$ 6,078
Utilities	C$ 2,508
Local education (one child)	C$ 8,700
Home education (one child)	C$16,298
Club	C$ 1,404
Medical insurance	C$ 2,480
Furniture storage	C$ 1,100
Air fares	C$ 6,065
Accommodation	C$29,000
Total	**C$73,633**

Figure 4.2 Senior executive salary calculation (Source: Employment Conditions Abroad Ltd)

Notes

1 The expatriate allowance is 15 per cent of notional UK salary.
2 The location allowance is specific to each country depending on an assessment of the inconvenience of the new location. The range is from 0 to 30 per cent. For Canada it is 0 per cent.
3 The UK national insurance contributions are assumed to be Class 1, contracted out. UK social security is payable for the first 52 weeks of employment in Canada, in addition to Canadian contributions.
4 It is assumed that free accommodation will be provided separately by the employer and that the posting is to Montreal.

Figure 4.2   Continued

The decision on what the level of supplementation should be can be contentious. It is therefore important to make that feature, as well as the income tax calculations, as uncontroversial and non-negotiable as possible. The best method is either to use the services of specialist consultants or official cost of living data to provide a precise index. It is important to recognise, however, that costs can vary sharply and much more quickly than any index number can register. It can be appropriate for the goods and services supplementation to vary monthly or quarterly rather than annually, as well as taking immediate account of some major incident, such as a revaluation of the local currency.

Hardship allowance is often paid to expatriates on the basis of real or assumed hardship in the host country. British employers are reasonably generous to their own nationals having to endure inconveniences such as a hot and humid climate, but are less likely to concede that the British climate may present hardship to those being expatriated from hot and humid climates to Britain, despite the British climate being the major source of grumbles by Britons desperate to escape it.

Hardship allowances of 5 per cent or zero are common for countries where the living conditions are similar or more pleasant, such as Australasia, North America and most parts of Western Europe. For other locations the hardship payment may rise to 30 per cent or even higher; the reference point being the basic salary. Among the features that are used to justify hardship allowances are:

- Unfamiliar and uncomfortable climate.
- Health hazards, such as the prevalence of disease, lack of sanitation, poor medical and hospital facilities, epidemics and poor health control facilities.
- Geographical isolation 'up country', particularly when communication, transport and similar facilities may be limited.
- General social and political conditions that are hazardous, such as civil war, street violence, risk of burglary, kidnap or mugging.
- Food shortage.
- Lack of cultural, recreational and social facilities.

The additional cost of housing can be considerable and the aim of the employer is to ensure that the cost of maintaining the home country *pied-à-terre* is neutral for the expatriate. One approach is to meet all the costs of overseas housing and leaving the employee to sell or rent the home country house as is preferred, with the employer playing no part. Other companies offer assistance with sale or rental.

It is unusual for housing to be purchased overseas by expatriates, so they rent. This usually comes in two stages. First there will be a period in temporary accommodation for a few weeks or months, while a more permanent home is being sought. Then the long-term accommodation is occupied and the employee receives an allowance to cover rental and a contribution towards the cost of running expenses, such as electricity and water.

All but the most munificent of companies place a ceiling on the level of rental that they are prepared to meet. The objective will be to meet the cost of accommodation that is appropriate to the family's personal needs and to the professional needs and expectations of the expatriate. In some situations there can be disagreements about what is reasonable. The biggest problem can be children's education. In a compact, well-developed location like Singapore an expatriate family would have little difficulty in locating excellent housing within easy reach of international schools. In other places it can be much more difficult, with a limited number of suitable houses in the vicinity and a large number of expatriates competing with each other for them.

An increasing number of companies pay the expenses of a pre-assignment visit of approximately one week, during which the prospective expatriate and spouse can find a house to live in. In some instances the pre-assignment visit is shorter with the sole purpose of general familiarisation with the territory and making some preliminary social contacts. House-hunting then takes place in the early weeks of the assignment. In either case the expenses connected with the house-hunting would be paid by the employer.

Expatriates with children will obviously be especially concerned about education allowances. Young children usually accompany their parents and attend a local school and will probably benefit considerably from the experience of being in a local state school, mixing with indigenous children. Alternatively they may attend a private school, where teaching may be in the home country language. As children get older, their parents are more concerned that they should follow the home country's curriculum and be prepared for qualifying examinations. Now the costs increase and are typically met by the employer, who will pay tuition fees and associated essential expenses such as books. It is less likely that the employer will meet the cost of additional items, such as violin lessons.

Older children usually have the option of continuing at a local school or moving to boarding school in their home country, so that they become gradually better prepared for the move into higher education or professional training. This may be a difficult decision for the parents to make, but most now opt for the boarding school, with the employer meeting the costs of tuition, boarding and books, as well as two or three return economy class air fares. One of the more quaint aspects of international air travel is to observe the scrupulous separation of parents from children, with the parents – only – enjoying the benefits of first or business class.

When children move into higher education, employer support usually ceases, apart from the return air fares, as the children are now adult and cost their parents no more and no less than any other children.

A further allowance is for home leave and travel. Most companies offer return air fares home for the family at least once a year, although the expatriate employee may have to visit more often for business reasons. It is not common for the costs of accommodation and subsistence during home visits to be met by the employer. It may be possible for the home leave travel allowance to be used not for the expatriate family to visit home, but for relatives or friends to visit them. There may also be an allowance for vacation travel within the host country region, but this is usually instead of, rather than additional to, the home leave. Where the overseas assignment is to a particularly grim or unfamiliar location, there may be short periods of paid 'R & R' for the expatriate family, rest and relaxation for a few days in a nearby city or resort that provides something more congenial than the comforts of home.

Income tax and Social Security

The tax and national insurance situation of the expatriate can be complicated – as well as expensive. If a UK employee remains out of the country for at least a year, and is paid abroad, there should be no tax liability, but there will be a liability to local tax at the place of assignment, and this can vary enormously. In Belgium, for example, the maximum marginal rate is 70 per cent, reached at a salary level of approximately £70,000. In Italy it is 62 per cent, reached at £280,000, and in Hong Kong it is 16 per cent reached at £21,000. The employer will have to neutralise these variations either by reimbursing the individual who would otherwise lose out, or by paying a net salary and meeting whatever tax obligations arise. Armstrong and Murlis (1991) describe a policy of tax equalisation:

> The tax equalization system offers a fairer global policy in that it reimburses tax excesses to those in high tax areas but makes a deduction from the total remuneration of those in low or zero-rated countries. Thus, all staff are maintained on a tax standard which reflects that of the home country. (p. 389)

The cost to the employer can be startling:

> in high tax countries the greatest challenge is tax effective compensation and reduction/avoidance of the pyramid effect of tax equalization. A senior executive earning $100,000 in Belgium, for example, could cost a company close to $1.0 million in taxes over a 5–7 year period. (Dowling and Schuler, 1990, p. 122)

The international manager

Most of the complexity in international payment arrangements refers to expatriates. The constantly travelling international manager described in Chapter 2 is normally a part of the home country salary and reward structure, with a heavy additional cost in expenses. There is, however, a potential for international managers to be paid on an international basis.

Everything so far in this chapter has assumed that the employee has a parent country, which remains the point of return and the point of reference. The acceptability and expense of salary and benefits all relate to whatever the home country is. As companies become more genuinely international, there may be no clear home country and international managers become truly cosmopolitan. That argues for a system of international base pay for this elite group, with them all on a common basis and all paid in a major reserve currency such as the Swiss franc or the Deutschmark. The country of assignment then becomes an irrelevance.

This superficially attractive idea has enormous problems attached to it, as individuals have to have nationality and citizenship, for such boring but unavoidable matters as income tax, pension entitlement, health care provision and so on. The gradual harmonisation of social security provision within Europe makes the vision more attainable, but it is still a long way off.

The engineer and the occasional parachutist

Those who travel abroad infrequently and for short spells are not likely to have any alteration in their normal salary arrangements, but there have to be arrangements about expenses and allowances that are acceptable, without getting out of control. The issue of control is important not only to monitor company expenditure, but also to ensure compliance with the income tax rules of the home country. If an occasional parachutist attends an important business meeting in Florida, it is reasonable that all expenses be met by the employer. If the meeting is followed by a week's holiday touring the Everglades, that expenditure should not be borne by the company. That is a simple example: it gets more complicated when there are accompanying spouses on business trips. Can their expenses be claimed if their role is to help with entertaining? Probably not. If they provide other types of assistance, such as secretarial or translation, then their expenses probably can be claimed.

Administrative control

The main means of administrative control is a policy framework to give general guidelines. This will probably be the responsibility of the personnel function to devise and update, although line executives will authorise and administer claims from members of their teams. The policy will specify, for instance, the appropriate class of air travel. It will not deal with other questions, such as why the only conferences that Bloggs ever needs to attend are always in Hawaii or Bermuda, and never in Frankfurt or Bratislava. The policy will usually contain the following features:

A designated travel organiser   In very large companies there will be a travel section to make arrangements such as booking flights and hotels. In others the work is done by a secretary in conjunction with a travel agent, who provides special terms. This single channel arrangement means that the work is undertaken, in compliance with the policy framework, by those with specialist expertise and at favourable terms.

Authorisation   Travel will need prior authorisation by a budget holder or a person with similar recognised authority. The main questions are:

> What is the journey for?
> Where is it to?
> How long will it take?
> Is there a cheaper, equally efficient alternative?
> Is the right person going?
> What will it cost?
> Who is paying for it?
> Is the cost agreed?

Notice   Wherever possible, travel organisers ask for plenty of notice. This is not only to give them adequate time to make the arrangements and to have a range of options between which to choose, it is also to provide the best deal by taking advantage of the various discounts available to those who book in advance.

Class of travel   On long-haul flights it is usual for personnel to travel in business class, but the practice varies on shorter journeys so that economy class will usually be booked for journeys of two to three hours or less. In companies where only employees of a certain specified rank travel business class and others travel economy, a group will all travel in the class of person with the highest status. If someone entitled to a business class ticket wants to trade it for two economy tickets to allow a wife or husband to travel as well, this is not often allowed within the policy rules if the visit is a short one. If the period abroad is to be longer – say more than eight weeks – then trading one business class for two economy is more likely.

Cash or credit cards   Although the airline ticket will be paid by the company before departure, and possibly hotel room charges as well, travellers incur considerable expenditure while away. The normal travellers' arrangements of cash and travellers' cheques are one way of dealing with these charges, but of growing popularity is the company credit card, issued to the employee on departure and recovered on return. This avoids the problems of carrying large amounts of cash or cheques and provides a convenient way of authorising the actual items of expenditure *post hoc*.

Car hire   When an employee is going to use a hired car while abroad, there will obviously need to be the appropriate checks on the status of the licence, the possible need for an international licence, adequate insurance and so forth. If the arrangement can be made in advance the cost will probably be less than if booked on the spot.

Insurance   With the possible addition of car insurance, what is required is insurance cover similar to that taken out by most holiday-makers: insurance against sickness and related expenses, including the possibility of emergency travel home, and insurance of baggage and personal belongings.

Managerial discretion

The suggestions about the elements of the policy framework may seem trivial, yet many an occasional parachutist will know that of such things are office rows made. The length of journey that justifies business class rather than economy needs to be precise, known and adhered to. The length of time you have to be away before you can convert your one business class ticket into two economy tickets again needs to be clear and relatively inflexible.

There will always, however, be cases at the margin requiring discretion of two types. First, there is the discretion of the individual engineer or occasional parachutist confronted with an unexpected dilemma. The last flight has been cancelled: do you go by a longer route or stay overnight in the airport hotel and take the first flight out in the morning? The customer with whom you had a firm date for your meeting will not be back from Toronto for three more days: do you wait or come back and fix another date later? These are not situations for which you can produce rules, so you rely on the judgement of the person on the spot, even if it costs you an extra £500.

Second, there is the discretion of the all-powerful people who authorise the expense claims. Was it necessary for Blenkinsop to hire a Porsche? Surely a Volkswagen would have been adequate? It is surprising how anxious people become about the expense claims they submit, and surprising how belligerent they become when they hear about Blenkinsop.

References

Armstrong, M. and Murlis, H. (1991), *Reward Management*, 2nd edition, Kogan Page/IPM, London.

Dowling, P. J. and Schuler, R. S. (1990), *International Dimensions of Human Resource Management*, PWS-Kent, Boston, Mass.

Pinder, M. (1990), *Personnel Management for the Single European Market*, Pitman, London.

Reynolds, C. (1986), 'Compensation of overseas personnel', in Famularo, J. J. (ed.), *Handbook of Human Resources Administration*, 2nd edition, McGraw-Hill, New York.

Teague, B. W. (1972), *Compensating Key Personnel Overseas*, The Conference Board, New York.

CHAPTER 5

Communication through individual behaviour and organisational systems

Any business survives by effectiveness in communication. Twenty years ago management courses were almost entirely taken up with features of the communication process and any management problem was all too often construed as a problem of communication. Although management education has become much more diverse, effective communication remains a pre-eminent requirement for success. This means care with organisational structure, for what is an organisation chart except a statement about responsibilities, status, channels of communication and job titles? It requires an appreciation of organisational culture, an effective set of systems, procedures and drills and also personal competence in members of the organisation, especially managers.

The challenges of communication multiply when a business is operating internationally, but the richness and fascination of the management job multiply also.

The process of communicating

A hackneyed, but well-established, method of understanding communication is the analogy with telecommunications, comparing the human process with the electronic. Figure 5.1 shows how communication begins with some abstract idea or thought in the mind of the person seeking to convey information. The first step is for the central nervous system of that person to translate the abstractions through the vocal organs into speech or some form of written or other visual message. The sounds, words or images are then transmitted by the sender to be received by the ears or eyes of the receiver and conveyed as nervous impulses to the brain. The message is unscrambled in the central nervous system of the receiver, which then instructs the listener to understand; the final stage comes when there is registration and the receiver understands.

Through these various stages of translation from the mind of one to the mind of the other there are a number of points at which error is possible, even likely. It is almost impossible to know whether the abstract idea in the mind of one person has been transferred accurately to the mind of the other. One essential element in the whole process is feedback. This completes the circuit so that there is some indication

Noise

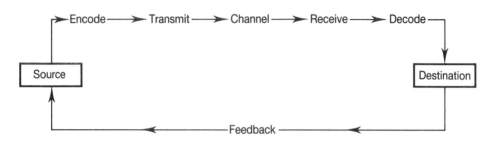

Figure 5.1   The telecommunications analogy

from the listener of having received and understood, the feedback response giving some indication to the transmitter of the quality of the message that has been received.

In communicating across national and cultural boundaries, feedback is especially important both to check and develop understanding between the communicators. Take the example of the British marketing director talking to the Danish marketing manager of a Scandinavian subsidiary. The Briton opens with:

> 'I think it would be a good idea to see what scope we would have for marketing this line to older people.'

The Dane could develop feedback in a variety of ways. One would be for clarification:

> 'What do you mean by "older people"?'

Another response would be to provide information that the sender of the original message did not have:

> 'Yes, but remember that our retirement age is different from yours. We retire at 67.'

A further possibility is to develop the idea:

> 'If we do that, we could find that this age group have uses for the product that are different from our existing customers, and it is a big market. The number of retired people is increasing rapidly throughout Scandinavia.'

There are other responses, such as disagreement, offering alternatives, or redefining the message. All develop the nature and depth of the exchange and are important across national boundaries because of the limited understanding each will have of the other's situation, to say nothing of the cultural and linguistic uncertainties that feedback can help clear up.

The foregoing example assumes that feedback will be provided related directly to the content of the message, but the feedback may be provided for a different purpose. Mead (1990, p. 47) provides the illustration of hotel managers in South East Asia, who will say 'yes' to a question such as 'Can the refrigerator in my room be repaired today?' even if it cannot:

His cultural priorities tell him to give a pleasing answer and to satisfy immediate needs; the long-term problem can be resolved at a later date or may disappear. The guest may decide that he doesn't need to use the refrigerator; or will change his travel plans and move out that day; or can be accommodated in another room.

Remembering Hofstede's analysis of cultural variations, described in Chapter 3, we must realise that people from cultures with a wide power distance are not likely to provide feedback which is other than straightforward assent. They are inhibited by the feeling that their questions will indicate criticism.

Feedback is not only on-the-spot, one-to-one in interpersonal exchanges; it is also a feature of formal communication arrangements. Brandt and Hulbert (1976) studied organisational feedback in a number of multinational companies that had their headquarters in Europe, Japan and the United States. They found that the American organisations had many more feedback reports and meetings between headquarters and subsidiaries than their European or Japanese counterparts. In contrast, Pascale (1978) found that Japanese managers in Japan used face-to-face contacts more than American managers as well as more upwards and lateral communication. Japanese managers in America used communication in the same way as Americans.

A further element in the communication process is that of 'noise'. This is used as a generic term to describe anything which interferes in the transmission process: inaudibility, inattention, physical noise and so forth. Noise impairs the quality of both transmission and feedback.

In international dealings, noise is most commonly found in the problem of an unfamiliar accent, or the use of idioms that do not translate readily.

Barriers to communication

It is the listener or reader who determines how well a message is understood. What we hear, see or understand is largely shaped by our own experience and background. Instead of hearing what people tell us, we hear what our minds tell us they have said – the two may be different. There are various ways in which expectation determines communication content and all can impair the accuracy of message transmission.

The frame of reference and the power of the group

Few of us change our opinions alone. We are influenced by the opinions developed within the group with which we identify: our reference group. If a particular group hold certain values in common, individual members of that group will not readily modify their values unless and until there is a value shift through the group as a whole. This is perhaps most apparent in the relative intractability of opinions relating to political party allegiance. There are certain clearly identifiable social class groupings who tend to affiliate to particular political parties and a change in that affiliation by an individual is rare and difficult.

Managers frequently direct to an individual a message, a request or instruction which would elicit a more positive response if it were mediated through a representative of the group of employees rather than being directed at an individual.

Whenever a matter is being discussed the people among whom it is being considered will view it from their particular personal frame of reference reflecting the interests of the group with which they identify. Where the frames of reference of transmitter and receiver differ widely, there may be substantial difficulties in accurate transmission of messages and even greater difficulties in ensuring the response of the receiver is that which the transmitter intended.

The sharpest example of contrasted frames of reference is when international expansion is by the route of acquisition. Employees in the acquired company will feel a greater sense of community with each other than with those who have acquired them. They will see corporate affairs from their own standpoint and will tend to be cautious in their behaviour and suspicious in their interpretation of what they hear from their new owners. Even when that initial suspicion begins to unwind, there are still difficulties. For example:

> *Rivalry*   Despite the Herculean attempts to forge a common identity, companies in different countries will take pride in their own accomplishments and disparage (informally, of course) the accomplishments of other nationality groups. As long as this stimulates healthy competition, rivalry can benefit the company, but it quickly becomes destructive, like the situation of the car assembly plant in Britain which constantly rejected and returned gear boxes made by the same company in Germany.
>
> *Distorted perceptions*   National boundaries produce distorted ideas about the 'other' people, whose achievements are underestimated and undervalued in comparison with the achievements of your own group, which may be overestimated.
>
> *Resource allocation*   Allocation of resources between competing interests is always problematical, but becomes even more difficult in international comparisons. A company in a vulnerable situation may go as far as to provide disinformation about a rival in order to win additional resources.

The stereotype

An extreme form of letting expectation determine communication content is stereotyping, where we expect a particular type of statement or particular type of attitude from a stereotype of a person. It is for instance quite common for the English to expect certain types of behaviour and intention from the Irish ('Never stop talking and always ready for a fight'). Equally, there is a stereotype expectation about the Scots, that they will be mean or at least extremely careful with money. They continue: Germans are thorough and unimaginative, the French are romantic and obsessed with status, the Chinese all look the same, Americans are loud and brash, the English are reserved and aloof, Arabs are fatalists, Spaniards are haughty . . .

Our chapter on culture was partly an account of national stereotypes and exemplifies the problem: we need to understand general differences in behaviour and attitude that are rooted in cultural diversity – otherwise we will be misunderstood in what we say and will misinterpret what we hear – but we must avoid the trap of assuming that all nationals conform precisely to a single model. Not all the Irish are loquacious and not all the Scots are mean – really they aren't!

The effect of stereotyping on communication is that if you meet someone for whom you have a stereotype, you will begin hearing what the person says in the light of the stereotype that you hold. It will be some time before your listening, understanding and evaluation will adjust to the actual exchanges in which you are involved, in contrast to what you expected.

In all types of human encounter stereotyping is a basic method of making sense. When stopping your car to ask directions from a passer-by, you do not ask someone at random, you choose a likely prospect on the basis of a snap appraisal. You will probably avoid people who are too young or too old, as well as passing by those who look wild, frail, drunk, impatient or who are locked in a passionate embrace. You will look for someone who seems friendly, relaxed, intelligent, approachable and not touting for business.

In dealing with foreigners, some well-informed stereotyping can avoid initial offence and misunderstanding, but it must give way to more sensitive behaviour as the other person is evaluated and better understood.

Cognitive dissonance

Another area of difficulty which has been explored so extensively by Festinger (1957) and others is the extent to which people will cope successfully with information inputs that they find irreconcilable with what they already know. If someone receives information which is consistent with what they already believe, they are likely to understand it, believe it, remember it and take action upon it. If, however, they receive information which is inconsistent with their established beliefs, then they will have genuine difficulty in understanding, remembering and taking action.

A Portuguese manager of a small company in Bombay received an instruction from his head office about closing one of his plants, so he called in the manager of the plant and showed him the letter. He was baffled when the plant manager begged him to destroy the letter. The Portuguese saw this as a pointless symbolic act; the Indian saw it as a way of making the instruction void. A young Swiss woman in London was equally baffled when paying for an item in a store by using a cheque, she was told to cross the cheque. Having tried folding it in half, she required great persuasion to draw two straight lines across the face of it. This seemed to her not only strange, but was directly counter to her previous experience and beliefs.

Cognitive dissonance does more than lead to misunderstanding; it can also distort or inhibit action. Not only do recipients of information find it difficult to understand, remember and take action, they will also grapple with the dissonance that the problematical new information presents. One of the ways in which they do this is to distort the message so that what they actually hear is what they expect to hear and can easily understand rather than the difficult, challenging information that is being put to them. A further twist is that people with a cognitive dissonance block are not likely to disagree with you, as they have convinced themselves that their understanding is correct. They say 'yes' to what they believe you to mean, but it will still be 'no' to what you really mean.

A British manager of a factory making miners' lamps in Madras was dismayed to see the workmen sitting cross-legged on the floor, rather than standing at a workbench like his compatriots in Lancashire. He explained that it was not good that the Indian workmen had to sit on the floor, so he would arrange for them to be supplied with workbenches. This was greeted with broad smiles and enthusiastic nodding of heads. When the benches arrived, the manager went to see how things had improved and found that the workmen were now sitting cross-legged on the benches.

The halo or horns effect

A slightly different aspect of expectation determining communication content is the halo or horns effect, which causes the reaction of receivers of information to move to extremes of either acceptance or rejection. When we are listening to somebody in whom we have confidence and who has earned our trust, we may be predisposed to agree with what they say because we have placed an imaginary halo around their head. Because of our experience of their trustworthiness and reliability we expect that what they say will be trustworthy and reliable. On the other hand if we have learned to distrust someone, then what we hear them say will be either ignored or treated with considerable caution.

Perhaps the most common example of this is the reaction that people have to political leaders. Margaret Thatcher, Fidel Castro, Jean-Marie le Pen and Nelson Mandela are very different people, yet have in common the ability to excite extremes of popular support or disapproval. In commercial organisations, managers in one country may develop a high degree of rapport with a particular member of the head office team from another country, which is not a function of that person's hierarchical situation. That will be the most appropriate person to go to see them with bad news, or with a difficult message.

Semantics and jargon

One difficulty about transferring ideas from one person to another is that ideas cannot be directly transferred because meaning cannot be directly transferred. Communicators have to rely on words or symbols as the vehicle to convey their meaning, but unfortunately the same symbols may suggest different meanings to different people. The meanings are in the hearers rather than the speakers and certainly not in the words themselves. A simple example of this is 'quite ill' which could have a variety of weightings according to how it was heard and the circumstances in which the comment was made.

The particular nuance of a word or phrase may be untranslatable from one language to another. 'Glasnost' and 'perestroika' are two Russian words that are universally understood outside the Russian-speaking peoples, because of the intensive coverage of the extraordinary political events at the time the words were first heard, but never translated. The Germans still do not bother coining a word to translate 'manager' and the French increasingly use the word because they have no direct equivalent. In their chapter on Shell, Cynthia Haddock and Basil South describe the Shell practice of 'flocking', which is a wonderfully precise term to express the nature and purpose of the gatherings that take place. French and German people have great difficulty in understanding the nuances of the term, because neither language has an equivalent that distinguishes between, for example, flocking and herding.

We can also fall into the trap of misunderstanding a word which is not what it sounds as if it should be. An example which causes many problems on bedroom taps is the Italian 'caldo', which means 'hot'. Here are a few French words that do not mean what one might think:

achever	*means*	to finish
eventuel	*means*	possible
lard	*means*	bacon
partition	*means*	musical score
prune	*means*	plum
truculent	*means*	realistic
veste	*means*	jacket

The problem of jargon is where a word or a phrase has a specialised meaning that is immediately understandable by the cognoscenti, but meaningless or misleading to those who do not share the specialised knowledge. The Maslovian hierarchy of human needs is by now quite well known in management circles. On one occasion a lecturer was describing the ideas that were implicit in this notion and was surprised some months later in an examination script to see that one of the students had heard not 'hierarchy' but 'high Iraqui'. The unfamiliarity of the word 'hierarchy' had been completely misinterpreted by that particular receiver, who had imposed her own meaning on what she heard because of the need to make sense of what it was that she received. Professor Eugene McKinna relates how he was lecturing on the same subject of motivation, describing job enlargement and job enrichment. After the lecture a puzzled student asked him, 'What exactly was the job in Richmond?'

The value of jargon in international management is that the jargon quickly becomes universally understood by the experts, no matter what their nationality. Botany, medicine and chemistry are fields where a specialist can probably understand a technical paper no matter what the language may be. Management is moving in that direction, with JIT, QWL, TQM and the rest.

Non-verbal communication

Life would be simple if all our communication were verbal: it would also be very dull. Managing across cultural boundaries requires an appreciation of how we communicate non-verbally; first, as we try to convey an impression that is not the truth, second, as we reveal an attitude we would rather conceal. Sigmund Freud made the comment in 1905: 'No mortal can keep a secret. If his lips are silent, he chatters with his finger tips. Betrayal oozes out of him at every pore.'

In describing the way in which people express themselves, Goffman (1972) draws a distinction between the expression that people give and the expression that they give off. The first involves direct attempts to communicate and to inform. The expression that the individual gives off is more involuntary and covers a range of actions and signs by which people give clues to their real feelings about the situation as they attempt to sustain the performance they are presenting. We appear generally to be more able to learn how to interpret the involuntary impression given off by those with whom we are conferring than we are able to manipulate and control the expressions we ourselves give off. Although the human in communication is a dissembler, there are two types of such dissembling. To some extent we express an artificial self to others quite deliberately and we are aware of the truth at the same time as we express the image. There is also, however, an extent to which we delude ourselves about the reality. In presenting a performance, we come to believe that the performance is the reality.

While communication is taking place there are various other things going on as well as speech. We can usually see the person with whom we are interacting and this itself adds a major dimension. When people are conferring in a language with which they are not completely familiar, non-verbal behaviour becomes even more important as it is used as a substitute for words. A remarkably high level of communication can be achieved between two people who have no common ground in spoken language. An interesting exercise is to watch people speaking on television with the sound off and see how much of the conversation can be understood. If you were able to interact, wordlessly, with the people on the television screen, you would greatly increase your understanding by looking puzzled, seeking confirmation, repeating a gesture with a different emphasis, showing understanding and so forth.

Bodily contact

It is relatively uncommon for people to communicate via bodily contact in working situations in Britain, Scandinavia, North America and Germany. Such communication is much more common in Mediterranean and African countries, where the embrace is more familiar and where there is more widespread use of kissing on both cheeks at welcome and parting.

In Britain bodily contact as communication is limited almost exclusively to the handshake. There is a mysterious folklore attached to the handshake which decrees that somebody shaking hands with a palm that is dry and a grip which is firm indicates a strong and reliable personality, whilst a handshake that is relatively limp and moist indicates a personality of low quality which is generally not to be trusted. Despite the ease with which a handshake can be manipulated in the direction of firm dryness, the folklore continues but is almost unknown to people of other cultures.

In South East Asia a slight bow is more common, accompanied by the 'wai' of placing the palms of the hands together in front of the face. The positioning of the hands in relation to the face and the accompanying lowering of the eyes have a series of subtle gradations according to the relative status of those greeting each other. Koreans and Japanese bow deeply to each other in greeting, with the depth of the bow indicating the degree of respect. Physical contact is almost taboo.

Proximity and critical space

We take up a position in relation to the other person which will enable us to feel comfortable. This of course only applies when the two or more parties to an encounter have freedom of control over their relative positioning, and the lack of such freedom is one of the many contributors to the feeling of uncertainty and discomfort which is experienced, for instance, by candidates in selection interviews.

We tend to get slightly closer to those people whom we like and in whom we have confidence, and to move slightly away from those people whom we suspect or distrust. If our suspicions are allayed, then we might move nearer again. There are many situations in which people experience an acutely uncomfortable degree of proximity. The most familiar is travelling in a lift, which produces proximity so unnatural as to cause discomfort to most people making the journey.

Those from the Middle East and South America move in closer during conversation than most North Americans or Europeans find comfortable. This leads to the problem that one party to the conversation is made uncomfortable by the close proximity, while the other feels a sense of being pushed away and being denied any sense of emotional sincerity in the exchanges.

A further aspect to the use of space is in offices. Western managers communicate power and status by the size and splendour of their office accommodation, as well as its remoteness. The person with the most prestige will have the biggest office and it will be at the top of the building. The superiority of the mighty has to be declared in this way because the power distance (in the Hofstede sense) is narrow in the culture. An oriental manager, from a culture of wider power distance, would not have this need and would probably use quite a small office or share with colleagues.

> In a wide power difference culture, the superior demonstrates his or her authority in relations with subordinates; perhaps they lower their eyes when speaking and remain standing, sit in obedient silence at meetings and negotiations, show deference at every opportunity. Then the superior has far less need to symbolise authority by size and position of office space. (Mead, 1990, p. 149)

In some Japanese offices there is the intriguing phenomenon of the 'window people'.

> In this collectivist culture, where employment may be guaranteed for life, they cannot be dismissed without creating loss of face or conflict. Nevertheless, the employee moved to a window desk is being discreetly told that his or her services are no longer crucial, and that if he or she should decide to find some other job in

preference to fruitless hours spent staring out of the window, this would not be regretted. (ibid.)

Gesture

Gesture can be considered in two ways. First of all it can be used to emphasise and underline speech, so that speakers who can control their gestures can use them directly as a manipulator. Alternatively and frequently, gestures derive from an emotional state and may involuntarily indicate that emotional state to a keen observer.

An example of the first aspect of gesture would be the stabbing forefinger of the orator who is seeking to compel the attention of the audience. Very common examples of gesture to emphasise speech are beckoning, waving, nodding and shaking the head. Not all gestures are universal. Most Europeans will beckon or point something out using the forefinger, but Malaysians will use the thumb laid across curled fingers. There is a very narrow difference between the European and American wave. An American waving 'goodbye', with the full palm and fingers facing front, may be construed as saying 'no'. If you are trying to park your car in a narrow space with the help of a local national, the helping gestures would vary according to the nationality of your helper. Northern Europeans and North Americans would signal with one or two hands, palm up and with the gesture relying mainly on movement of the wrist. Most southern nationalities would have the palm down, the wrist firm and only the fingers moving.

The second type of gesture is harder to read. Sweating usually indicates anxiety, shivering can indicate either cold or nervousness. Krout (1954) conducted some experiments in America which suggested a link between certain types of involuntary gesture and specific attitudes:

> Steepled fingers indicated suspicion
> Hand to nose indicated fear
> Fingers to lips indicated shame
> Clenched fists indicated aggression
> Open hand dangling between the legs indicated frustration

. . . but this, of course, was only for Americans.

Eckman *et al.* (1971) studied the similarities and differences of gesture and facial expression between different nationalities. They found that most emotions could be identified cross-culturally, but the intensity of emotion was much harder. It is easy to tell that someone is angry, but hard to decide how angry.

Posture

Height tends to make one person dominate another, due to childhood conditioning when parents are always taller than their children during the formative years. Frequently height is emphasised by artificial devices such as the rostrum for the public speaker, or high-heeled shoes. Relative shortness is seen as an interpersonal disadvantage and frequently short people try to compensate by emphasising other dominating characteristics such as aggressiveness. Some short people feel they interact more effectively when sitting, which reduces the height differential. Conversely, tall people deliberately seek dominance by standing.

Scandinavians are on average taller than all other nationalities, but the average height of those from all northern countries exceeds that of those from the south, so those travelling south need to remember that they may appear dominant to those they are visiting, unless they find ways to de-emphasise their height.

Furthermore, posture can be an indicator of emotional state, somewhere between the very tense and completely relaxed. At one extreme there is the 'open' posture, where the person leans back comfortably, perhaps with hands behind the head, legs apart and muscles slack. At the opposite extreme there is the 'closed' posture, where the legs are crossed or pressed tightly together. The closed posture stems from ancient behaviour in preparing to be attacked and can be compared with the stance of a boxer.

We cannot, however, take these extremes simply on their face value, as it is necessary to interpret the degree of tenseness for each individual. The naturally tense person may be very thin, and will exhibit an open posture less often than the normally more tranquil person, who may be pleasantly plump. Again there are marked regional differences – Asians will never show the soles of their feet, shod or unshod, to another person, as it is regarded as offensive: the idea of putting one's feet up on the desk, or on the despatch box in the House of Commons, is utterly unacceptable.

Gaze

Generally we look at other people to obtain information and also to obtain feedback, and we look at the other approximately three times as much while listening as while talking (Argyle and Dean, 1965). Long periods of looking can be interpreted as a desire to be friendly and we tend to look at the other more when we are further apart, to compensate for the separation, whilst looking is quite threatening when people are very close. This is something with which the public speaker will be familiar. It is relatively easy to maintain eye contact with one member of a large audience for a sustained period, as when that person is asking a question, whilst such eye contact would not be sustained so comfortably if the person were closer.

Shifts of gaze can also be used to synchronise speech between people, so that a speaker will usually give a prolonged look at the other before ending a statement to indicate that it is becoming time for the other person to speak.

In Asian and Middle Eastern countries it is usual for a subordinate to look away from a superior in order to show respect, but this can be disconcerting for Britons and Americans who tend not to trust those 'who won't look you in the eye'.

Dress

Managers wear uniform. It is not as identical as military uniform, and there are seldom house rules about how managers should dress, but a marked degree of uniformity helps everyone feel comfortable. For both sexes, it is what goes round the neck that seems to be the most universal signifier.

Men of most nationalities wear a tie, often with a white shirt, although only the British recognise the significance of the old school or regimental tie. Europeans, Americans and Japanese are also likely to wear a suit, although blazer and slacks are not uncommon. Because of the identification of commercial success with Western societies, those from Africa, the Middle East and Asia are likely to follow this pattern, at least while they are moving between air-conditioned offices, cars and hotels and in foreign countries. For both climatic and cultural reasons, they may adopt different dress in their own countries, but the uniform principle will still apply. In Malaysia, for instance, a long-sleeved batik shirt is more formal than either a Western shirt and tie or a short-sleeved batik shirt. In India it seems that those of high status can appear without a tie, while those of lower status are still expected to wear ties.

Western women, and other women taking Westerners as role models, are likely to wear a suit with a white blouse or shirt, but with a colourful tie or scarf at the neck. Orthodox Muslim women will wear traditional costume, with all its subtle variations.

Spreading the word

A quite different aspect of communication for the personnel specialist in the international company is the need for propaganda or public relations; disseminating information and other messages within the organisation to help develop corporate culture, a sense of collaboration across national boundaries in order to integrate the business.

Most managers have to think globally but act locally and the dissemination of information throughout the organisation helps that type of global thinking, so that members of the different units in the business understand why a company has been acquired in South America, even though it seems to threaten the livelihood of some parts of the parent organisation. Comprehensive communication can raise awareness of the wider market and the opportunities that are waiting to be grasped. Foulds and Mallet (1989, p. 78) suggest the following as purposes of international communication:

> to reinforce group culture so as to improve the speed and effectiveness of decision taking;
> to encourage information exchange in internationally related activities and prevent the 'reinvention of the wheel';
> to form the background to the succession planning activity – certain cultures demand certain types of people;
> to establish in people's minds what is expected of them by the parent company;
> to facilitate change in a way acceptable to the parent company;
> to undermine the 'not invented here' attitudes and thereby encourage changes;

to improve the attractiveness of the company in the recruitment field – particularly where the subsidiary is small and far from base;
to encourage small activities, which may be tomorrow's 'cream', and give such activities a perspective within the international activities.

There is a need for constant communication throughout the organisation to disseminate information and to sustain changing values. The organisation must operate holistically. It is not the sum of its parts: the whole exists in every part, like the human body. If you are ill a doctor can obtain information about your illness from any part of you. A sample of your blood or the taking of your temperature is just as good wherever it comes from. If you are to be protected against cholera, which attacks the intestines, you have an injection in your arm. If you are about to be shot in the chest, your entire body will shiver in fear.

Customers have a holistic view of the organisation. If your breakfast is late in the Hilton Hotel, your impression of the whole hotel, or the whole hotel chain, is unfavourable. Managers cannot work effectively in their part of the business without understanding its simultaneous relationship to the whole. Businesses function holistically and holism is a function of constant, efficient communication, like the bloodstream and the central nervous system.

Relentless communication will develop a sense of corporate identity that entices customers to buy, but also entices prospective employees to seek jobs and causes them to feel commitment to the organisation:

> research demonstrates that a good organisation which is well known is admired more and liked better than an equally good company which is not so well known. It will attract more and better people to work for it, can more readily make acquisitions and more effectively launch new products: it will perform better.
> (Olins, 1989, p. 53)

Communication in any organisation mainly follows the work flow, in that members communicate with each other in connection with their work, first between members of a particular work group, then between one work group and another which is adjacent in the work flow, and then between departments. In a hotel, for instance, there will be a great deal of communication between different members of the kitchen staff and a certain amount between members of the housekeeping staff, but relatively little between kitchen and housekeeping except where there is a work flow link, such as constant disagreements about who collects breakfast trays from bedrooms. Both departments will, however, have frequent contacts with personnel and cashiers.

When a company is operating internationally the work flow pattern may be very clear and provide the logical main channel for communication. If a washing machine is produced by manufacturing electronic components in California, sub-assemblies and wiring harnesses in Korea and final assembly in Scotland, there is an easy sequence to follow. Job instructions, guidance notes, queries, telephone calls, specifications, requisitions, authorisations, order forms are some of the many ways in which groups of people communicate with those before and after in the work flow, or critically adjacent to the process – like personnel. Among the most effective international communicators are airlines, as their entire business is moving not only customers but also staff constantly across national boundaries to different organisational outposts of the business: the business activity creates the communications.

When the company is operating not serially but in parallel, organisational communication becomes much more difficult. Reverting to the hotel analogy, the hotel in Manila is a complete operation in just the same way as the hotel in Copenhagen that is part of the same group: guests are not bedded in one and passed on to another to be fed. The work flow communication link is missing.

All international businesses require centralised, co-ordinated communications to create common purpose and to share ideas and benefits, but those that do not have a natural work flow link across national boundaries will have this need more highly developed.

IHRM and communication

As in any organisation, the communications management challenge for international human resource management is at two extremes. At one extreme is the personal behaviour and skill of individual organisation members in making themselves understood, persuading others to do things, negotiating agreements with people from different cultural backgrounds, overcoming language barriers, appreciating different frames of reference and developing heightened sensitivity to varying behavioural norms and conventions. Communication is an individual activity, reflecting personal style, and the HRM requirement is for cultural awareness and perhaps language training. In this type of communication the manager is a skilled solo performer.

The other extreme is impersonal and systemic, more concerned with channels of communication than with individual behaviour, and more concerned with systematic distribution of carefully chosen information and the organisation of communications opportunities. In this type of communication the manager both writes the score and conducts the orchestra.

Although the forms of communication are so different, they are also linked. Organisational communication is only as good as the quality of interpersonal communication that is taking place.

> consistent patterns of interaction begin to develop when a group of individuals, in response to certain characteristics and needs of the environment, create a system of patterned activities for the accomplishment of a specific task. The process by which these relationships are formed and maintained is interpersonal communication. (Baskin and Aronoff, 1980, p. 7)

It is not practicable for employees to develop confidence in a communications system; they can only acquire confidence in what the system produces and in those other members of the organisation with whom they interact. That confidence is built by the substance of what people say and do, but also by a climate in which people feel encouraged to express ideas, make suggestions and question the validity of decisions they cannot understand. Communications and behaviour are so closely interlinked that everything which influences behaviour also influences communication.

This chapter closes with a recent example from Associated Press in Prague of a government edict:

> Because Christmas Eve falls on a Thursday, the day has been designated a Saturday for work purposes. Factories will close all day, with stores open a half day only. Friday, December 25 has been designated a Sunday, with both factories and stores open all day. Monday December 28, will be a Wednesday for work purposes. Wednesday, December 30, will be a business Friday. Saturday, January 2, will be a Sunday, and Sunday, January 3, will be a Monday.

Perhaps it has lost some of its crispness in translation.

References

Argyle, M. and Dean, J. (1965), 'Eye contact, distance and affiliation', *Sociometry*, vol. 28, pp. 289–304.

Baskin, O. W. and Aronoff, C. E. (1980), *Interpersonal Communication in Organizations*, Goodyear Publishing, Santa Monica, Calif.

Brandt, W. K. and Hulbert, J. M. (1976), 'Patterns of communication in the multinational company', *Journal of International Business Studies*, Spring, pp. 57–64.

Eckman, P., Ellsworth, P. and Friesen, W. V. (1971), *Emotion in the Human Face: Guidelines for research and integration of the findings*, Pergamon Press, New York.

Festinger, L. (1957), *A Theory of Cognitive Dissonance*, Stanford University Press, Stanford, Calif.

Foulds, J. and Mallet, L. (1989) 'The European and international dimension', in Wilkinson, T. (ed.), *The Communications Challenge*, Institute of Personnel Management, London.

Goffman, E. (1972), *The Presentation of Self in Everyday Life*, Penguin Books, Harmondsworth.

Krout, W. H. (1954), 'An experimental attempt to determine the significance of manual symbolic movements', *Journal of General Psychology*, vol. 51, pp. 121–52.

Mead, R. (1990), *Cross-Cultural Management Communication*, John Wiley, Chichester.

Olins, W. (1989), *Corporate Identity*, Thames and Hudson, London.

Pascale, R. T. (1978), 'Communication and decision making across cultures: Japanese and American comparisons', *Administrative Science Quarterly*, March, pp. 91–110.

CHAPTER 6

Consultancy and consultants

Management consultancy has developed as an essential feature of contemporary management practice because of the ever-increasing amount of specialist expertise that is needed in the running of any enterprise, and because of the move towards flexible manning of organisations, where there is a core workforce and a peripheral workforce. Those in the core are those on whom the distinctiveness and drive of the organisation depends. 'These are the people who are essential to the organization. Between them they own the organizational knowledge which distinguishes that organization from its counterparts. Lose them and you lose part of yourself' (Handy, 1989, p. 72).

Those on the periphery are those whose input is essential, but not specialised to the organisation itself. The company medical officer, the driver of the heavy goods vehicle or the legal adviser are all people of valuable expertise, yet the value of that expertise to you, the employer, lies partly in the fact that it is *not* unique to you. Charles Handy (pp. 72–81) describes a form of organisation that is like the three leaves of a shamrock. One leaf represents the core workers, one represents the flexible labour force of part-time and temporary workers who, for instance, cope with the longer hours of opening of most retail stores. His third leaf is the sub-contractors: self-employed professionals and technicians, who are paid fees, not salaries, for results, not time.

Consultants fit into this third category and are especially important in international management because of the abundance of detailed matters on which advice is needed to deal in unfamiliar cultures and different economic systems. As we have seen in the preceding chapters, international HRM issues are among the most complex and specialised of all management challenges, so that need for expert local knowledge is paramount. But it is not simply local knowledge. There is also a need for the independent perspective of someone who knows the organisation well, but who is always on the outside. In Chapter 14 Cynthia Haddock and Basil South describe the Shell practice of their operating companies always having one member from another country to avoid too narrow a perspective. In other companies this feature may well be provided by a consultant.

Management folklore is full of horror stories about expensive projects that failed, of impressive 'front men' coming to sell the service to be followed by ineffectual 'junior consultants' who were supposed to be doing the job, but who lacked experience or any particular ability. Frequently consultants are associated with bad news, in the sense that their assignment is often to make possible something that is unpleasant, such as organisational change that reduces the number of people employed. It may, indeed, be a very sensible management strategy to use consultants to take the flak for unpopular initiatives.

The reservations are becoming less common as the range of consultant services widens and becomes more expert, but every consultant has a first task of winning the confidence of those among whom the consultancy assignment is to be carried out. Using consultants on international aspects of HRM is less controversial than on domestic aspects because the need for specialised expertise is more obvious and is less likely to generate problems of acceptability, although the need for skill and thoroughness in recruiting and briefing the consultant will be of a very high order indeed.

Consultants are not only expert strangers who come in from outside, they can also be expert insiders with a specialist role within the organisation because of their deep knowledge of the business as well as specialised expertise that will be needed in different areas at different times. The 'occasional parachutists' described in Chapter 4 are often of this type. A consultancy mode of operating is now widely adopted by personnel specialists in fulfilling their management function, and it is one of the keys to their organisational effectiveness and authority. The personnel manager who cannot perform the consultancy role skilfully is in danger of having only a marginal role in organisational affairs.

In international HRM the personnel manager has to make sound selections of external expertise, to brief external consultants so that they deliver what is really needed and to operate as an internal consultant in a way that managerial colleagues will respect.

This chapter considers first the use of consultants and advisers, then the question of how to be an effective consultant. Finally, there are comments about specific consultancy methods. An excellent introduction to the state of the art in consultancy is in the book by Bennett (1990) and a helpful guide to most aspects of using consultants is in the work commissioned by the International Labour Organisation (Kubr, 1976).

What consultants can do

Duncan Wood (1983) calculated that there were about a thousand people in the United Kingdom who could be described as personnel consultants, of whom half were genuine specialists with expertise concentrated in one area, such as recruitment, pay or communications, while the remainder offered more general services. He asked senior representatives of 14 well-established consultancies to rank seven reasons for their use in personnel work and the result was:

First	To provide specialist expertise and wider knowledge not available within the client organisation.
Second	To provide an independent view.
Third	To act as a catalyst.
Fourth	To provide extra resources to meet temporary requirements.
Fifth	To help develop a consensus when there are divided views about proposed personnel changes.
Sixth	To demonstrate to employees the impartiality/objectivity of personnel changes or decisions.
Seventh	To justify potentially unpleasant decisions. (p. 41)

In international matters the essential need for consultants is to provide assistance in the first four areas.

Specialist expertise and wider knowledge

In this chapter on compensation there was an example of the work of Employment Conditions Abroad, a specialised consultancy that provides an information service which very few individual organisations could match. In the chapter on cosmopolitans and expatriates there were several references to the need for specialist advice in all sorts of areas from cultural awareness and language instruction to personal taxation. The emphasis is therefore on *resource* consultancy, which is transferring knowledge and understanding from the consultant to the client, or simply getting a job done for the client, like engaging 10 engineers to work on a project in the Persian Gulf and sorting out all the details of transport, pay, accommodation and so forth.

An independent view

In contrast, *process* consultancy is developing the capacity of the client organisation to deal with unfamiliar situations by acquiring new skills in analysis and diagnosis. The advantage of the consultant may be as simple as hearing a different point of view from someone who, first, has some specialised expertise that gives validity to their opinions and who, second, has sufficient interpersonal skill to be an effective counsellor. In Chapter 15 Heather Lussey, an Englishwoman, describes the French company GSI, where she has worked for several years as an independent consultant, providing a general commentary on organisational affairs and an occasional detailed critique of some specific management initiative. All consultancy relationships of this type require the careful development of mutual trust and respect. That, in turn, is based on ethical standards of behaviour. Rosbeth Moss Kanter has suggested that what she calls the 'business athletes' of the future will have to operate with the highest ethical standards, because things will move so quickly that high trust will be essential in the same way as it has always been, for instance, in diamond trading. Her comment is just as appropriate for consultants:

The doing-more-with-less strategies place an even greater premium on trust than did the adversarial-protective business practices of the traditional corporation ... The trust required for new business strategies is built and reinforced by a mutual understanding that each party to the relationship will behave ethically, taking the needs, interests and concerns of all others into account. (Kanter, 1989, pp. 362–3)

The catalyst

A catalyst speeds up a reaction without undergoing any change itself. Every manager in a business (a core worker) has a substantial personal investment in it: career prospects, personal power, resources, stimulating working relationships and an arena in which to achieve a degree of personal fulfilment. All of these add up to a significant vested interest that may not be consistent with the vested interest of colleagues. Despite all the lofty contemporary talk about change being the only certainty, managers are profoundly cautious about changes which appear to threaten their personal interests. International ventures can appear very threatening and frequently represent a serious real threat to some people in influential positions. The consultant can reduce the level of anxiety of some and strengthen the enthusiasm of others by working through the opportunities that a particular initiative represents. This can hasten the decisions which implement the change.

Another type of consultant-catalysis often mentioned is the financial commitment of engaging the consultant in the first place. A management team that cannot decide what to do may call in a consultant as a way of deferring a decision, but having committed the expenditure, they put themselves under some pressure to take action on the proposals!

Extra resources

Managements doing more with less will often need additional, expert help at times when they are hard-pressed. If they can use consultants, they avoid all the baggage of a permanent appointment and the commitment to the development of the appointee's career. The consultants arrive, they are briefed, they do the work and then they leave.

Working with consultants

Wood (op. cit.) estimated that there were more consultants working in the area of personnel and HRM than any other area of management, but until recently personnel specialists had little experience of using them for international aspects of HRM, as it is so recent a development. In a comprehensive survey of 350 senior personnel specialists in 1986 (Torrington and Mackay, 1986a) there was not a single respondent who mentioned international aspects in questions about employing consultants. The research probed practitioners' views of consultants more thoroughly. This is reported fully elsewhere (Torrington and Mackay, 1986b), but the aspect of interest here is that confident and competent personnel managers readily called on the services of outside experts without fear of jeopardising their own position, and they can specify closely what they require. Where the personnel function is under-resourced or where the personnel manager lacks professional expertise, then consultants will be used reluctantly, with a poor specification of requirements and the likelihood of an unsatisfactory outcome for both client and consultant. We now review the steps towards achieving a satisfactory consultancy.

Choosing the consultant

There are two professional bodies for British-based consultants:

> The Institute of Management Consultants,
> 32 Hatton Garden,
> London EC1 8DL.

> The Management Consultancies Association,
> 11 West Halkin Street,
> London SW1X 8JL.

An enquiry to one or the other will produce a list of consultants who might suit your needs. The Institute is a professional association of individual consultants and it provides a free advisory service as well as a complaints procedure should a consultancy assignment by one of its members be unsatisfactory. The Association is slightly different in that it is an association of approximately 30 large consulting firms which employ several thousand individual consultants between them. Every member must have been in business for at least five years and have to comply with a code of professional conduct. One provision of this code is the prohibition of consultants charging fees based on results. There is, again, a complaints procedure.

This does not exhaust the supply of people who may be just what is needed for a company's specific international requirements. Linguists, for example, or researchers with detailed knowledge of the workings of a foreign economy may be best located through a university, most of which now have an apparatus for dealing with such enquiries. The Department of Trade and Industry and other agencies of government will have specialist facilities, as well as the consulates of a country in which you are interested.

The best way is by experience. The number of people working as consultants is increasing, partly as a result of redundancy and partly because of people choosing to work with that degree of independence. Every manager will have a network of contacts and it is worth adding potential consultants through recommendation from a satisfied customer, through hearing an effective presentation at the meeting of a professional body, through reading an article or through considering ex-employees who have opted for the consultancy life.

Approaching the consultancy assignment

If you want the assistance mainly as an independent point of view, you will logically leave the formulation of the approach partly to the consultant, as you may feel that you are not able to formulate it yourself without losing the potential benefits of the independent advice. This next section, however, assumes a consultancy assignment to provide particular expertise or extra resources.

Deciding whether or not to use a consultant at all, and then devising the commission to the selected firm is best approached by a series of steps, as follows:

1. CHECK THE EXPERIENCE OF PREVIOUS CLIENTS

In deciding which source of assistance to use, it is always useful to ask the opinion of previous clients. Consultants themselves will readily supply the names of these, but your personal network of contacts may be a better source. Also, an independent professional body, like the Institute of Personnel Management, may be able to put you in touch with people with experience of working with a particular consultant. It is helpful to ask specific questions, such as:

- What exactly was the consultancy assignment? How was it performed? How long did it take? Were there any surprises?
- What was the pay-off for the client? How was this calculated? How did it compare with expectation?
- Did the consultant keep within the estimated budget? How often were bills submitted and how was expenditure detailed?
- Would the client use the same consultant again? If so, what changes in briefing, monitoring or staffing would be made?

2. DESCRIBE WHAT YOU WANT DONE

What is the matter about which you might seek external advice? This may not be obvious, as worrying away at an issue can show that the real matter needing to be addressed is not what is immediately apparent. If, for example, the marketing manager (Western Europe) leaves abruptly, the immediate problem will present itself as 'We must find a replacement'. So the first thought is to ring up the executive search consultant you used when you needed someone for the Middle East in a hurry. However, working away at finding a correct description of the problem could suggest that the presenting cause is easy to deal with because Robinson has been waiting for just such an opportunity for months, has just completed a European MBA and all the signals suggest that Robinson would be an ideal marketing manager (Western Europe). But why did the marketing manager leave? Trying to answer that question could establish that the reason was beyond the company's control, so that appointing Robinson is all that is required and the commissioning of a consultant is unnecessary. On the other hand, it might establish that the remuneration arrangements are all wrong, or that there are no clearly defined career prospects for people working overseas, or any of a host of matters needing attention – possibly with the assistance of external expertise – before deciding whether or not Robinson should be appointed.

3. FORMULATE AN APPROACH

The next step is to rough out an approach to the problem, with the emphasis here on 'rough'. If you knew the answer you would not need any further advice; if you have no idea of the possible solutions you cannot brief a consultant (but you might unwittingly authorise some expensive, relevant advice). What is needed is a clear, but not inflexible, strategy so that you can go through the remaining stages of making up your mind without putting the consultant, and yourself, in the wrong framework. If you decide that the problem behind the departure of the marketing manager is a combination of succession planning and remuneration policy, the approach you would then formulate would be based on ideas about how those two issues could be tackled, without an absolute commitment to a single approach.

4. WORK OUT HOW YOU COULD DO IT WITHOUT EXTERNAL ASSISTANCE

Having formulated an approach to the matter, you next decide how it could be tackled by using your own existing resources, how much it would cost, how long it would take and what the repercussions would be, such as stopping work on something else, and engaging consultants to work on *that*. Some potential consultancy assignments become unnecessary when thought through clearly at this early stage.

5. OBTAIN PROPOSALS FROM CONSULTANTS

Assuming your initial enquiries have identified a few possible consultancy firms to help you, it is now time to obtain proposals and estimates from them on the basis of the work you have already done in steps 1 and 2 above to specify the assignment. It is important that each consultant quotes for exactly the same thing, so that you can compare the estimates you receive in terms of the results that will be achieved, how long they will take and how much they will cost. A key part of the specification will be to detail the assistance that the consultant will receive from you, whether key information is readily available, not known or – perhaps – withheld. Bennett (1990, p. 36) says that the consultant's proposals will normally include:

  (i) a statement of the consultant's perception of the problem that needs to be solved,
 (ii) how the consultant will approach the job,
(iii) a schedule of the intended work,
 (iv) details of duties/research to be performed by the consultant (and by the client),
  (v) materials and equipment to be supplied and
 (vi) who will provide secretarial and other assistance.

You would also need to see a draft contract that would require careful scrutiny.

If the problem is not correctly described there may be bids for the wrong things and if the approach is not accurately formulated, the consultant will be obliged to carry out a preliminary study, at your expense, to formulate an approach for you. When this happens, you are beginning to lose control of the operation.

6. DECIDE BETWEEN THE ALTERNATIVES

A set of alternatives between which to choose gives you the opportunity to compare relative costs, times and likely outputs, as well as implications. In making the final decision, consider the following points:

- Does the proposal meet your requirements specifically? If not, how significant are the variations?
- What are the specific achievements and pay-offs claimed in the proposal for your assignment? Are there any unexpected additional benefits (such as access to the consultant's database)?
- How will it be possible to assess the consultant's performance as the assignment proceeds? Are there clear stages in the suggested work schedule for you to check on progress?
- Who will actually be doing the work, what are their qualifications and experience, and to what extent will they be working also on other assignments at the same time?
- What exactly are the costs and when will they be levied?

The most important point to remember is that the responsibility is inescapably yours. If the consultant can produce the 'best' outcome, have you the resources to implement it? Can you wait? If you can save £10,000 by relying on your own staff and time, will you produce an outcome which adequately meets the needs of your rough-and-ready approach? The eventual outcome is all that matters.

Commissioning consultants is an increasingly important part of the general personnel role:

> The personnel manager is a general practitioner in personnel, dealing with many issues, running many programmes and producing many plans. Sometimes there is a need for special skills the personnel manager does not possess or have available; then the consultants are called in or 'the patient' is referred to a training school, assessment centre, or some other source of special treatment. The personnel manager orchestrates the use of these skilled resources, and that requires a high degree of expertise. (Torrington, 1989, p. 65)

In international matters the required expertise is greater, the costs will probably be higher and the range of consultants available may be fewer, so that a very thorough and clear-headed specification of requirements is essential. Also, the degree of trust reposed in the consultant will be considerable as you have less scope to check and verify credentials.

Acting as a consultant

Following the analogy of the last paragraph, the general practitioner has to have considerable and wide-ranging expertise in order to brief the right consultant to investigate the real problem. There is also a need to have some of the consultant's skills.

The development of joint ventures between Western business and the previously closed economies of the communist world has recently given point to the long-standing problem of cultural differences in business. The expertise of the 'advanced' countries in the West is needed, but how can it be transferred? The following comment after exhaustive research among German expatriate managers in China illustrates how difficult this is:

> Despite differences in leadership style, we could not prove the impact of cultural values on that of West German expatriate managers in China. This is of particular interest in regard to the contradiction we found between the results reported in this study and our previous interviews on the leadership attitudes of West German expatriates (unawareness of the importance of culture in leadership style, insecurity in finding the appropriate leadership style in China, lack of knowledge about the behaviour of Chinese employees). (Domsch and Lichtenberger, 1990, p. 83)

Increasingly, personnel specialists are being involved in knowledge transfer and consultancy in HRM matters. While it may be wise to limit some activities – like local recruitment – to local experts, there are many more where the need to transfer company standards is important. In the opening chapter of this book there was the comment by Chris Hendry on the way in which HRM issues may be the main remaining form of centralisation. The later chapters by Reg Carr and Cynthia Haddock and Basil South demonstrate the clear need for this sort of activity. Among the best-known recent examples have been the establishment of Euro Disneyland in France where large numbers of young people from many different countries were inducted into the Disney way of life, and the establishment of McDonald's in Moscow:

> a large number of Soviets are employed in an almost exact replica of a U.S. workplace . . . The restaurant offers not only burgers and fries, but a little piece of the U.S.A., right down to service and cleanliness. Being a part of that is what is transforming the lives of McDonald's-Moscow employees. (Cascio, 1992, p. 4)

There is an increasing requirement for personnel specialists to develop expertise in the consultancy process itself, as well as acting as a buyer and monitor of consultancy services. How do you become an effective management consultant? There are two well-tried approaches.

Harold Leavitt: The Alcoholics Anonymous analogy

Harold Leavitt (1972) suggests that the best approach to consultancy is to follow the pattern of Alcoholics Anonymous (AA), an organisation with considerable success in enabling individuals to overcome alcohol addiction. He first summarises the AA approach:

> One finds no threat, no command, no surreptitiousness in the process. The alcoholic stops drinking; he is not stopped. He is helped to change himself. He is

helped by being shown alternative means, substitute behaviours, new sources of faith – by anything that will fit his needs. This is a predominantly augmentative, supportive process in which responsibility never actually leaves the change. (p. 159)

The approach of helping someone to change, by whatever means suits the individual, and only when that individual is ready and willing, is obviously different from consultancy in business in significant ways. The consultant cannot, for example, simply wait until people feel disposed to change what they are doing; it is not usually possible for managers to solve their own problems in their own way, there has to be some conformity to organisational norms and time constraints. The personnel specialist acting in a consultancy mode cannot simply allow people to do things differently if they feel like it. It is the local managers who must make the changes, and must first own them. This requires good data, clear presentation and effective interpersonal skills.

Whilst displaying the limitations of this method in the management situation, Leavitt suggests a general set of conditions for bringing about behaviour change in continuing relationships at work. A is the consultant, B is the person who has to do things differently:

1 A perceives a problem. A will not be able to wait for B to see the problem, so it will have to be pointed out, either by a simple statement or by producing persuasive evidence. A must not, however, suggest that B is the problem, nor should B perceive A as the problem!

2 B takes responsibility for finding solutions to the problem, but realises that A could be a useful source of ideas.

3 A and B evaluate alternatives and their implications. As B now sees A as a potential source of help the alternatives can be evaluated to make sure that a change is likely to be an improvement, rather than simply different.

4 B decides on an alternative that A can accept. The responsibility for making and implementing the decision remains with B, even though it will need to be acceptable to A; it does not have to be ideal.

5 B tries the changed method and A provides support, help and reassurance. The early stages will be the time of greatest difficulty for B and the time for a positive contribution from A. It is not helpful if A disclaims responsibility or joins the critics.

6 B either consolidates the change in behaviour or abandons it in favour of another. A may also be abandoned if seen as the source of unhelpful advice.

This sequence can be a useful framework for those forms of personal consultancy that are close to coaching and can be especially relevant in some international work where the consultant knows the business but does not know local custom and practice. It assumes a close, personal working relationship between two people with time for that relationship to develop a high degree of trust and mutual respect, with A being seen as a counsellor rather than a consultant.

The Blake and Mouton consultation approach

The inventors of the famous managerial grid also produced an interesting, if rather difficult, analysis of the consultation process as a form of contracting. They suggest the following five alternative forms of contract between the consultant and client (Blake and Mouton, 1976):

1 The *acceptant* contract is one of the classic helping approaches of psychotherapeutic counselling. The emphasis is on listening, being supportive and not evaluative of the client's behaviour.

    Acceptant consultation attempts to aid a client through sympathetic listening and empathic support. It might seem that any good friend of the client can do this just as well – but . . . the consultant avoids certain actions that friends might take. For example, the consultant does not adopt a partisan point of view and help the person justify the reasonableness of his or her own positions and feelings – the client's behaviour cycle must be broken not perpetuated. (Blake and Mouton, 1976, pp. 14–15)

2 The *catalytic* contract is similar to the process in chemistry where a reaction is speeded up by adding a catalytic agent to other substances. The consultant aids the process of change by providing new information and assisting in problem diagnosis. To do this it is necessary to get inside the frame of reference of the client, so that the assistance is provided to solve the problem the client has already identified. The consultant does not provide answers, only information, interpretation and diagnosis.

3 The *confrontation* contract is a much more direct challenge to the validity of what a client is doing, where expressed values contrast starkly with actual behaviour. The consultant brings the client's underlying values into focus and shows how values influence behaviour. An example could be that belief, expressed in a policy statement, that there is equal employment opportunity for all racial and ethnic groups may be false in practice if the values of an individual manager produce behaviour which invalidates the policy. By demonstrating the dissonance between belief and behaviour, the consultant may induce some change in belief which leads to a change in behaviour.

4 *Prescriptive* contracts are the most obvious as they are where the consultant explicitly tells the client what to do, deploying an authority to which the client's compliance is expected. There may be occasions for this approach in modifying behaviour, but the simpler examples for personnel managers are in advising people of standard reporting procedures, which have to be followed. An inescapable pre-condition is that the consultant has some specialist expertise that is not available to the client.

5 *Theory/principles* contracts are very similar to prescriptive contracts in that they rely on the consultant teaching the client theories or principles that the client will then apply to problems being experienced. The difference is that prescriptions says, 'do this and you will be able to . . .' while the theories/principles consultant says, 'Learn this and you will be able to work out how to . . .'

The personnel specialist working internationally may well need to adopt all of these strategies at different times, according to the nature of the assignment and the cultural background of the client. Leavitt, Blake and Mouton were all Americans, writing for an American audience and throughout this book we see how cultural assumptions in one country cannot readily be transferred to certain others.

Methods for consultants

Having decided the appropriate approach to be adopted, the HRM consultant then uses various methods in carrying out the assignment.

PROBLEM IDENTIFICATION

Whether preparing a brief for an external consultant or coming to terms oneself with a problem that has been presented, there is a need for some device to describe the problem as a preliminary to trying to solve it. Priestley and his colleagues suggest a simple '5 W–H' method which is: What? Who? Where? When? Why? and How? (1978, p. 28). A typical problem could be approached like this:

What is the problem?
Communications between head office and subsidiary X are poor.

Who is involved?
All sections, but most problems are at the middle management level.

Where is it worst?
In accounts and in the sales office.

When is it worst?
At the end of each month and at the end of the head office financial year.

Why does it happen?
Because of an erratic flow of work between the two departments which is worst at those times.

How could it be solved?
By drawing attention to it and getting the middle managers to tackle it themselves, smoothing out the flow of work, helping them to appreciate the effect of their work flows on the other department and appreciating the problem of two different financial years.

This is a straightforward problem, with a minimal number of questions and does no more than illustrate the method. Each question would probably have dozens of supplementaries in order to fill out the details of a complex problem.

The main value of the consultant at this stage is the ability to raise questions that those close to the matter have not thought about. This is not because consultants are cleverer, but because they have a different pattern of experience and take for granted different things than those who are looking at the presenting problem every day.

INFORMATION GATHERING

In all consultancy a prime means of gathering information is by *interviewing*. Priestley has three simple suggestions:

1 Listen to what the person being interviewed is saying . . . Listening also implies not talking too much. In assessment the interviewer should not be talking for more than 10 per cent of the time.

2 Be courteous . . . One good way of doing this is to treat interviewees as though they were slightly more intelligent, slightly older, possibly of the opposite sex, and of slightly higher status than yourself . . . unless, of course, you encounter someone who actually fulfils all these conditions: the best thing to do in those circumstances is to try to treat such a person as an equal.

3 Be confident. You are not on show and are just doing your job to the best of your ability. (*op. cit.*, p. 181)

Kubr (1976, pp. 353–60) contains a section on person-to-person communication in consulting which examines this process in more detail. There is also valuable guidance in Guirdham (1990).

Although interviewing is the most common method of gathering data that consultants use, they will also analyse documents and observe their surroundings. The following two forms of observation could be used:

1 *Non-participant observation* is where the consultant is acquiring information through observing what is happening in the place where the consultation is being carried out. The novelist Christopher Isherwood expressed it like this: 'I am a camera with its shutter open, quite passive, recording, not thinking.' Much understanding of organisational dynamics and working relationships comes from this process of noting the small incidents and tensions, the modes of dress and address and the various minutiae of behaviour that in some way provide explanations of what has to be understood. Isherwood's comment about not thinking is important. Consultants do not make snap judgements about organisational problems on the basis of the graffiti in the lavatories, they first collect data for *later* evaluation to develop their understanding.

2 *Structured observation* is a more specialised and difficult technique that records for subsequent analysis the working behaviour and activities of people as they occur. It has the advantage over interviewing that the researcher is not dependent on the willingness or ability of the subject to respond to questions. This method is very common in efficiency and productivity studies, but has also been used in studies of management work (for example, Mintzberg, 1970) and as a preliminary to improving time management, where the observer records the frequency of changes in activity. The difficulties are the uncertainty of knowing the extent to which the observation alters the normal behaviour of the person observed and the likelihood that those willing to be observed are not typical of all those in the category whose work is to be reviewed (Hensen and Barlow, 1976, p. 99).

Questionnaires are sometimes used by consultants to collect information that is precise and factual or dealing with clear preferences. Questionnaire design is not difficult but requires great care. The main points are these:

1 How can the subject be presented to respondents to achieve a high response? In-company investigations have fewer problems with response rate than those conducted among the public at large, but even a small proportion of refusals can reduce the reliability of the results.

2 What is the best order in which to introduce topics? It is helpful to begin with questions that are easy for respondents to understand and reply to accurately, as well as getting them 'on the wavelength' of the inquiry before proceeding to more complex questions.

3 What wording of questions will produce precise data? There is a need to use words that are not only unequivocal, but also where the meaning is not likely to drift with the respondent. Another consideration is the distinction between questions to obtain facts and questions to seek opinion. These are best separated.

4 How long can the questionnaire be? The need to know has to be balanced with the ability of the respondent to reply. Some respondents will not be willing to spend long periods working through a questionnaire, others will have difficulty in maintaining concentration and others will have much more to say than the questionnaire provides for.

5 What is the best layout of the survey forms?

PROBLEM ANALYSIS

When the data are gathered they have to be assembled and analysed in order that alternative courses of action can be developed. Methods of analysis vary greatly, according to the nature of the study and the discipline within which it is set. Whatever method is used, satisfactory analysis depends on effective organisation of the raw data. Ideas for grouping and categorising material will be suggested by the type of information gathered and by the previous experience of the consultant. One of the hardest aspects of consultancy is making sense of an amorphous mass of material so that the argument develops logically and convincingly.

It is important to start writing early and to write often. This cannot be emphasised too strongly. Part of the skill that is developed in consultancy is the organisation and compression of material into succinct summary and analysis. This requires considerable reworking of the material to make it clearer and clearer.

When problems have proved to be intractable there is usually a need to generate better solutions based on a fresh interpretation of the data. One method of generating alternatives was devised by Kepner and Tregoe in 1965 and has recently been re-presented (1982). A more popular method is Edward de Bono's lateral thinking (1982), which aims both to enable people to find new solutions to problems and to escape from old solutions to which they may have become attached.

When working with a group of other people, rather than working individually, the brainstorming technique can be used to generate a large number of fresh ideas, some of which may be worth further development. A drill for conducting a brainstorming session is as follows:

- Decide the purpose of the session.
- Appoint someone who can write large and fast as note-taker.
- Ask group members to call out any idea that comes into their head.
- Note-taker writes all ideas on blackboard or large sheet of paper that all can see.
- Encourage group members to develop the ideas of others ('hitch-hiking') as well as 'sparking' in different directions.
- Stop judgements by anyone: all ideas are valid, however bizarre, even if they seem to be repeating what has already been said.
- Keep the group going.
- Stop after no more than 30 minutes; probably 20.
- Classify the ideas into five or six groups.
- Rank the ideas in each group.
- Decide how to follow up any of the ideas that are worth further consideration.

Implementation

> The implementation is the most important step in the process and is the area where consultants are the weakest . . . it is no use to present a brilliant solution to a problem and not be able to implement it throughout the organisation. (Chickillo and Kleiner, 1989, p. 29)

The decision to adopt a change must be the client's decision, as it is the client who has to live with it and make it happen, even though the consultant may provide an intitial shove. The consultant can explain alternatives and ask the client to pick between them, or can recommend a course of action, but it is still essential for the client to believe in the rightness of that course of action and to take ownership of it.

References

Bennett, R. (1990), *Choosing and Using Management Consultants*, Kogan Page, London.

Blake, R. R. and Mouton, J. S. (1976), *Consultation*, Addison-Wesley, Reading, Mass.

Cascio, W. F. (1992), *Managing Human Resources*, 3rd edition, McGraw-Hill, New York.

Chickillo, G. P. and Kleiner, B. H. (1989), 'Skills and roles of consultants', *Journal of European Industrial Training*, vol. 14, no. 1, pp. 26–30.

de Bono, E. (1982), *Lateral Thinking for Management*, Penguin, Harmondsworth.

Domsch, M. and Lichtenberger, B. (1990), 'In search of appropriate management transfer: leadership style of West German managers in the People's Republic of China', *International Journal of Human Resource Management*, vol. 1, no. 1, pp. 73–86.

Guirdham, M. (1990), *Interpersonal Skills at Work*, Prentice Hall, Hemel Hempstead.

Handy, C. B. (1989), *The Age of Unreason*, Business Books, London.

Hensen, M. and Barlow, D. H. (1976), *Single Case Experimental Designs: Strategies for studying behaviour change*, Pergamon, Oxford.

Kanter, R. M. (1989), *When Giants Learn to Dance*, Simon & Schuster, London.

Kepner, C. H. and Tregoe, B. B. (1982), *The Rational Manager: A systematic approach to problem-solving and decision-making*, McGraw-Hill, Maidenhead.

Kubr, J. (ed.) (1976), *Management Consulting: A guide to the profession*, International Labour Office, Geneva.

Leavitt, H. J. (1972), *Managerial Psychology*, 3rd edition, University of Chicago Press, Chicago.

Mintzberg, H. (1970), 'Structured observation as a method to study managerial work', *Journal of Management Studies*, vol. 7, pp. 87–104.

Priestley, P., McGuire, J., Flegg, D., Hemsley, V. and Welham, D. (1978), *Social Skills and Personal Problem Solving*, Tavistock, London.

Torrington, D. P. (1989), 'Human resource management and the personnel function', in Storey, J. (ed.) *New Perspectives on Human Resource Management*, Routledge, London, pp. 56–66.

Torrington, D. P. and Mackay, L. E. (1986a), *The Changing Nature of Personnel Management*, Institute of Personnel Management, London.

Torrington, D. P. and Mackay, L. E. (1986b), 'Will consultants take over the personnel function?', *Personnel Management*, February, pp. 34–7.

Wood, D. (1983), 'Uses and abuses of personnel consultants', *Personnel Management*, October, pp. 40–7.

CHAPTER 7

Competence:
its acquisition and development

Acquiring the competent people your organisation needs for its *international* operations is an activity rooted in a *national* legal and social framework. Developing the competence of the organisation's people to work in an international mode is partly nationally rooted in the same way – as education systems differ widely, as do perceptions of management and the perceptions of role in the business from one country to another. There is, however, a further dimension to developing competence that is centrally driven: developing and sharing the values, fostering a corporate sense of participating in the organisation as a whole and not just a single geographical location.

Recruitment and deployment strategy

The recruitment process is largely determined by the conventions and legislative requirements of the country in which it takes place. In Germany there is a statutory obligation to seek the agreement of works councils on a number of aspects of recruitment such as the documents used and the guidelines to be followed in making the appointment. In Greece,

> the culture of recruitment and selection seems to sanction a greater degree of inquisitiveness about personal circumstances than in the UK. Certainly a manager would expect to be asked about family background and origins, and a woman about her marriage and family plans – questions which would be technically illegal and to which candidates could exercise a 'right to lie' elsewhere in the Community. (IDS, 1990, p. 98)

Because of this diversity of legislation and convention, the recruitment of people to work in their own country is normally undertaken by local managers, possibly working with the assistance of a consultant. If the parent company has a well-established local subsidiary, there should be no difficulty. Establishing the local presence in the first place is more problematic as it is essentially a process of recruiting a small number of key people to create the new local corporate entity.

Establishing the core

Methods of getting started in a new location vary from buying an existing business to sending a lone expatriate.

Buying an existing business involves buying a controlling interest in a local company that would benefit from the extra investment or increased product lines of the parent company. Although the objective in making such a purchase is to expand the business, it has the by-product of providing the basic management apparatus and local expertise to carry out any further recruitment that is needed. Evalde Mutabazi's chapter on Rhône Poulenc includes a description of how that company bought a part of the American Union Carbide.

This type of initiative gives the parent company control, but it often produces local political resistance as there is the risk that the benefits of the operation will be greater to the country of the parent company and less to the local community, with the possibility of driving out local enterprises. In Chapter 13 Reg Carr describes a similar process in the development of ZENECA, when it was still ICI (Pharmaceuticals):

> In many territories markets were extended by acquisition of a local company into which the business put increased resources as the sales performance improved . . . The philosophy has always been to staff the local Pharma companies, whenever possible, with nationals of that territory as the business believes better links are possible with governmental agencies and there is a better understanding of the culture . . . (see page 203)

A joint venture is where two or more partners own and control a business in the country of one of them. They will share both control and profits, although the shares may not be equal. Their respective contributions will be complementary, so that a company with little cash but considerable international experience might team up with a company that is cash-rich but short of international experience and networks. This reduces both the commercial risks and the risks of destructive internal rivalry. This approach has been particularly popular as a means of Western businesses setting up operations in the emerging market economies of Eastern Europe. From the point of view of recruitment and selection it confers the same benefits as the wholly owned business, as the local partners provide the management apparatus and local expertise.

Licensing and franchising are modes of international operation that move the recruitment responsibility further away.

> A license is an agreement that allows one party to use an industrial property right in exchange for payment to the other party . . . a typical arrangement . . . is to use a patent, trademark or proprietary information in exchange for a fee . . . Franchising is a business arrangement under which one party allows another to operate an enterprise using its trademark, logo, product line, and methods of operation in return for a fee. (Hodgetts and Luthans, 1991, pp. 102–3)

In these arrangements recruitment is completely the responsibility of the licensee or franchisee, but the involvement of the licensor or franchisor may be considerable in training and perhaps also in recruitment. Burger King and Kentucky Fried Chicken have, for instance, expanded worldwide by franchising, with a training scheme being a significant part of the franchise package.

Direct export may be the only possibility for small- to medium-sized companies as they expand: it is most unlikely that they will have the expertise or finance for the other methods described so far. They will need to appoint a local agent, probably using the assistance of their embassy, and this could provide the kernel of a local presence if the business develops sufficiently to justify a joint venture or similar development.

The deployment of a *lone expatriate* is rare and usually it is to work in conjunction with a local agent, unless the expatriate has extensive earlier experience in the country.

Once there is a managerial core established in a country, recruitment of local nationals to work in that country becomes their responsibility because of their familiarity with local laws and customs.

Recruiting and deploying expatriates

Although Chapter 2 contains our main treatment of employing expatriates, we need here to consider the overall strategy to be adopted in using these very expensive employees to ensure the appropriate distribution of competence in the business. British firms regard this as one of their greatest problems. Hugh Scullion interviewed senior executives in 45 British and Irish companies to find out their main anxieties about international affairs, and 80 per cent of the respondents felt that the main challenge was to secure an adequate supply of expatriates, mainly because individual managers were reluctant to undertake the mission:

> The reduction in international mobility was attributed to several factors, including continued rationalisation in the UK which created uncertainties regarding re-entry, the growing unwillingness to disrupt the education of children, the growing importance of quality of life considerations, and finally, continued uncertainty regarding international terrorism and political unrest. (Scullion, 1992, p. 66)

The attraction of using expatriates is that they are completely familiar with the parent company products, processes, conventions and control systems. Many expatriates are also appointed because of their technical expertise. When starting a new venture in a strange land, it is comforting to have your 'own man on the spot'. The drawbacks of expatriates are that their employment costs are high, as shown in the chapter on compensation, and there can be some expensive failures. Harvey (1983) has estimated that the direct cost of employing American expatriates is three times their domestic salary plus the expenses of relocation. The level of failure by expatriates is especially high among Americans, who have been more reluctant than Europeans and Japanese to entrust key positions to local nationals. Rosalie Tung (1982, p. 61) compared the proportion of senior management positions held by local nationals in American, Japanese and European companies operating in different regions of the world:

| | Percentage of senior management positions held by local nationals in firms with parent companies in: | | |
	United States	Europe	Japan
Latin America	44	79	83
Middle East	42	86	67
Far East	55	85	65
Africa	36	75	50

Source: Tung, R. L. (1982).

In a later analysis Tung (1987, p. 117) also demonstrates that the failure rate of American expatriates is double that of the Europeans and Japanese, although nearly half of the European companies reported failure rates between 6 and 15 per cent for their assigned expatriates. The cost represented by each failure can be enormous. It is tempting to move towards the simple strategy of reducing the number of expatriates to nil, but that is an unsatisfactory solution if it undermines the need for integration. Bartlett (1986) and Kobrin (1988) both argue that the future will be a time in which multinational corporations will need both to fragment and to integrate to a greater degree than has so far been necessary:

> even the most integrated strategy must be executed by national sub-units. Effective management of a diversified MNC entails exploiting the strengths and knowledge of the subsidiary within the context of a global system. Furthermore, optimization at the system level is more complex than a simple sum of local optima; the subsidiary's role is to maximise its contribution to worldwide objectives rather than local returns . . . there may well be a conflict between achieving local and system wide objectives. (Kobrin, 1988, p. 69)

A reduction in the use of expatriates in a company means that the majority of managers in the global business identify with a single, local unit. This may be desirable from the point of view of the local economy and may provide enhanced autonomy for local managers, yet they all depend on the effectiveness of the business as a whole: integration as well as fragmentation. Furthermore, the continued effectiveness of the global business will depend crucially on the experience and expertise at headquarters. Here there is theoretically an understanding of, and identification with, the business as a whole. That understanding will be limited if the personnel concerned lack international experience, especially as expatriates, and if there are no foreigners represented. This point is made most clearly by Cynthia Haddock and Basil South in their account of Shell.

The well-publicised drop of IBM from their position as market leader is attributed to a number of causes, one of which was their continued dominance by American cultural stereotypes. Berenbeim, (1983, p. 16) calculated that only 15 per cent of top executives in American multinational companies had international experience. The multinational company needs international experience in its personnel in order to maintain its international competence. There are three alternative approaches: colonies, protectorates or federation.

The *colonial* approach is to fill all key positions with nationals from the country of the parent company. This provides common managerial and technical expertise from people with similar experience, as well as close links and tight control from headquarters. If there is lack of local expertise, this approach may be inescapable and may be welcome in the local country because of the potential for technology transfer that it could involve. The problems are that promotion prospects for local nationals are curtailed, the expatriates may take some time to adapt to local circumstances, especially if they do not speak the language, and their relatively privileged living conditions may be resented by local managers. It is probably a satisfactory approach only while the operation is in its early stages.

The *protectorates* approach pursues the colonial idea in a different way. British protectorates, like Aden and Zanzibar at the end of the imperial era ran their own affairs, with Britain being responsible for their defence. In multinational companies the parallel to this approach is for nationals of the parent company to fill all the positions at corporate headquarters, while subsidiaries in other countries are managed entirely by their own nationals. This overcomes the main difficulties of using expatriates in the subsidiaries – cost, language, lack of promotion opportunities locally, and the need for acclimatisation – and provides the benefits of continuity in management, as there is not the artificial constraint of the expatriate contract, which is rarely more than two to three years. Also, the parent company is distanced from the local political situation and local 'conventions' which would embarrass it: in the early 1980s the Western press was full of stories about payments from 'slush funds' that large companies had to make in certain countries in order to win contracts. The potential drawback is the extent of the fragmentation, so that integration becomes harder, with many short visits from headquarters to subsidiaries and back again.

The *federal* approach relies on appointing the best person for the job from anywhere in the company, regardless of their nationality. This method is a most effective integrator as it develops a movement of people in all directions, not simply from headquarters out and back again. It is probably, however, a method that can only be used effectively in a mature company that has spent some time developing its methods of appraisal and pre-assignment preparation. Headquarters will need a databank of prospective expatriates, but can only establish and maintain such a facility if there is a company-wide system of appraisal and career development that identifies appropriate talent and then makes the necessary investment of training and experience that will both prepare a cadre of prospective transnational appointees and then make the appointments.

There can be a number of problems, like the reluctance of most Western countries to provide work permits for foreign nationals when it would seem that an adequate number of indigenous personnel are available. Also, the control of who works where is centrally located rather than distributed. In a mature organisation this will be accepted and perhaps welcomed. In organisations with less well developed procedures and conventions the managements of local companies may resent not being able to make their own appointments.

Developing international competence

Developing the competence of the organisation's people has many features which do not change whether the company is international or not, but we consider here some of the needs and methods of competence development that companies have to tackle in order the sustain effectiveness as international players. Barham and Wills (1992, p. 51) suggest that there are a number of things that managers in international companies have to be able to *do*, with effective communication across language barriers being the most obvious. They then have to develop the sort of people they *are*, in terms of being psychologically mature and intellectually adroit, at the same time as thinking of what they can *become* through further learning and development.

Language

The importance of linguistic competence is frequently underemphasised in English-speaking countries, partly because it is a difficult competence to acquire and there seems to be the easy excuse of saying that English is the language of international business anyway. This fails to recognise that language fluency does not simply aid in negotiating with partners or dealing with colleagues but is essential if one is to acquire any real understanding of the foreign culture. Mendenhall and Oddou (1985 and 1986) explain further advantages. There is improved access to information about a country's economy and market opportunities and any degree of fluency increases confidence in being able to make oneself understood and to be socially accepted.

For those who are not cosmopolitan, in the sense used in this book, there may still be value in linguistic competence, for instance for scientists and engineers. These specialists share another universal language, that of mathematical formulae, so that it requires not too great a degree of understanding of the foreign language to be able to identify a journal article or item in the trade press that would benefit from expert translation:

> many engineers and managers in Japanese computer companies have a sufficient command of English to enable them to understand English-language trade journals and conference presentations, often sources of valuable business intelligence. In contrast, their English-speaking counterparts employ only a handful of engineers capable of following Japanese-language materials and of making the proper inference between publicly available information and its underlying strategic significance – a task that an outside translation service is not equipped to handle. (Dowling and Schuler, 1990, p. 104)

The need to extend one's linguistic ability varies according to one's nationality. The Dutch have a native language spoken by hardly anyone else but themselves so they have become accustomed from an early age to the usefulness of acquiring other languages, even if it is only to understand the television programmes. They also have a central geographical position in Western Europe, common borders with France, Germany and Belgium and a long tradition as an international trading nation. Familiarity with English and either German or French is common. In contrast, the Japanese have a language that is unlike any other except Korean, but this uniqueness has not led them to acquire multilingual fluency in anything like the same way. Their export achievements are all the more remarkable when one realises the extent of their linguistic insularity.

The British and Americans are renowned for an inability to speak any other language and enjoy the dubious benefit of almost everyone else being able to speak English. In many ways the most linguistically adept are those nations across Asia, from India to Borneo who have acquired English as well as their native tongue and who have also acquired confidence in making themselves understood in what are often multilingual societies.

The best way to learn another language is to start as early as possible – certainly before adulthood – and much has been expected from educational institutions, but a 1992 survey of British courses in international management reports very limited language training:

> the languages being studied are still French, German and Spanish; virtually all programmes provide only one language other than English. The future of business lies as much in the Far East as in Europe, but British business schools have made little response to this so far . . . it is not sensible that all schools should try to specialise in Asian languages; but it is disappointing that so few have been prepared to make the commitment. (CNAA, 1992, p. 26)

The common method of language training used in international companies is to employ the services of a specialist commercial company, such as Berlitz, or facilities at a local educational institution. Manchester Business School has a language unit, where it is possible for managers to undergo intensive language training by a combination of one-to-one tuition, language laboratory methods and interactive methods, such as group conversation classes and study of film and video footage shot in the country where the language is spoken. The languages available are Arabic, Chinese, Japanese, Russian and all major European languages.

Cultural sensitivity

Leaning a language is best done in conjunction with getting to know the culture, customs and taboos of the country where the language is to be spoken. This makes the language learning much less tedious and mechanical and adds the essential dimension of cultural awareness to the knowledge of the language. It may also be necessary for other members of the organisation who are not going to learn the language, but still need to have a sensitivity to the culture of a country they are going to visit or whose nationals are visiting them. There are many potential pitfalls relating to religious practice, political allegiances, the social position of women, food, clothing and many more. Cultural variance does not prevent misunderstandings even when people share a common language. Recently a Canadian manager visited Britain for the first time and was accommodated in his English managing director's house. On the first evening there was an excellent dinner and the Canadian thought he was adjusting very well until it was time to go to bed, when the parting words from his host's wife were, 'I do hope you sleep well and don't bother to set your alarm. I'll knock you up in the morning.'

One method of developing cultural sensitivity is to read about the culture of the people with whom you have to deal, or watching films made with the specific purpose of explaining cultural variations. A refinement is for employees of the organisation to prepare case studies on their experiences abroad. This is a feature of training at NEC, as Nigel Holden explains in Chapter 10:

> These case studies are designed to provide to those who come after them illumination about problems of handling non-Japanese personnel. Some of these case studies are translated into English and are used by foreign-language trainers – Tokyo-based American employees – to sensitise employees to the pitfalls of cross-cultural misunderstandings whilst enhancing their knowledge of 'on-the-job English'. (see page 136)

If the degree of local interaction is to be modest and the period of working there only a few weeks or months, then these methods should suffice. If the period is to be longer and the degree of interaction greater, Mendenhall and Oddou (1985) suggest that there should be up to four weeks' full-time training, or as much as eight weeks if the new culture is a particularly unfamiliar one. The methods of training will then benefit from becoming participative, with role plays of typical business and social situations and perhaps a short acclimatisation visit to the new country.

Although some managers believe that all their training should be related to business situations, role plays of social situations of a traditional nature are ideal learning methods, as cultural conventions are at their most explicit. It would probably be too bizarre to organise a role play of a wedding or a funeral, but a traditional family meal would contain many of the key features of local cultural behaviour. Ronen (1990) suggests a 'host-family surrogate' as a feature of the preparation of an expatriate family. The prospective expatriates spend time with a family from the culture they are to visit who reside in the country of the expatriate and who are paid a fee from the employer to set up and run a series of acculturation experiences. The value of this method is that it is as realistic as possible and the learners have to respond in a whole variety of different situations.

An alternative was devised in the early 1970s and called a cultural assimilator (Fiedler, *et al.*, 1971). The learner reads through a brief statement about a situation of cultural puzzlement and then is asked to choose one of several interpretations of what was happening. If the correct choice is made, the learner proceeds to the next episode; if not, there has to be a further choice until the correct interpretation is picked. Figure 7.1 shows an example.

Harry Brown has just completed his first working day in Malaysia. He has found it pretty irksome as the people he met seemed more interested in making agreeable conversation than getting down to business. He has just got back to his hotel and feels he would like a good drink in the lounge before going up to his room for a shower. He rests a weary foot on the edge of a low table while he slumps in an armchair and flicks his fingers for a waiter. Unable to attract attention, he calls out, 'Service here, please' and points to a member of the hotel staff, who then speaks to a waitress who comes to Harry's table and takes his order. Harry notices that she seems very embarrassed.

Why is the waitress disconcerted ?

1 Because she realises that she was not attending to her duties properly.
2 Because Harry's behaviour was what Malaysians regard as impolite.
3 Because she was about to go off duty and has been delayed.
4 Because Malaysian waitresses do not expect to be asked
   to wait at table when the customer is a single male.
5 Because drinks are not normally served in hotel lounges,
   but a waitress would not wish to point that out to a
   European visitor.

The correct choice of interpretation is 2, as it is considered insulting to show the soles of your feet to someone, or to point your feet towards another person. Pointing with the finger is also regarded as impolite: Malaysians point or beckon with the thumb laid across the forefinger. It would also be most unusual for voices to be raised to attract attention.

Figure 7.1   Example of a cultural assimilator

The less intensive methods of acculturation will be needed at all levels of the parent company, so that employees understand the range and variety of the company as a whole, rather than being interested only in their own patch. Meeting people employed in subsidiary or associated companies abroad, receiving news about overseas activities and about the lives of people in those countries can all aid understanding. It is perhaps important to remember that ideas about certain overseas countries can be distorted through popular television programmes, which emphasise, for instance, street violence in the United States and widespread use of martial arts in Hong Kong. Academics in British and American universities regularly enrol research students from the Middle East and the Far East, who arrive with bewildering, stereotyped views about the societies they are entering.

Developing cultural sensitivity is very difficult among employees who feel that their jobs are threatened by the internationalisation process. It is incontestable that many people in Western nations have lost their employment through their employers moving parts of their operation to other regions of the world where labour costs are lower. This can lead to a form of protectionism when there is a belief that the competition is 'unfair' in the sense that there are, for instance, illegal immigrants in other countries that can be employed at extremely low rates. If it is possible to demonstrate how those employed on similar work in other countries are achieving impressive levels of productivity by 'fair' methods, it can have a stimulating effect.

On a more limited scale, cultural awareness training that includes personal exposure to unfamiliar cultural situations, either simulated or real, can slightly reduce the problem of managerial reluctance to take on overseas assignments.

But what competences are needed?

Apart from languages and cultural sensitivity, what are the competences that are needed for an international business? Are there any, apart from those two, that can be identified as generally necessary? There has been some discussion in the literature about the *characteristics* of the successful manager of an international business (e.g. Barham and Devine, 1990; Tung, 1982) but less on the more specific idea of competences.

In writing about ZENECA in Chapter 13 (see page 204) Reg Carr provides us with a practical answer by setting out the competences considered to be key in that company:

Conceptual thinking	Concern for standards
Strategic thinking	Concern for impact
Cultural adaptability	Strategic influencing
Flexibility	Results orientation
	Development orientation

Despite the large number of different lists of competences (or competencies) there is no general agreement on what are generally needed in any aspect of international work, so companies need to develop their own lists. One appropriate method of doing this is to use an approach which concentrates on the type of change that should be brought about. Kandola and Pearn (1992, p. 66) provide an example:

from	*to*
Technology-led	Marketing-led
Tactical and short-term	Strategic and long-term
Internal focus	External focus
Try to do everything	Specialised target markets
Parochial outlook	Company commitment
Procedure-bound	Innovative and open-minded
UK focus and export	Global competition

Competences is an idea that has taken the world of management training and development by storm, as well as camouflaging some extremely woolly thinking. The basic idea of competence-based training is that it should be criterion-related, directed at developing the ability of trainees to perform specific tasks directly related to the job they are in or for which they are preparing, expressed in terms of performance outcomes and specific indicators. It is a reaction against the approach to training as being a good thing in its own right, concerned with general preparation of people to deal with general matters.

The most influential piece of research on competences is by Richard Boyatzis (1982), although it has been criticised on methodological grounds and many trainers find it too complicated to put into operation. Boyatzis carried out a large-scale intensive study of 2000 managers, holding 41 different jobs in 12 organisations. He defines a competence as: 'an underlying characteristic of a person which results in effective and/or superior peformance in a job' (p. 21):

- It may be a TRAIT, which is a characteristic or quality that a person has, like efficacy, which is the trait of believing you are in control of your future and fate. When you encounter a problem you then take an initiative to resolve the problem, rather than wait for someone else to do it.
- It may be a MOTIVE, which is a drive or thought related to a particular goal, like achievement, which is a need to improve and compete against a standard of excellence.
- It may be a SKILL, which is the ability to demonstrate a sequence of behaviour that is functionally related to attaining a performance goal. Being able to tune and diagnose faults in a car engine is a skill, because it requires the ability to identify a sequence of actions that will accomplish a specific objective. It also involves being able to identify potential obstacles and sources of help in overcoming them. The skill can be applied to a range of different situations. The ability to change the sparking plugs is an ability only to perform that action.
- It may be a person's SELF-IMAGE, which is the understanding we have of ourselves and an assessment of where we stand in the context of values held by others in our environment. For example: 'I am creative and innovative. I am expressive and I care about others.' In a job requiring routine work and self-discipline, that might modify to: 'I am creative and innovative. I am too expressive. I care about others and lack a degree of self-discipline.'
- It may be a person's SOCIAL ROLE, which is a perception of the social norms and behaviours that are acceptable and the behaviours that the person then adopts in order to fit in.
- It may be a BODY OF KNOWLEDGE.

Some of these characteristics can be developed, some can be modified and some can be measured, but not all. Although not developed specifically for international applications, the Boyatzis framework provides a useful reference for thinking about what is required in international training.

IHRM *and competence*

The international dimension of competence acquisition and deployment lies largely with the strategic question about the amount of international exchanges of personnel. Despite the high cost of these moves, and the reluctance of many people to undertake them, such exchanges are essential to the overall development of the international business. Without them the need for the business to fragment can never be balanced by the complementary need for integration. The mature organisation will be able to adopt the federal model that has been described, but organisations in an earlier stage of development will probably have to take the protectorate or colonial route to integration while maturity is being attained.

The development of international competence in all the members of the organisation will have cultural awareness at its centre, so that the misunderstandings that stem from the mystery of cultural dissimilarity can be reduced. Cultural awareness will be a powerful integrating force at all levels of the operation, especially including those who never work away from their home site. For the travellers and others who look outside the organisational boundary, the development of language goes together with understanding a different culture: language is the way cultural variety is most frequently expressed and cultural experience is the most amenable way to acquire a grasp of language.

Apart from language and cultural sensitivity, the other aspects of competence required in the international organisation will be for each business to decide for itself, but the comprehensive framework prepared by Richard Boyatzis will make a useful point of departure in identifying what those competences are.

References

Barham, K. and Devine, M. (1990), *The Quest for the International Manager*, Ashridge Management College, Berkhamsted, Herts.

Barham, K. and Wills, S. (1992), *Management Across Frontiers*, Ashridge Management Research Group, Berkhamsted, Herts.

Bartlett, C. A. (1986), 'Building and managing the transnational: the new organizational challenge', in Porter, M., *Competition in Global Industries*, Free Press, New York.

Berenbeim, R. E. (1983), *Managing the International Company: Building a global perspective*, The Conference Board, New York.

Boyatzis, R. (1982), *The Competent Manager*, John Wiley, New York.

Council for National Academic Awards (1992), *Review of International Business and Management*, CNAA, London.

Dowling, P. J. and Schuler, R. S. (1990), *International Dimensions of Human Resource Management*, PWS–Kent, Boston, Mass.

Fiedler, F. E., Mitchell, T. and Triandis, H. C. (1971), 'The cultural assimilator: an approach to cross-cultural training', *Journal of Applied Psychology*, April, pp. 90–9.

Harvey, M. G. (1983), 'The multinational corporation's expatriate problem: an application of Murphy's Law', *Business Horizons*, January–February, pp. 71–8.

Hodgetts, R. M. and Luthans, F. (1991), *International Management*, McGraw-Hill, London.

IDS (1990), *Recruitment*, European Management Guides, Institute of Personnel Management, London.

Kandola, R. S. and Pearn, M. A. (1992), 'Identifying competencies', in Boam, R. and Sparrow, P. (eds), *Designing and Achieving Competency*, McGraw-Hill, London.

Kobrin, S. J. (1988), 'Expatriate reduction and strategic control in American multinational corporations', *Human Resource Management*, vol. 27, no. 1, pp. 63–75.

Mendenhall, M. and Oddou, G. (1985), 'The dimensions of expatriate acculturation', *Academy of Management Review*, vol. 10, pp. 39–46.

Mendenhall, M. and Oddou, G. (1986), 'Acculturation profiles of expatriate managers: implications for cross-cultural training programmes', *Columbia Journal of World Business*, Winter, pp. 73–9.

Ronen, S. (1990), 'Training and international assignee', in Goldstein, I. (ed.), *Training and Career Development*, Jossey-Bass, San Francisco.

Scullion, H. (1992), 'Strategic recruitment and development of the international manager: some European considerations', *Human Resource Management Journal*, vol. 3, no. 1, pp. 57–69.

Tung, R. L. (1982), 'Selection and training procedures of U.S., European and Japanese multinationals', *California Management Review*, Fall, pp. 57–71.

Tung, R. L. (1987), 'Expatriate assignments: enhancing success and minimizing failure', *Academy of Management Executive*, Summer, pp. 117–26.

CHAPTER 8

Co-ordination to integrate the fragments

> To operate as an effective strategic whole, the transnational must be able to reconcile the diversity of perspectives and interests it deliberately fosters, integrate the widespread assets and resources it deliberately disperses, and coordinate the roles and responsibilities it deliberately differentiates.
> (*Bartlett and Ghoshal, 1989, p. 166*)

We have already seen how managers believe that they have to pursue both fragmentation and integration simultaneously (Kobrin, 1988). The above quotation expresses succinctly the way in which managers give themselves major problems of co-ordination by adopting the measures they see as necessary for business success. The challenge is to find ways of doing this which transcend conventions that have worked so far. Many IHRM activities, such as recruitment and negotiating with trade unions, are rooted in local, national practice and sensibly stay that way. Approaches to co-ordination may have been culturally determined in the past, but must increasingly move to a more intercultural style, as the dominance of the parent company nationality declines in favour of the multinationality of the global business. Co-ordination is the way to synergy, so that the global business does more and better together than it could possibly achieve as a number of independent units.

Traditional approaches to co-ordination

To explain how methods of co-ordination tend to vary with the nationality of the parent company, Bartlett and Ghoshal describe what they see as the three broad approaches to co-ordination that have been used so far, the Japanese, the American and the European.

Japanese centralisation

The typical Japanese approach is where a strong headquarters group maintain for themselves all major decisions and frequently intervene in the affairs of overseas subsidiaries. This appears to stem from their difficulty in dealing with foreigners, as Nigel Holden explains in his chapter on NEC:

> a major strategic challenge for Japanese firms is to accept that non-Japanese must somehow be given more direct responsibility and opportunity for genuine promotion within the company at the local level . . . there has to be letting-go from the centre. But this is no easy thing. For companies must overcome severe impediments associated with wariness, distrust and lack of knowledge about the world beyond Japan. (see page 127–8)

American formalisation

The American approach is described as formalisation. Power is vested not in headquarters or in the managers of local companies, but in formal systems, policies and standards, so that it is the systems that drive the business. Many American businesses went international at the time that the use of control systems were being rapidly developed to cope with the large size of businesses. The idea of delegation and holding others accountable by means of extensive computerised information systems seemed eminently suitable for operating the increasing number of overseas units, especially when one remembers the apparent unpopularity of overseas postings among American managers that we have already seen (e.g. Tung and Miller, 1990).

European socialisation

In European companies the approach to co-ordination is described as socialisation. There has been a reliance on key, highly-skilled and trusted individuals. These people were carefully selected and developed a detailed understanding of the company's objectives and methods. Their personal development included the establishment of close working relationships and mutual understanding with colleagues. Once groomed these key decision-makers were despatched to manage the subsidiaries, so that the headquarters and the subsidiaries were both strengthened.

> because it relies on shared values and objectives, it represents a more robust and flexible means of co-ordination. Decisions reached by negotiations between knowledgeable groups with common objectives should be much better than those made by superior authority or by standard policy. (Bartlett and Ghoshal, 1989, p. 163)

These three different approaches or emphases worked best for companies headquartered in those three regions of the globe. As the world becomes smaller and companies become more diverse with subsidiaries that are fully mature, more sophisticated methods are needed: companies are not international, but global.

Extending the range of co-ordination methods

A company will not suddenly cease to be Japanese or American as a result of managerial decree, and the strength of the three contrasted approaches should not be underestimated. Any management will, however, benefit from considering additional means of achieving co-ordination. Some will fit well with their current practice and will add to their strength, others will not seem suitable yet, others will not seem suitable at all.

Evangelisation

The first suggestion is summed up, with some hesitation, by using the word evangelisation, to describe the process of winning the acceptance throughout the business of a common mission and a shared purpose. The idea of needing to win hearts and minds has been a common thread in management thinking for most of this century, but it takes on particular significance in the international or global business because of the number of barriers to be surmounted in co-ordination, especially the barriers of language, culture, national boundaries and parochial self-interest. It is indeed a remarkable management team who will be able to commit themselves with enthusiasm to closing down their local operation on the grounds that the business as a whole will benefit if an operation in another country is developed instead.

Evangelisation is used hesitantly to describe this process because it is the language of religion. Using it in relation to business will be heretical to some and irrelevant to others, but the processes of evangelisation contain many of the methods that are needed in co-ordination and evangelists confront the same barriers as those dealing in the world of global business. One of the most successful of all the great international companies has been Matsushita, the founder of which established in 1932 a development plan that was set out to cover a 250-year period. All employees undertake a programme of cultural and spiritual training and all worldwide units of the company have a daily assembly ritual. The very thought of a 250-year plan is inconceivable to most managers, but the fact of over 60 years of business success makes their mouths water. At the time of writing the example of the American electronics giant IBM is less happy, but throughout its years of market leadership, the company had some evangelistic features, including the IBM hymn, which caused one team of French analysts to describe it as 'la nouvelle église' (Pages et al., 1979).

Co-ordination through evangelisation works through *shared belief*. The beliefs may be interpreted in different ways and may produce varied behaviours, but there is the attempt to promulgate relatively simple doctrines to which members of the organisation subscribe and through which they are energised. Some readers of this book will have learned their catechism as children, or will have studied the Thirty-nine Articles defining the doctrinal position of the Church of England, or will know the Gettysburg Address by heart. Although this may seem inappropriate to the business world, the Matsushita case provides at least one example of its current application in commercial circles. In the 1970s a British company, Vitafoam, was established by a man who required his senior executives to copy out his annual policy statement by hand, three times, before handing it back to him. It is now commonplace for companies to have mission statements, which come close to being unifying articles of faith:

> At the top is the mission statement, a broad goal based on the organization's planning premises, basic assumptions about the organization's purpose, its values, its distinctive competencies, and its place in the world. A mission statement is a relatively permanent part of an organization's identity and can do much to unify and motivate its members. (Stoner and Freeman, 1992, p. 188)

Evangelisation also works through *parables*. We all love a good story and religion flourishes as tales of the founder and of current heroes are recounted and we learn from the message that the parable conveys. Ed Schein (1985, pp. 237–42) identified 'stories and legends' as one of the key mechanisms for articulating and reinforcing the organisation's culture. In pursuing the religious analogy, it is interesting that almost every Western-based multinational company will have one or more voluminous documents, colloquially known as 'the Company Bible', yet it is invariably a set of rules and procedures, rather than stories, legends or articles of faith.

The company house magazine partially serves the purpose of circulating the good news about heroic deeds in all parts of the company network. Better are the word of mouth exchanges and accounts of personal experience. Those who visit another country have to be fully exploited when they return. Returning expatriates have stories to tell to all members of the company to which they are coming back, not just to the senior managers conducting the debriefing. There are many problems in repatriation, but one of the best ways of getting re-established is to share one's overseas experience widely (with as many people as possible) and fully (covering the full gamut of experience). 'Occasional parachutists' and 'engineers' also need to be encouraged to 'evangelise'. They return with important technical understandings that need to be shared, but they also return with all sorts of other awareness of the visited company which can contribute to the bonding between units. On a tedious flight between Istanbul and Singapore, an Australian businesswoman spent over an hour sorting through a large number of holiday snaps, explaining that she regarded them as the most important present she could bring back. Her male colleagues brought back photographs of machine parts, warehouse layout, operational equipment and production processes. These were used at debriefing sessions with fellow managers. She took back pictures of people and places, of food and mealtimes, of cluttered offices and what was put up on the office walls. These were handed round and explained in casual encounters over coffee, on the way to and from meetings and at dinner parties.

Evangelisation can use *apostles*, ambassadors sent out to preach the faith. These are the 'international managers' described in Chapter 2. Because of their frequent movement they know the worldwide organisation well and can describe one component to another, explaining company policy, justifying particular decisions and countering parochial thinking. They can also move ideas around ('In Seoul they are wondering about . . . What do you think?') and help in the development of individual networks ('Try getting in touch with Oscar Jennings in Pittsburgh . . . he had similar problems a few weeks ago').

At times of crisis, apostles are likely to be especially busy, countering rumour and strengthening resolve. In mature companies apostles will have home bases in different regions, just as expatriates will move in various directions and not simply from the centre out, but before maturity is reached it will probably be important that most of the apostles come from headquarters and have personally met, and can tell stories about, the founder. Anita Roddick's Body Shop is an organisation that grew rapidly on the basis of working in a way that was markedly different from the conventions of the cosmetics industry that it was challenging. Its growth seemed to need people in all parts to identify closely with the vision and personality of the founder:

> The inductresses' eyes seem to light up whenever Anita's name is mentioned. We are told, in semi-joyous terms, the great tale concerning that first humble little shop in Brighton. And . . . one of our inductresses uses the phrase, 'And Anita saw what she had done and it was good'. (Keily, 1991, p. 3)

Standards and norms

Co-ordination can be improved by the development and promulgation of standards and norms. Many British companies have sought the accreditation of BS 5750, which is the British Standard for quality, others claim to be equal opportunity employers. Global companies will wish to set standards for many aspects of their operation. Cynthia Haddock and Basil South in Chapter 14 describe how the Shell centre are charged with developing and maintaining standards relating to alcohol and drug abuse. If standards are adopted throughout a global company, they become a form of co-ordination. Furthermore it is not necessary for all of them to be developed at the centre. Decentralised standard formulation can enable different parts of the global business to take a lead as a preliminary to universal adoption of the standard they have formulated: an excellent method of integration.

Few businesses will be able to develop universally applicable standards in all aspects of human resource management. While researching equal opportunity some years ago, this writer found an interesting situation in an American computer company with a rapidly growing British subsidiary. The company had a high-profile commitment to 'positive action to seek out and employ members of disadvantaged groups'. This was reinforced in the annual appraisal system for managers, who had to indiciate what they had done in the last 12 months to implement a 'programme of employment and development for minorities'. The company annual report made a claim that this initiative was advancing in all international locations. In Britain, however, it was found that:

> Without exception, all managers to whom we spoke ignored that part of their

appraisal . . . They put a line through the offending clause and wrote 'not applicable in the UK' . . . despite the corporate objective of 'citizenship', applicable in the UK, requiring recruitment officers to seek out the disadvantaged in the community . . . Suggestions by the researchers that such an active recruitment policy was an obligation on the part of the management . . . invoked the reaction, 'we're not a welfare organisation.' (Torrington *et al.*, 1982, p. 23)

This particular example may have been an oversight, or an aspect of employment practice that had not yet been developed, but other aspects of IHRM strategy would be much more difficult to standardise. Many manufacturing developments in Asia have been for the explicit reason of being able to enjoy the benefits of low labour costs. It is most unlikely that the American/European/Japanese parent company would develop a company-wide standard on the level of pay rates in manufacturing. In contrast, a company-wide standard set of terms and conditions for expatriate assignment would be much more feasible. The Institute of Personnel Management Library in London has just such a document from IBM in the form of a sample letter of 24 pages!

Systems and procedures

There is obvious scope for co-ordination through systems. Many global businesses are dominated by a single system, which reaches every part of the business. Singapore Airlines, which Ling Sing Chee describes in Chapter 11, has a ticketing and booking system which links thousands of computer terminals in order to operate the airline. At a booking desk in Penang you can book a seat on an aircraft travelling from Istanbul to Manchester. The system is only useful if it provides the global link, and providing the systems link constantly reinforces with all personnel the interrelationship of the activities in all countries where the airline operates. Although that is a specialised example, all businesses have systems and they can be developed to avoid duplication and overlap, so that in one country a team develops a spare part retrieval system that is quickly adopted for use throughout the business, while in another country they concentrate on an aspect of accounting procedures or systematic advice on training opportunities.

Capability

A similar approach is to consider the concentration of *capability* by seeking to encourage the development of particular expertise in different locations, but for group-wide application and exploitation. Bartlett and Ghoshal (1989, p. 106–7) offer the intriguing example of how Teletext was developed by Philips. Because of an interest from the BBC, the British Philips subsidiary began work on the possibility of transmitting text and simple diagrams through a domestic television set. Within Philips generally it was regarded as 'a typical British toy – quite fancy but not very useful'. Despite little encouragement and sales that were initially disappointing, the

British persisted. Ten years after starting work, there were 3 million Teletext receivers in use in Britain and Philips had established a world lead in a product for which there was initially only a British market.

Philips have pioneered this type of development, settling activities in places where culture suits the activity:

> their centre for long-range technology developement was recently moved from the United States to the Far East, where the time orientation was seen as more conducive to innovations than the 'quick fix' mentality of North America. Some major research departments are located in Italy, which is seen by other firms as an impossible country for important facilities. Yet their Italian research laboratories are highly successful, as are the important R & D facilities of IBM and DEC in the same region. All of them run in a uniquely Italian way, and are left to do so since this appears to lead to their success. Manufacturing plants are likely to be located elsewhere – Germany, for example. (Evans *et al.*, 1989, p. 116)

The corporate Olympics

The scope for co-ordination in a transnational, global business is perhaps summed up by the analogy of the Olympic Games. This is an activity which unites almost every country of the world. The heroes are young men and women far from the decision-making bodies, the youth of some countries appear more skilled and are more numerous than the youth of others, yet they are all equal in contest, observing the same rules and striving to achieve the same standards. There is rivalry and intense competition, which produce levels of achievement that can rarely be reached without the stimulus of the high-profile contest. Competitiveness creates rather than destroys performance. As it moves around the globe every four years, it is accepted that not all participating countries can act as host. This extraordinary event is energised by the ideal of worldwide sporting competition, and it is co-ordinated by detailed rules and conventions that are readily observed. Although there is an international managing committee, this has considerable power over only a small range of decisions. The conduct of the events is left in the hands of a national committee that changes for every Olympic celebration. The international Olympic movement is a triumph of international human resource management.

The global company will be energised by an ideal (such as the world's favourite airline, the largest motor company, the world's most luxurious hotels) and it will be co-ordinated by a range of processes which provide precise high standards throughout the company, when these are needed, and which constantly distributes responsibility for company success to different parts of its corporate body. Stories of the founder will be retold and there may be rituals that are repeated with the solemnity and symbolism of lighting the Olympic flame, but the company will not be rooted in a single, geographical location. The modern Olympic Games were established by a Frenchman and the headquarters of the International Olympic Committee is in

Geneva, but no one would say that the Games are French or Swiss. Rosbeth Moss Kanter has also used the Olympic metaphor in a slightly different way:

> Successful managers in the corporate Olympics must not only be good negotiators, seeking the best deal for 'their' unit, but also understand when and how to share resources, to combine forces, to do things that benefit another group – in the interests of superior overall performance. (Kanter, 1989, p. 362)

The challenge of co-ordination in the international company is the stiffest test that human resource management has to face, and success in international human resource management is fundamental to the development of the international companies of the future.

References

Bartlett, C. A. and Ghoshal, S. (1989), *Managing Across Borders: The transnational solution*, Random House, London.

Evans, P., Lank, E. and Farquhar, E. (1989), 'Managing human resources in the international firm: lessons from practice', in Evans, P., Doz, Y. and Laurent, A. (eds), *Human Resource Management in International Firms*, Macmillan, London.

Kanter, R. M. (1989), *When Giants Learn to Dance*, Simon & Schuster, London.

Keily, D. (1991), 'Body Shop blues', *The Sunday Times*, 8 December, London, p. 3.

Kobrin, S. J. (1988), 'Expatriate reduction and strategic control in American multinational corporations', *Human Resource Management*, vol. 27, no. 1, pp. 63–75.

Pages, M., Bonnetti, M., de Gaulejac, V. and Descendre, D. (1979), *L'Emprise de l'organisation*, Presses Universitaires de France, Paris.

Schein, E. H. (1985), *Organizational Culture and Leadership*, Jossey-Bass, San Francisco.

Stoner, J. A. F. and Freeman, R. E. (1992), *Management*, 5th edition, Prentice Hall, Englewood Cliffs, NJ.

Torrington, D. P., Hitner, T. J. and Knights, D. (1982), *Management and the Multi-racial Workforce*, Gower Press, Aldershot.

Tung, R. L. and Miller, E. L. (1990), 'Managing in the twenty-first century: the need for global orientation', *Management International Review*, vol. 30, 1990/1991, pp. 5–18.

PART II

IHRM *in action*

CHAPTER 9

Ferranti-Thomson Sonar Systems
An Anglo-French venture in high tech collaboration

ANN P. MORAN

In 1990, a large French-domiciled international company bought a 50 per cent stake in a small division of a British engineering company and a joint venture was formed. This case study reviews the changes in human resource management practice that were needed during the first few years of the new company. The sudden move to internationalisation in management practice was stimulated by the trauma of a well-publicised fraud that rocked the international business community. The subsequent fundamental reorganisation of the company required major changes in attitudes to, and methods of, communication and company structure.

Accompanying the changes was the development of language training. This was only one of the several changes in orientation that Ferranti employees have had to undertake, together with a reshaping of the human resource function, as differences between the French and British conventions are gradually reviewed to find scope for increased harmonisation.

Company background

Ferranti-Thomson Sonar Systems (UK) Ltd which is based at Stockport, near Manchester, was the sonar systems division of Ferranti Computer Systems Ltd until June 1990.

More than a century ago Sebastian Ziani de Ferranti invented a unique alternator revolutionising the power industry and went on to found the company which is now Ferranti International. In 1987, Ferranti merged with the US company International Signal and Control (ISC) with the aim of gaining access to the US military market. One of eight companies forming the new Ferranti International was Ferranti Computer Systems Ltd, one division of which was sonar systems. The company's expertise is in civil and military computer systems.

In September 1989, a major fraud was discovered within ISC which led to a substantial reassessment of the company's assets. Legal proceedings were started by Ferranti International against several of ISC's senior managers. In 1990, in order to ease the financial situation, Ferranti sold various parts of the company. In particular, Ferranti Defence Systems was sold to GEC, and the sonar systems division of Ferranti

Computer Systems was formed into a joint venture with Thomson CSF, an international defence electronics company.

Thomson CSF, with headquarters in Paris, is a member of the Thomson Group, the world's largest non-US electronics corporation, dealing in defence, consumer and semi-conductor electronics. It participates in major R & D and industrial co-operative programmes around the world. The French government holds a controlling interest in the Group.

Expected benefits of the Ferranti-Thomson sonar joint venture included pooling of R & D programmes and use of the worldwide marketing capabilities of Thomson CSF. There was also a general move at this time in a contracting defence industry towards a concentration into fewer but larger groups of companies.

The joint venture was specifically with Thomson Sintra Activities Sous-Marines (TSASM), based at Valbonne in the south of France with other offices at Brest and Arcueil. The joint venture company was named Ferranti-Thomson Sonar Systems (UK) Ltd (FTSS). Thomson CSF have also formed a joint venture with the UK company, Pilkington Optronics (optical systems) based in Wales and Scotland. Other Thomson companies in the United Kingdom are Link-Miles (military simulators) and MEL Communications Ltd (military communications). Thomson CSF have also acquired a major part of Philips' European defence activities in Holland, Belgium and France.

Because of its geographical location at Stockport and at three other small ex-Ferranti sites in the United Kingdom, the new joint venture company started life with a strong Ferranti culture which was affected by the recent unsettling times in the company. Initially all employees were ex-Ferranti. By the end of 1991, the company had 650 employees at four sites with over 400 staff at the Stockport site. The ways in which the international Thomson influence has increased and to some extent has replaced the Ferranti culture at Stockport will now be examined.

Changes in communication channels

General communication

The area in which there has been the greatest need for personal adjustment is that of communications. Managers are now finding that because of cultural differences between themselves and other parts of Thomson, they need to check and double-check to be sure that what was intended has actually been communicated. The communication may need to be repeated and re-emphasised. Thus the interchange of information is much greater than it would be in a similar British-only company. One manager estimates that the effort needed to communicate has doubled. The French expect a response from the person to whom a communication was sent and not from a delegated person. To reply otherwise is taken as a slight. The non-executive board is now multinational, half British and half French, whilst the executive board remains

100 per cent British. Communication with the two groups on the non-executive board takes up more of the senior managers' time. The two groups have different priorities and want different information presented. For example, the French board members wanted a 10-year plan for the company which had not been prepared before.

More upward and more complicated communications are needed whilst keeping within the formal hierarchical framework that is normal in French companies. Open questioning of superiors by the French is not common.

Because the company is an Anglo-French joint venture, the UK Department of Trade, which were involved in the setting up of the company, still show great interest in its progress. There is thus continuing communication between the Department and the company. There is now direct communication with officials of foreign countries and with UK political figures – something which did not happen before.

There have been invitations for company representatives to attend cultural events at the French embassy but, at a local level, the company wishes to emphasise its independence at present rather than to be thought of as a French implant. There is a preference to be active in local social events.

General international company information is communicated through its publicity functions. Press releases are exchanged and various English language Thomson monthly and quarterly journals are circulated including *Thomson World Round-up*, published by Thomson Corporate Communication Department. A quarterly journal called *BIC* informs the Thomson Sintra affiliates of each other's activities. The Ferranti International journal is sent to Thomson. Publicity photographs and videos are exchanged. Ferranti-Thomson does not as yet produce any such literature in French. Altogether, FTSS staff have found the Thomson journals to be a very helpful introduction to the international company.

Meetings

The style of meetings held with French counterparts in Thomson is considerably different from that of meetings held with British companies. The British are at an apparent advantage here as there are contractual obligations in some joint projects to conduct all communications in English. These international meetings are held for the purpose of exchanging joint project, financial, technical and contract information.

A difficulty for many managers attending these international meetings is coming to terms with the surprisingly unstructured approach of their French colleagues who do not feel constrained to follow the agenda and sometimes walk out of the meeting for private discussion. This makes the meetings much more difficult for a British chairperson to control. Important decisions are often made by the French outside the meeting rather than in it. However, it has been found that important information is sometimes passed on between managers in the French company only in the circumstances of formal meetings and they are known to find it difficult to understand the British decision-making process. More time must therefore be allowed for decisions to be made and more information must be made available. Accurate communication of technical and strategic points between the British and French can be difficult and managers at these meetings have to be sure that they have been clearly understood.

Ferranti International is now active in different business sectors from FTSS but Thomson Sintra is in the same sonar business. Thus whilst many of the senior managers hold regular meetings with their opposite numbers in Thomson Sintra, similar meetings are not held with Ferranti opposite numbers. This type of communication is found to be relatively easy between managers because although Thomson Sintra is four times the size of Ferranti-Thomson, it is a parallel business and there is good synergy between staff. However, some staff feel that these meetings should always be held with an internationally experienced person present. Those in FTSS who speak some French converse in French with Thomson staff whenever possible, although it has been found that Thomson international representatives speak very good English.

Many smaller top-level meetings are now held by tele-conferencing as it has been found increasingly difficult to arrange for all participants to come together. To date, video-conferencing has not been used.

A monthly meeting of a business opportunities committee decides how business opportunities already identified are to be approached. The full technical abilities of all parts of the international company are now taken into account and these 'bricks of technology' are used to construct the best approach to a successful bid for a contract. Whereas before the joint venture was set up only Ferranti technical abilities could be considered.

Finally, the traditional French business lunch, starting late, finishing late and progressing very slowly, may still be part of a French business trip. Many significant decisions can be taken during such lunches and a good knowledge of French cuisine and culture is therefore important for British managers.

Reporting

Reporting requirements have changed and expanded, especially in the financial area, as a result of the international aspects of the joint venture. Top-level financial and management reporting is to both parent companies, the reports requiring different emphases for each company. The resultant much enlarged workload of report preparation can wrongly be seen to be counter-productive by some staff. Timing and content of reports now have to fit in with Thomson requirements. Whilst in many ways the local management have more autonomy, more stringent reporting requirements are now placed on managers. The French expect more detailed and analytical planning, whereas the British tend to plan more generally and then compromise or adapt.

Information technology

Thomson is a strongly financially aware company and since the existing system was inadequate for its requirements a new management information computer system, covering all aspects of company finances, has been installed.

Ferranti-Thomson is now buying communications equipment compatible with Thomson equipment so that programme plans and documentation can be exchanged on joint projects. The marketing databases have been overlaid and the bigger marketing network of Thomson can now be accessed. This support gives Ferranti-Thomson added strength in this area. Publicity styles and software packages are being made compatible. Managers now have to take international implications into account when selecting software.

The adjustment of the company's information technology has progressed slowly in the area of personal computers in the two years since it became part of an international group, but has progressed relatively quickly in the area of management information systems. There is some concern that the sharing and exchanging of computer data may lead to an excess of information.

Changes in company structure

As a result of becoming a joint venture, the company board now consists of half Ferranti members and half Thomson members with a rotating chairperson. The company executive managers are nominated half by Ferranti and half by Thomson. The company chief executive officer (CEO) who was previously head of the sonar division has found that his job has changed completely. Thomson expect stronger management control and have increasingly dominated the joint venture. A French-speaking finance director has been appointed. Managers, especially the CEO, now have to think of the international impact of programmes, projects and R & D.

Below the executive manager level, the departments that have been affected by internationalisation are finance, sales, marketing and publicity. Initially there was some overlap in function in the sales area, which led to a small reduction in sales staff. Use is now made of Thomson's large internationally based sales force. The FTSS sales force operate so as to be compatible with Thomson's international style and also look after Thomson's UK interests. Thus there has been a reduction in autonomy but an expansion in product range covered by the sales staff. Marketing has moved from a UK-based operation to become a combined international effort. The range of quality standards that has to be addressed has increased. Moving from a position of competition with Thomson for sales to co-operation and consultation has been difficult and has taken some time to accomplish. There have been no other job losses as a result of becoming an international company.

Informal links have been made between senior technical managers in FTSS and their counterparts in Thomson Sintra. However, the functions of design and development are not yet carried out jointly. It is likely that the first staff secondments and interchanges will be in non-technical areas such as finance, sales, marketing and personnel. The fact that the company is a joint venture rather than wholly owned by Thomson makes interchanges more difficult. However, this issue is currently being reviewed by the CEO and it is hoped that opportunities will be provided for staff at many levels in the company in the near future.

Language training

French language tuition started in Ferranti at Stockport during 1989 before the joint venture was set up. Now up to 25 people out of approximately 400 at Stockport are learning French, paid for by the company. Two managers who commenced employment with FTSS after the joint venture was set up are fairly fluent French speakers, one existing employee in the sales area was already fluent and two managers who started tuition in 1989 are now fairly fluent and feel this has had a significant impact on their role in the company. Those learning French include the executive managers and the CEO, the publicity manager, sales managers, security manager, receptionist, senior technical and project managers and those senior staff involved in joint projects.

A senior secretary who is bilingual holds occasional lunchtime French conversation classes that are open to anyone in the company.

It has been noticed that whilst there is much keenness to gain proficiency in the language and many managers thought it very important for French tutorials to be available, the time and long-term application needed can be considerable. Some rather overstretched managers have not been able to keep up with the tuition. Out of 26 senior managers questioned 21 had the British qualification GCSE or O-level French but only a few had made serious attempts to maintain their language ability. To move from very little knowledge to a useful fluency is not easy, especially for technically biased staff. A disturbing trend is that the younger technical staff have less background linguistic training than staff in their late 30s or 40s.

Staff felt that it was generally important and socially useful to be able to speak some French to cross cultural bridges and also for travelling although they could get by without it. It could put French colleagues at ease if there was some attempt to use their language. Some thought that at least one person from every area of the company should be able to speak French and that a total lack of French in a senior manager was now a disadvantage. In future, senior secretaries who can speak French will be preferred.

Board meetings consist of half Ferranti members and half Thomson members and translators are present. Technical meetings can sometimes be difficult but many technical words are English. However, it should be remembered that whilst Thomson is a French-owned company, it has worldwide operations. Over half its staff are not French and are more likely to speak English.

Language training is not necessary for everyone but will continue where it is needed. During the last few years, the two areas of major training expenditure in FTSS have been language tuition and training for the new computerised management information system. Thomson provides an intensive French language tuition course which may be used. Opportunities provided by Thomson's other training facilities for staff to gain more understanding of French language and international culture will be used. FTSS staff need to be developed to meet the communication needs of the French connection.

Effect of internationalisation on employees

The average employee has been affected more by the company becoming small and independent than by it becoming an international joint venture. Only the company board members, the management executive, a few senior technical managers and those staff involved on joint projects have been affected by the internationalisation. The company's top management is now locally based and the decision paths are noticeably much shorter. The CEO has to undertake more international travel and has a bigger and broader workload because of different cultural and reporting requirements of the joint venture. Much of the CEO's previous workload has been delegated to the executive managers. The main effect on other senior managers is that they now have to think of the international effect of their actions and have to work to international standards. The finance director has employed a bilingual secretary. The increased emphasis on finance is partly due to the company becoming a stand-alone joint venture and partly to it becoming part of an international company.

From a personal point of view, most staff felt that their security of employment had increased by becoming part of a large, successful government-sponsored international company. However, due to a reduction in defence business, there was a reduction exercise carried out during the first year of the joint venture which involved non-voluntary redundancies. Since then the feeling that being part of the Thomson Group is an advantage has returned. In particular, it provides additional dimensions to job satisfaction. There are now increased opportunities for travel, for developing linguistic expertise and for first-hand international experience. Some jobs in the company have become significantly more attractive and there is the hope of increased international job opportunities. The effect of having two parent companies, even if one has had severe financial difficulties, is perceived as giving more financial security.

It is felt that being an Anglo-French (or if you are French, a Franco-British) joint venture is rather 'fashionable'. Customers also like the international aspect of the company, which gives them more confidence.

Senior managers have increased authority to take decisions whilst being required to maintain a balance between the parent companies' requirements. FTSS staff are exposed to Thomson's business methods and are forced to think internationally. In the future, the company must be able to sell its products in the international market.

Increases in job opportunities for staff have in fact been slow to materialise. Postings to other parts of the company were thought by managers to be very important for management training. From a sample of 26 managers questioned only 8 have had previous international experience, none of which has been in France. One major problem that has not been resolved to date is that the defence nature of most of the work makes exchange of staff difficult. This also affects the level of information exchange. A Thomson project representative with limited access to FTSS company information was based in Stockport at an early stage in the joint venture and more recently Thomson have transferred a new sales manager, who is British, to Stockport. FTSS sent a fluent French-speaking sales representative to France two years after the start of the joint venture.

It is difficult to separate the new ways of thinking in the company caused by internationalisation from those caused by the many changes in the company over the last four years. The main change is that not only Thomson Sintra but other parts of Thomson have to be taken into account in all commercial decisions. Managers have to be much more aware of Europe. The crisper, more commercial and competitive Thomson business methods are filtering into the top layers of management. The general need to change has increased.

It is felt that there is a need for the company to have a small elite group of staff that understands how the large international parent works. They should be aware of the company culture and politics, who is empowered to do what, who to approach with certain problems, who to deal with. Acquiring this knowledge can take a considerable amount of time for those managers who only have occasional interaction with the international company. Most staff who have worked in the company for several years already know and understand how Ferranti, the other parent company, works.

The perceived advantages of the joint venture with an international company are the new areas of business, better business opportunities, the use of Thomson's selling expertise, expanded market areas, the increased and better product range. The company is now in a position to bid for larger and more complex contracts.

The perceived disadvantages of the joint venture include a dichotomy of priorities in the characteristics of the two parent companies. One parent, Ferranti, was recovering from a financial crisis when the joint venture was formed, whilst the other, Thomson, was wanting to press ahead with a long-term aim of obtaining a greater market share in the sonar business. Differences in opinions have to be resolved across the cultural divide.

It is felt that initially the company was not sufficiently resourced in certain areas to encompass the international standards now required. The increased reporting, referral and bureaucracy cause fear that a quick response to the customer may be endangered. Because there is now more interaction with people from another country, business is generally more difficult. However, this does increase management experience and ability, with managers having to take more care and time thinking about the effect of their communications.

The joint venture and internationalisation have been generally welcomed and supported by staff at all levels and continue to be viewed in a positive light.

Effect of internationalisation on the human resources function

The role of the personnel executive manager has changed considerably since the company became international and he is finding the international involvement with

Thomson exciting and invigorating, bringing extra ideas and facilities and a more determined go-ahead approach. There is more interest and emphasis on human resource management from Thomson. A broader human resource view is now needed with an insight into the style of European human resource management. The personnel executive manager is on the Thomson advisory committee on training where an international view of training is taken. The job has a much wider scope and has grown in status within the company. As in other areas in the company, policy decisions need to be assessed for their impact on the larger Thomson Group.

The personnel manager now makes a special point of attending meetings on international issues and international conferences run by the Institute of Personnel Management. There is daily contact with his opposite number in Thomson Sintra and monthly contact with the personnel function at Thomson CSF HQ in Paris when there is an exchange of knowledge and discussion on topics such as job evaluation and job assessment. The company is encouraged to use various human resource tools already used by Thomson. The Thomson international training programme which is now available to the company includes the Thomson University, Thomson three-year convention and transatlantic and transpacific seminars. The aim of this training is to develop global management within Thomson and blend people with different cultural backgrounds.

International employment laws have had no effect on the company as yet but it is expected that European directives will need to be taken into account in the near future. There has been some consideration of the benefits of joining an international pension fund but at present staff belong to the Ferranti pension scheme.

Significant connections have been made with opposite numbers in other Thomson UK organisations and FTSS has hosted Thomson UK subsidiary human resource meetings where there has been a high level of interest and interaction beneficial to all participants. The Ferranti human resource influence, whilst still strong historically, is declining relatively and the Thomson international human resource influence, which is viewed in a positive light, is increasing. However, human resource procedures are still very locally oriented.

Thomson likes to benefit local industry and the community and most of their contracts have some local involvement. This preference has yet to have its effect on FTSS. Historically, Ferranti has been a major employer in the Manchester area and had many local educational and cultural links. However, the position changed in the late 1980s with the company's financial crisis and the reduction in the workforce. Attempts are now being made to renew the links and to build on the respect the Ferranti name still commands in the local community.

Few personnel exchanges have occurred to date as a result of the joint venture. At an early stage FTSS took part in the Thomson 'Olympics', sending a team of staff with athletic ability to the south of France to take part in a series of games. This was felt to be a great ice-breaker and was viewed as being very successful, especially as FTSS won the games overall. The company has looked at language exchanges for employees' children and is attempting to overcome the security problems in order to organise further staff exchanges.

Thus at present there are two inputs of ideas from the two parents, but neither can force their methods onto the joint venture. The personnel manager thus has a lot of local autonomy and can use ideas from either company if he feels they are beneficial.

Recruitment policy changes

The successful company manager of the future will need to have better communication skills since there is more communication in an international company. This is necessary for the top managers and also for those lower down the organisation. Those that succeed in the future will be able to accommodate to change easily and take up the opportunities that an international company can offer, i.e. they will be European-style people. There will need to be a change towards being more accepting of other styles of approach and operation, and more awareness of differences in standards.

When questioned, today's managers thought that it would be important in the future for the company to recruit people with European experience and language ability although few felt their own management style had changed as yet. Top managers of the future are likely to be bilingual, more commercially oriented and possibly not from a Ferranti background. More tact and diplomacy will be needed to make progress within the international structure and to be able to deal with the French opposite number. A tough but not confrontational style is appropriate for international communication. This can fail, especially over a complex subject, even if both sides are speaking English. Subtleties and feelings need to be understood. This calls for a particular type of person of which there are few in the company at present. Middle managers in the company need to be exposed to the international situation perhaps via the Thomson training facilities. They need to become Euromanagers, Eurocommunicators.

There have been no direct changes to recruitment policy but early top appointments went to people with French language ability and an understanding of France who would be able to fit in with the international scene in Thomson. Appointments in the finance, sales and marketing and executive areas have been influenced by Thomson. There is now some consideration of recruitment from other Thomson subsidiaries within the United Kingdom and also from international sites but security problems are inhibiting transfers from the French partner at present. Student exchanges and placements are under consideration. Two years after the setting up of the joint venture there have still not been any management transfers or exchanges, but this is likely to happen first in the finance and sales areas.

Anyone within the company who already has European experience and French language ability is in an advantageous position as regards future opportunities within the company. This is a significant change in approach. Although half of a sample of managers knew nothing about how a French company was run they did not anticipate any major problems in this area.

Payment structures and salary administration have not yet been affected by the internationalisation and are still negotiated locally, but approval for payment packages is needed from the joint board. There has been encouragement to use performance-related pay and job evaluation. Although the FTSS appraisal scheme has recently been changed, the Thomson appraisal system is also being looked at.

Management incentives have not been changed to date although performance-related management incentives are being looked at. It has been found that the Thomson opposite numbers have fewer company cars but higher pay. Thomson's long-service awards are also being compared.

Future developments

Looking to the next few years, it is expected that FTSS will move closer still to Thomson international business methods and that there will be an increased exchange of ideas. The personnel manager expects the human resource role to become more international with probably more time spent in France. Many facets of this role will assume more importance. It is expected that there will be increased emphasis on performance-related reward policies. However, the company will still be tied to British legislation and security. The top management in general will need to become more internationally oriented.

Future human resource initiatives will include more use of the international training available and more joint activities such as the 'Olympics'. These opportunities will be available to a range of staff throughout the company, with the main aim of getting people to meet people. Management weekends are being arranged so that senior managers can build up relationships with their opposite numbers from a work and social point of view. It is expected that the number of staff exchanges will increase substantially.

Internationalisation of the company has been gradual and has affected only the senior managers in the company who have generally welcomed it for the opportunities for new business experience. It has been found that the quality and quantity of communication have needed to increase. Language ability and international experience will be viewed as extremely important for future progression to the top of the company. The human resource function at executive level continues to increase in influence with a widening scope. The extra input of human resource ideas from the international company will continue to be invigorating.

CHAPTER 10

NEC
International HRM with vision

NIGEL HOLDEN

Introduction

NEC is one of the world's largest manufacturing organisations and belongs to that pantheon of Japanese electronics companies which have helped to place Japan, in Dower's (1985, p. 316) crisp phrase, 'at the cutting edge of management and technology'. It is a leading international supplier of communication systems and equipment, computers and industrial electronic systems, electron devices and other products relating to TV and domestic electronic goods. In Japan NEC has a network of 60 consolidated subsidiaries, 62 plants and 400 sales offices. Domestic operations account for three-quarters of NEC's total business. NEC, in Japan and overseas, has a total of 100 000 employees.

The scope of its international operations is summarised as follows:

- 26 manufacturing companies in 15 foreign countries.
- 45 sales and service companies in 23 countries.
- Representative offices, including R & D facilities, in 25 countries.
- Sales offices in most of the 148 countries where NEC does business.
- 24 000 foreign employees throughout the world.
- 26 per cent of NEC's total business comes from overseas sales.

All the company's activities are underpinned by the concept of 'C & C' (computers and communications) which foresees the synergistic integration of computer and communication technologies. Not only does the concept of 'C & C' determine NEC's long-term technological thrust, it also serves, as we shall see, as a principle for internationalising NEC staff. In support of its extensive international business operations, NEC has evolved sophisticated education systems for internationalising its personnel at all levels. But, as with other Japanese company practices, international management education has features which are decidedly Japanese in philosophy and orientation and which are, therefore, unusual according to Western theory and practice.

This case study will concentrate on international education in NEC, which is seen as one of the major instruments for internationalising the attitudes, competencies and outlook of company personnel. Before the detailed examination of current practices in NEC, it will be necessary to set the scene with a backdrop comprising the following elements: concepts of company education in Japan; internationalisation and cross-cultural communication issues; challenges besetting NEC in the globalisation (i.e. international extension) of its activities; and NEC's distinctive international vision. Attention will then turn to the development of international education in NEC, focusing on the period between 1974 and 1987, which saw the establishment of new company-wide internationalisation schemes and management structures to support them. The final sections will focus on current practices and challenges. The case study will conclude with a review of discussion points for HRM specialists for whom Japan still remains an awkward clash and fusion of traditionally Japanese and borrowed Western management theory and practice.

But a word of caution. The practices of NEC should not be taken to be generally characteristic of international management education in major Japanese corporations. First of all, NEC has a reputation for being forward-looking and experimental in its approach to company education. Second, the corporation is special in that it is an electronics-based concern with a highly distinctive worldwide vision. Third, NEC looks upon international education in strategic terms for overall organisational development and for forging its international business networks.

Concepts of company education in Japan

There is a long-standing acceptance in Japan that business success is closely related to education and that life, in each and every endeavour, is a ceaseless process of learning (Daito, 1986; Gow, 1988; Holden, 1990a; Reischauer, 1984). There is furthermore a conviction among the Japanese that 'self-betterment (means) national betterment' (Meech-Pekarkik, 1986, p. 120). Self-betterment can be seen as something promoted by companies for their own ends, but also put by the companies at the disposal of the most important group of all: Japan itself. For, as Rohlen (1974, p. 44) points out, there is in Japan a general acceptance that 'the company succeeds only if the national system succeeds, and the nation depends on the contribution of companies'.

According to the management scientist, Sasaki (1984, p. 41), the immediate purpose of company education is 'to stimulate creativity, to promote an aggressive spirit and to promote the spirit of the company man'. But company education is also a continuation of the general education system which inculcates into all Japanese the necessity of behaving harmoniously – i.e. with due deference to elders and betters – in the groups and circles in which they move or might move. It might, therefore, be said that company education systems in Japan reinforce the Japanese propensity for this learning for harmonious interaction.

All in all, therefore, the shape, scope and orientation of company education in Japan have psychosocial underpinnings that lie outside Western experience. Not only that, company education is perceived as a major means of creating long-term organisational development. In this sense it has a strategic remit that largely falls outside the more functionally-based Western company training. To explain: the Japanese as a race like to organise and be organised, to plan and to be regimented. Japanese companies, it seems, cater for this psychological need on a long-term basis in such a way as to achieve their economic objectives. It is indeed as if major Japanese corporations create their entire organisational development programmes around this evidently deeply ingrained need.

These various points about organisational development become manifest in Figure 10.1 which shows the 'professional ability development programme' of one of Japan's leading computer companies, but not NEC. Note that the development programme is for all employees and spans a 42-year cycle!

Although major Japanese corporations are replete with departments and personnel responsible for organisational development and company education, one of the striking characteristics of Japanese practice is on-the-job training (OJT). The essence of OJT is that those who have knowledge and experience pass them on to those who lack them (Gow, 1988, pp. 32–4). Those with the all-important knowledge and experience are longer-standing members of the company, and the OJT system allows them to nurture or, as the Japanese are wont to say, 'take care of' junior colleagues.

OJT can be informal, be integrated into various in-company programmes or performed outside the company, as when new recruits are called upon to 'understudy' field sales managers. It is mainly through OJT that younger company members both learn about the entire company system: its visions, philosophies and business object-ives, on the one hand, and its human and technological capabilities, on the other.

These various points about Japanese company education systems must of course be seen in conjunction with the fact that Japanese employees tend to remain all their working life with one company, and are socialised through the calculatedly integrative and even paramilitary character of education programmes. The elements that come to the fore are:

1 A tradition which explicitly links education with business success.
2 A belief in education as a means of self-improvement in its own right.
3 A conviction that senior members of the company should 'take care of' younger members.
4 A propensity, on the personal level, to learn anything that may be beneficial to the members of any group one is involved with for a productive or social purpose. In the company context this predisposes people to share learned information and knowledge for the perceived corporate good.
5 A concrete aim to produce an exclusive (i.e. 'outsider-shunning') corporate culture, which will facilitate and sustain the bonding process among all members of the same company.
6 The necessarily long-term nature of company education, coupled with management behaviour that naturally spreads decision-making, permit the Japanese to do what they are particularly good at: *the planning and organisation of activities on a grand scale with other Japanese.*

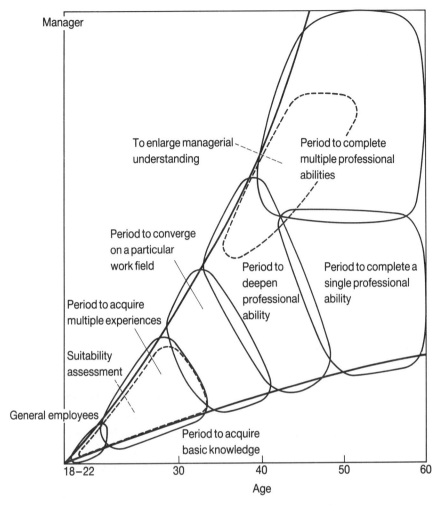

Manager

To enlarge managerial
understanding

Period to complete
multiple professional
abilities

Period to converge
on a particular
work field

Period to
deepen
professional
ability

Period to complete a
single professional
ability

Period to acquire
multiple experiences

Suitability
assessment

General employees

Period to acquire
basic knowledge

18–22   30   40   50   60

Age

Figure 10.1   Professional ability development programme of a major Japanese
computer company (Source: Institute for International Co-operation/Japan International
Co-operation Agency, 1988; reproduced from Dore (1988))

The globalisation of NEC

The terms 'globalisation' and 'internationalisation' appear to be used interchange-
ably. The terms certainly overlap, but they are by no means synonymous. In this case
study globalisation will refer to activities which extend international operations: the
setting up of overseas sales offices, manufacturing facilities, the hiring of foreign
personnel. Internationalisation, the more troublesome word, will refer to policies and
practices to equip company personnel with attitudes and outlook which transcend a

narrowly ethnocentric world-view. But, as will become clearer in due course, internationalisation actually means more than this in the Japanese corporate context: it shields a Japanese wariness and anguish about how best to handle relationships with foreigners. At the same time 'internationalisation' is something of a loaded term used by the Japanese to camouflage, and deflect criticism of, the Japanisation of the world economy (van Wolferen, 1989, p. 415).

First, though, we take a brief look at globalisation: at the general problems and challenges thrown up by the international business environment and which impede the globalisation process. According to company sources in 1988, the major problems and challenges facing NEC are:

- Unstable exchange rates.
- Trade friction.
- Competition from other Asian countries.
- Competition from giant electronics companies in Europe and the United States.
- Changes in the global electronics market (information technology is now available for home as well as company use).

These challenges remain intact, but NEC's overall business position has in the last two years been exacerbated by other factors directly affecting Japanese computer manufacturers (see *The Financial Times*, 11 August 1992) as follows:

- Stagnant world-wide demand.
- Rapidly rising R & D costs.
- Fierce price competition.
- Home-market recession entailing substantial investment in computers by manufacturing industry and the financial sector.

But it is, of course, impossible to see these business problems and challenges in terms of economics, politics and technology. There is also a chalice of management challenges arising from Japan's interactions with foreign business cultures on a worldwide basis. NEC is a company that has devoted many years to the attempt to understand the nature of these challenges as part of its internationalisation strategy. One of the instruments in this strategy is the distinctive vision for the globalisation *and* internationalisation of NEC, associated with the legendary name of Koji Kobayashi, about whom more will be said shortly. First, though, we need to examine the problematical term 'internationalisation' in the Japanese context. It is also necessary to understand the nature of Japanese communication problems with the outside world. The following sections will deal with both difficult issues.

Internationalisation: a peculiar Japanese problem

To the Japanese the word internationalisation (Jap. 'kokusaika'), suggests procedures for integrating Japanese business systems with the rest of the world economy. But the word also implies that this process is not a smooth one and that Japan's global commercial ambitions are misunderstood and misinterpreted by other nations, especially by the United States and the EC countries. Virtually all major Japanese companies put 'internationalisation' very near the top of their corporate agenda, not only because of the Japanese dominance in several global sectors but also because they are being forced into becoming Western-style multinationals. This is creating awkward problems. As an article in *The Economist* in June 1989 explained:

> Reluctantly, but inevitably, Japan's big companies are learning to do what western ones did decades ago – to go multinational. Many Japanese firms have had factories and sales offices abroad for years. But their product development, marketing, financing and investment plans have been directed from Japan. That made them merely Japanese corporations with overseas subsidiaries. Traditional multinationals like Ford, IBM and Nestlé have tended to operate globally with regional headquarters making all the regional decisions. Learning to operate in truly global fashion is the biggest hurdle facing Japanese companies and one they could yet stumble over.

We find the same theme highlighted in a book co-authored by James Abegglen, founder of the Boston Consulting Group and distinguished chronicler of Japanese business and management (Abegglen and Stalk, 1985). It is worth quoting two connected passages at length (the word 'kaisha' is the standard Japanese word for company, but in this context refers to major corporations):

> The kaisha have some special handicaps in the effort to become international. First, they are based in a notably homogenous society, with little experience of differences in religion, race and culture. Second, the kaisha are notably integrated institutions. How does one integrate a non-Japanese speaking foreigner who is some thousands of miles from the company's main facilities, into the culture of Hitachi or Toyota or Nippon Kokan? Trial efforts at extended residence in Japan have been made – with the looming risk that after all the investment, the foreign employee will leave to work elsewhere. It is not clear that any Japanese company has yet developed a system to deal with these problems of personnel selection, training, and motivation as the kaisha move to be multinational. (p. 284)

Furthermore:

> To succeed abroad, a good deal of management authority has to be given to local management. But as local managements come to comprise an important part of the total kaisha, they need a voice in corporate affairs ... [The] inability to consider foreigners in the management of Japanese companies is a measure of the magnitude of the problem of the kaisha becoming multinational. (p. 284)

Abegglen and Stalk go on to say that the personnel issue is 'perhaps the most dramatic' of the challenges facing the big companies in their bid to internationalise.

Thus a major strategic challenge for Japanese firms is to accept that non-Japanese must somehow be given more direct responsibility and opportunity for genuine promotion within the company at the local level. In other words, there has to be letting-go from the centre. But this is no easy thing. For companies must overcome severe impediments associated with wariness, distrust and lack of knowledge about the world beyond Japan. As the German commentator, Gerhard Dambmann (1985, p. 16) points out, to the insular Japanese this is 'a strange, separate, other world, to which inner-Japanese norms and criteria are not applicable'.

Foreign language learning and communication malaise in Japanese corporations

The essence of the contemporary problem has been admirably summed up by Reischauer (1984, p. 398):

> Since the great majority of Japanese, including the leadership, live largely behind their linguistic walls . . . [they] are not aware that Japan is as intellectually isolated as it is or that to others it sometimes appears to be a tongue-tied giant or a sinister outsider on the edges of world society. Only slowly have they begun to realise the need for others to understand Japan better and for the Japanese to know more about the rest of the world. For both these purposes a great improvement in language skills is mandatory.

As far as company-sponsored language learning is concerned, the following attitudinal and intellectual factors exercise a considerable influence (Holden, 1990b):

1 The very idea of foreign-language learning in the context of Japanese organisations is synonymous with training for international communication. Japanese companies know that the very bottom line for international communication is proficiency in the English language; a Japanese firm without some kind of capability in the English language is severely handicapped in any kind of dealings with the rest of the world.
2 Language learning is closely bound up with the traditional aura in Japan about learning both as a means and end in itself (Dore, 1988); and the general Japanese belief that correlation exists between educational attainment and business success at some point in the future, however remote.
3 Language learning is linked to the quest to create an internationalised orientation; it is regarded, therefore, as an antidote to solving Japan's image problem – whilst maintaining (and ensuring) Japanese international competitiveness and, in some key sectors, outright dominance.
4 Japanese companies do not just see foreign-language ability as a means of sustaining and improving sales performance; it is continually required for two vital areas of Japan's competitiveness: enhancing the sophistication of international marketing research activity and economic intelligence

performance; and upgrading the 'cultural awareness' of managerial and other staff who are required to help run not just sales offices, but entire manufacturing operations on a worldwide basis.

5 The Japanese tend to take a politely flattering, yet fundamentally patronising view of foreigners' attempts to master Japanese (Miller, 1982; Reischauer, 1984). So, far from a knowledge of Japanese assisting contacts, it can on occasion be counter-productive, because 'though they are reluctant to admit it, nearly all Japanese are rendered even more uncomfortable by non-Japanese who speak fluent Japanese and have mastered the nuances of Japanese society and culture' (Christopher, 1984, p. 51). Here we encounter a central tenet of Japanese epistemology, which interlocks language, race and culture. For to the Japanese, their 'unique' language is not just one among many of the world's linguistic systems, but is a 'system of mystical experiences' (Miller, 1977, p. 21), which is 'unfortunately' beyond the understanding of foreigners.

6 Because, therefore, of the anxiety and uncertainty which many Japanese experience when dealing with foreigners at the personal level, it is not an exaggeration to suggest that as a race the Japanese suffer from a *communication malaise*. It can be tentatively suggested that the root of this anxious condition is an awareness that foreign languages are alien media for the expression of Japanese thoughts and ideas, and that the learning of a foreign language involves a certain loss of Japaneseness. Both factors are related to Christopher's point to the effect that many Japanese simply fail, or do not wish, 'to develop any real comprehension of the psychology' of non-Japanese.

7 Against all that, foreign-language capability is seen both as one of the principal antidotes to this condition and as a major means of entering the way of thinking of foreign business associates and customers.

In ways that foreigners find hard or even superfluous to grasp, the issue of language is central to any understanding of the social psychology of the Japanese and their perceptions of relationships with foreigners, and not least in business interactions. It is well worth heeding these remarks of the authoritative Reischauer (1984, p. 390):

Language is a fundamental tool in international relations, and the Japanese language is also a major subject in itself. It is what defines Japanese culture more distinctly than any other feature of their culture. At the same time, it is a major problem of their relationship with the outside world . . . Few people, in Japan or elsewhere, fully realise how great the language barrier is in Japan's international contacts.

NEC's distinctive international vision

It is against this somewhat perplexing background that one must examine the internationalisation of all Japanese corporations. In meeting these international business challenges, and transmitting its responses into management education philosophies and practices, NEC adopts a stance which has been strongly influenced by the impact of Dr Koji Kobayashi, who from 1964 to 1988 was president, then chairman of the corporation; and who in 1977 articulated NEC's 'C & C' business philosophy. Dr Kobayashi, in common with other great Japanese post-war business leaders, possessed: 'vision, understanding of institutional goals and purposes, knowledge of the substance of the basic work involved, and a genuine concern for human beings' (Wiesner in Kobayashi, 1986, pp. ix–x).

Kobayashi also had a burning ambition to attain for NEC truly global status, linked to an equally potent vision of NEC creating a new world order in which formal barriers of language and communication are dramatically reduced (Kobayashi, 1986; 1989; 1991). All this, of course, thanks to NEC's superior technology. According to Kobayashi (1989, p. 125), 'C & C is not merely a corporate goal of NEC, it is now being universalised as one of the global trends of the era.' It is noteworthy that Kobayashi's vision embraces the following decidedly Japanese elements:

- An idealistic striving towards a hitherto unrealised (even unrealisable) goal of unambiguous universal communication across boundaries of language and culture.
- A belief in technology as a promoter of worldwide progress.
- An inclination towards altruism.

Interestingly, however, Kobayashi's vision does not only aim to eliminate the scourge of the Tower of Babel from human affairs, it also offers to Japanese peoples, sticken with obsessive near-helplessness about themselves as cross-cultural communicators, the hope of communicating freely with all other cultures. In this sense his vision coincides with the quintessentially Japanese dream in which all the rest of mankind does not merely understand – and admire – Japan, but knows how to act in ways that harmonise with Japan's hopes and intentions (Holden, 1991).

In order to understand the NEC approach to internationalisation, it is of considerable importance to grasp both the essence and the scope of Kobayashi's vision.

International education in NEC 1974–87

The internationalisation of NEC began as far back as 1974 when an International Education and Training Centre was established to host trainees from abroad (Kobayashi, Koji, 1991, p. 180). Then, in October 1980, a new department was set up at NEC's Tokyo headquarters with direct responsibilities for internationalising all employees. The department had the academic-sounding title of NEC Institute of International Studies (Jap. 'Kokusai kenshujo'). Although it was integrated into a new structure in 1987, the Institute provided the basic system which underlies international management education in NEC in the 1990s. It is, therefore, instructive to examine in brief the workings of the NEC Institute of International Studies from 1980 to 1987, when it was reconstituted as the International Education Division of the NEC Institute of Management.

The key aims of the NEC Institute of International Studies were:

- To integrate company-wide international education.
- To develop and support overseas personnel.
- To provide management education in Japan to NEC's expatriate managers.
- To accumulate and make effective use of international management know-how.

The Institute integrated management development with foreign language training development; it also co-ordinated international education with the requirements of the personnel department.

The establishment of this new department was accompanied by two other important policy decisions to make the strategic shift of NEC from a globalised company to an internationalised one. The first of these abolished the distinction between domestic and international careers as far as promotion within the overall company was concerned. In most Japanese companies there was a marked tendency for people whose career had been largely in foreign locations to be less successful than stay-at-home careerists reaching for the top jobs.

The second of these initiatives ensured that every part of the company – 'even the domestic sales divisions' as a company report noted – was aware of this major reorientation in company thinking. This involved instituting a sophisticated company-wide system for selecting and monitoring personnel involved in working directly with other cultures.

This system still operates today and is run as follows. Every three years all employees of NEC, with the exception of production workers (unless nominated by their managers), are rated by two of their seniors using a 5-point scale on 10 factors associated with suitability for work in foreign environments. The set of factors remains confidential, but plainly the company will want to know about individuals' enthusiasm for learning foreign languages, their cross-cultural adaptability and their 'vitality' (meaning their unalloyed determination to put the company's interests first).

The data on employees are used by the company to help select personnel who, irrespective of their present position and function, look as if they have the potential to work well in foreign environments. The data are ultimately fed into the computers of the all-powerful personnel department which controls promotion and job rotation. Its task is to match an individual's 'internationalisability' with specific overseas opportunities which cover a vast spectrum of technical, commercial and personnel functions in all five continents. According to Mr Hajime Hasegawa, the senior manager who was initially responsible for implementing the new system, the NEC Institute of International Studies helped to eliminate '"undesirable practices" such as sending the same people overseas repeatedly or giving the impression that overseas assignment was a sort of "unlucky" assignment for one's career' (*Daily Yomiuri*, 1981).

NEC international education: goals and requirements

As noted above, the NEC Institute of International Studies was integrated with the NEC Institute of Management in 1987. This entity had been set up in 1983 as a wholly-owned subsidiary with responsibility for providing all NEC group companies with management education services.

The goals of international education in NEC must be seen in conjunction with the overall human resource development policy and supporting organisational structure. The main task of international management education is to nurture 'global business people', that is to say, to groom personnel who can actively promote a spirit of globalisation within NEC. The ideal for such personnel is that they possess 'superior perception and capability to act in the cross-cultural sphere'.

In practice this requires them to be effective in their own business area; to have good international communication skills, which entails more than just speaking English well and to be able to adapt to different cultures. In inculcating these competencies, international education at NEC emphasises – and therefore, incidentally, seeks in potential recruits – three key personal attributes: international outlook and sensitivity; a mental capacity for self-help; and a more flexible, more dynamic ability to perform tasks in different business cultures (Hayashi, 1991).

In practical terms international education at NEC concentrates on three main goals: internationalising of the whole company; supporting international operations; and creating an international ethos among NEC affiliates and offices worldwide. Consistent with the Japanese 'obsession with systemisation' of in-company training (Kobayashi, Kaoru, 1991), NEC breaks down its target groups for international education as follows: 'all staff'; 'staff handling overseas business'; 'staff likely to be assigned to overseas posts'; 'staff returning from overseas posts'; and 'locally hired staff in overseas offices' (see Figure 10.2 for an outline of international education at NEC). In order to suit the needs of each group, NEC has developed a suite of 10 broad education programmes (Hayashi, 1991) which are discussed next.

International education programmes

International communications programmes

The main focus of these programmes is on foreign-language training with English being by far the most widely taught language (see Appendix 1).

International management programmes

These programmes, which seek to improve the overall competence of NEC managers in foreign environments are becoming an increasingly important aspect of

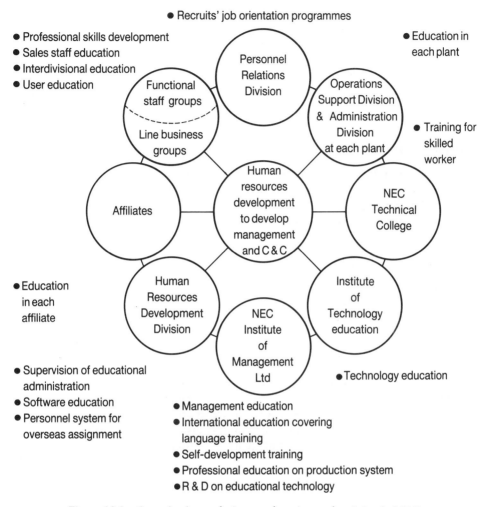

Figure 10.2 Organisations relating to education and training in NEC

international education. There are two main types of courses: (a) the Management Course for Staff Posted Overseas (for staff already appointed or likely to be appointed to overseas positions); (b) the Management Case Study Course. The former concentrates on developing skills and attitudes for overseas personnel management with contributions on issues such as health, religion, social and political developments.

International business programmes

These programmes aim to equip NEC personnel with nuts-and-bolts knowledge of international business. Topics include: trade practices, finance, insurance, law and contracts, accounting, marketing, overseas construction projects and production.

Area study programmes

The aim of these programmes is to provide appreciation of cultural, political and connected developments in given regions. NEC breaks up the world into six groups.

Orientation programmes for families of staff posted overseas

These programmes are aimed at the families – mainly wives – of NEC personnel destined for overseas postings, involving an introduction to NEC as well as information on the country concerned (uppermost in the wives' mind will be educational provision for children).

Programmes for staff on assignment overseas

These programmes take the form of correspondence courses for overseas personnel including local staff and cover topics such as production control, sales, accounting, personnel and industrial relations and even general education.

Returnees programmes

These courses are provided for personnel who, upon returning from an overseas assignment, need to be updated on company developments and reintegrated. NEC personnel are asked to write reports of their experiences in various locations. These accounts, written in Japanese and sometimes translated into English, are valuable information for future expatriates and are used in cross-cultural training (see below).

Overseas study

NEC sends roughly 40 people each year, mainly junior executives with 5 to 10 years' experience, to foreign universities and research institutes including MBA courses (mainly in the United States and EC countries), for 1 or 2 years. More senior executives attend short-term programmes at leading institutions such as Harvard Business School or IMD in Switzerland. Special programmes are also run in Japan with inputs from organisations such as McKinsey Japan or the International University of Japan.

Overseas operations training

Under this programme NEC also sends about 10 employees a year for on-the-job training with selected overseas subsidiaries. The purpose of these secondments is to help provide trainees with a wider international outlook.

Training for local staff in overseas operations

The first 9 courses are specifically for Japanese employees of NEC, but programmes for local staff, especially managers, are becoming increasingly important. The first such programme was run in 1977 (well before internationalisation became a big issue in Japan). Today, the company runs three courses in Japan for selected local managers. These serve as an introduction to Japan as well as to NEC and its operations.

A more recent development is the organisation of training programmes by local subsidiaries on a regional basis. Since 1989, NEC Electronics Inc. in California has been providing training on multicultural team-building and on developing relationships with Japanese counterparts. In Europe NEC (UK) initiated its first European training programme in January 1992 for 16 middle managers from the United Kingdom, Germany, Ireland, Spain and France.

Notable points about NEC's international education programmes

This description of international education at NEC took as its point of departure general concepts underlying company training and education in Japan. This approach helped to ensure that a Western overlay did not obscure some very significant features of NEC philosophies and practices. As a result, it is possible to isolate four features of NEC's international education activities, which plainly give it a distinctive IHRM orientation. These four features, which are discussed below, concern: the strategic remit of international education; foreign language and cross-cultural education; creation of NEC-specific case studies by overseas managers; the issue of the company's international vision.

Strategic remit

According to a recent survey on global human resource strategies undertaken by Ashridge Management College in the United Kingdom, the issue of internationalisation of management 'stormed to the top of corporate agendas everywhere in the world . . . [in] . . . the late 1980s and early 1990s' (Barham and Oates, 1991, p. 9). In the case of NEC, internationalisation as an active management principle can be said to have begun in November 1964, on the very day that Dr Koji Kobayashi took over the company reins. In his very first official pronouncement as president, he declared: 'I want to make NEC into an international corporation' (1989, p. 55).

However, internationalisation was not his first priority: undertaking company restructuring and the introduction of quality management systems (which extended, incidentally, into the human sphere, not just technical operations) were the first tasks. Nevertheless, both tasks were performed with a massive expansion of international business in mind. By the time NEC had established its first centre for international training in 1974, the need for creating a new type of Japanese manager, one able to perform internationally with cross-cultural adroitness, was already apparent. With the setting up of the NEC Institute of International Studies in 1980, it is true to say that internationalisation had become a central strategic issue because the goal was not just to inculcate key personnel with foreign language competence and cross-cultural skills, but in effect to internationalise – within reason – the entire company.

Foreign language and cross-cultural education

It is of major importance for the future well-being of NEC that it has plentiful staff who are 'effective' in English for a variety of purposes: international sales and marketing; acquisition and assimilation of relevant scientific and technical information; supervising expatriate employees in a wide range of technical, administrative and managerial functions. It will also be apparent how in NEC, as in other major Japanese corporations, English language training must inevitably be closely related to human resource development. It is not an exaggeration to say that a wide-ranging corporate capability in English is the *sine qua non* for both the internationalisation of NEC and for responding to changes in the world marketing environment. Because then it can be said that corporate capability in English is an indispensable factor in the ability to reposition the company internationally, English language instruction has strategic importance. This point is rarely if ever grasped by foreign writers on Japanese business and management because in their countries foreign language tuition in companies is either an irrelevant issue (as is frequently the case in the United Kingdom and the United States) or it is seen as an aspect of training. In other words, of all the major industrial countries, only in Japan can foreign language capability be considered as an element of international corporate strategy. Not for the first time Japanese corporations require us to pay attention to factors which fall outside Western concepts of organisation and management.

NEC-specific case studies

A notable practice of NEC, established well over 10 years ago, is to encourage expatriate managers to write short case studies on their experiences abroad. These case studies are designed to provide to those who come after them illumination about problems of handling non-Japanese personnel. Some of these case studies are translated into English and are used by foreign-language trainers – Tokyo-based American employees – to sensitise employees to the pitfalls of cross-cultural misunderstandings whilst enhancing their knowledge of 'on-the-job English'.

As a vehicle for cross-cultural education, these case studies may be effective. On the positive side, however, the practice of developing in-company case studies shows the seriousness with which NEC recognises the persistence of cross-cultural clashes and strives in a highly pragmatic way to transform actual experiences into material fit for study by others within the company.

International vision

Dr Kobayashi's vision for NEC, first articulated in the 1970s, is still central to the formulation and implementation of the company's corporate strategy for the 1990s and beyond. In fact, the NEC credo, promulgated by the company chairman and president in 1990, emphasises that the C & C philosophy will actively help to 'create an affluent and humanistic society' in the next century. Although it embraces a specific technological dimension, focusing on the integration of computer and communication know-how, the vision is unimplementable without its consistent honing of the core competencies of its employees. At the same time, of course, the vision, with its great psychological appeal to employees of whatever status and in whatever function, acts as a direction-giving catalyst of company energies.

In addition to the potency of the vision itself, the actual task of internationalising staff outlook and abilities is facilitated through two other influences: first, NEC provides an active, company-wide learning environment; second, it has created channels and mechanisms for personnel to communicate to others their experiences of interactions with other cultures. The first factor is strongly related to the Japanese propensity to learn anything which might be useful to the company (Holden, 1991). The second factor can be associated with a characteristic Japanese willingness to help others – others in the same group, that is – who come after them.

But to suggest to NEC that Kobayashi's grand vision is not really tenable is not the point. The power of the vision is such that it carries the company forward; and even it if is striving for the seemingly unattainable – unambiguous C & C-led interlanguage communication and reduction of Japanese communication malaise – the path ahead is one that will yield not just technologies and new product ideas, it will also create new organisational structures and new styles of management. In the meantime, the C & C vision will continue to ensure that for the foreseeable future NEC will remain one of the most popular destinations, if not the most popular one, as it was in 1982 through 1988, for Japan's best science and technology graduates (Ekusa, 1991).

Summary of the characteristics of international education in NEC

By now it is clear that the internationalisation of NEC, both in terms of policies and strategies, has features that are unusual from a Western perspective. Before examining in the next and final section of this case study the practices of NEC in relation to current thinking on IHRM, it will be as well to summarise the key characteristics of the company's international education philosophy and activities as follows:

- Positioning overseas careers as one of the most valuable career paths.
- Internationalisation attempts are not confined to headquarters, but seek to reach all employees of NEC.

- Long-term organisational development is seen to be closely related to the identification and selection of personnel particularly well suited for work in foreign environments.
- Commitment to foreign-language learning, with constant emphasis on English.
- Development of the close relation between the international character of NEC products and grooming of a company-wide international outlook.
- Attempts to integrate expatriate managers' experiences into teaching input for other employees.
- Use of the company vision to underpin internationalisation and international education policies.

NEC and developments in international HRM

It is now time to examine NEC practices in the context of issues surrounding IHRM as a worldwide management preoccupation. It was suggested earlier (in the section on strategic remit) that NEC was already involved with internationalisation, first as a corporate aim, then as an active element of company development, well before internationalisation became fashionable as a management issue in the West.

This can be decisively illustrated with reference to a recent survey by the Ashridge Management Research Group which found that 'international HRM issues, including management development, vie with customers, alliances and organisational designs as top priorities for the future' (Barham and Oates, 1991, p. 20). This study listed 11 major IHRM concerns as follows:

1. Identifying and retaining highly qualified people.
2. Ensuring sufficient quality and quantity of management at the appropriate time.
3. Ensuring management succession.
4. Sustaining and improving performance at all levels in all areas of business.
5. Increasing the depth of talent in the organisation.
6. Making sure that people have the technical and managerial skills to compete.
7. Making the management competencies and culture that are required sufficiently clear to people.
8. Total quality management and changing people's attitudes to quality.
9. Establishing training as part of management culture.
10. Gaining top management and line management interest in human resource development.
11. Linking HRM to strategic objectives.

To NEC (and quite possibly other major internationally operating Japanese corporations) *these issues are not new.* In fact many of them were dealt with automatically by long-tried philosophies and practices years before they 'exploded' on corporate agendas in the West. This suggests that a Western priority-based strategic framework for international HRM may be at best only partially applicable to Japan – which is only another way of saying that Japanese companies have different priorities. It is not easy to be categorical about the nature of this divergence, but the case of NEC provides answers and insights.

The crucial difference between the Japanese and Western stance seems to arise from a Japanese tendency to see international HRM as strengthening the organisation and a Western tendency to emphasise international competences primarily with respect to individual managers. This may be, up to a point, stating the obvious, but it is the implications of this divergence of approach that we should dwell on.

First, as noted above, NEC has established IHRM as a core issue of its global strategic vision. In furthering this aspect of internationalisation, NEC has created structures, now subsumed under the NEC Institute of Management, for co-ordinating training activities on a company-wide basis in Japan – no mean feat of management in its own right. Second, in NEC there is a clear concept of how training programmes fit into corporate strategy and, related to this, a very detailed examination of international needs for specific overseas functions. Third, in NEC, as in all Japanese corporations, there is at all levels a potent urge to learn for the company.

As for the future, the real test for NEC, to prove that it is a genuinely internationalised company, will be to integrate Japanese and non-Japanese policy – and decision-making inputs into the principal management systems of the company in Japan and at subsidiary level throughout the world. This will be hard: it will involve the 'de-Japanisation' of control of NEC as a global concern, and that will mean developing strategies and programmes for multicultural teamworking across all the national boundaries embraced by NEC worldwide.

Acknowledgements
I am greatly indebted to the NEC Corporation for their kind assistance to me in 1989 and in 1992 in the preparation of this study and an earlier one published by *The Economist* Intelligence Unit. In particular my thanks are due to Mr Hajime Hasegawa, Senior Vice-President and Director of the NEC Institute of Management (and first General Manager of the NEC Institute of International Studies) and to Mr Shuichi Hayashi, Manager of Education, NEC Institute of Management.

Appendix 1

We should note that many courses are concerned with developing proficiency in business English. For example, NEC has introduced a course in technical writing, which is aimed at technical personnel who require to write specialised documentation, such as manuals, in English or who need an appreciation of editing technical texts. In order to gauge proficiency in spoken and written English, the company employs TOEIC, test of English for international communication (a standard English-language proficiency test). NEC is basically interested in three thresholds: 470, which means that employees (to use the words of one of NEC's training managers) 'can go abroad, but need support'; 630, which means that they 'can go abroad without assistance'; and 740, meaning that they are able 'to negotiate with foreigners'. All employees are required to take TOIEC tests. By 1992 approximately 80 200 of NEC's Japanese employees had taken TOIEC tests, which suggests something of the scale of company-sponsored learning of English. It should also be noted that a certain proportion of employees volunteer to take English on a basis that might be termed 'company-related self-betterment'. Another consideration is that English serves as the medium of instruction for a course in cross-cultural communication.

The English language tuition comes under a suite of courses called 'international communication'. Instruction in English relates to the following topics: conversation; writing; documentation; presentation (i.e. making presentations). Languages other than English are also grouped under 'international communication'.

In addition to English, which is dominant in NEC's foreign-language training programmes, the following languages, among others, are taught on a limited basis: Chinese, Korean, Thai, French, German and Spanish. NEC does not employ its own instructors for the teaching of these languages, but hires them from specialist commercial language schools. In some cases university teachers will be invited to run courses.

As noted above, NEC employees are either seconded to learn (more) English or they can request permission from their managers who will either grant or deny the opportunity. The same principle applies to the 'non-English' languages, but it is the case that company students of these languages learn them at the instigation of their managers. The basic course in these 'non-English' languages is 60 hours, tuition normally taking place in blocks of 2 or 3 hours once a week. Thus the basic course will last between 3 and 4 months. The basic course can be followed by an intermediate course which is 45 hours long.

The purpose of these courses is to prepare people for 'daily life' in the countries concerned. As stated earlier, the starting point for all Japanese conceptions of international business communication is that the English language is universal. However, problems arise in a variety of countries where cross-sections of the entire population, such as taxi drivers, tradespeople and shop assistants, have little or no knowledge of English. In addition to basic knowledge to help with daily practicalities, NEC stresses the importance of this knowledge to demonstrate courtesy and commitment to particular markets.

References

In addition to the works cited in this chapter and referenced below, I have been able to draw on various material supplied by NEC – not just various annual reports and public relations documents, but also back issues of *NEC Management News*, a strictly in-house publication in English produced by the NEC Institute of Management.

Abegglen, J. C. and Stalk, G. (1985), *Kaisha: The Japanese corporation*, Basic Books, New York.

Barham, K. and Oates, D. (1991), *The International Manager*, Economist Books, London.

Christopher, R. (1984), *The Japanese Mind: The goliath explained*, Pan Books, London.

Daily Yomiuri (1981), 'NEC strengthens training for overseas assignments', 21 May.

Daito, E. (1986), 'Recruitment and training of middle managers in Japan, 1900–1930', in Kobayashi, Kesaji and Morikawa, H. (eds) *Development of Managerial Enterprise: Proceedings of the conference on business history 12*, University of Tokyo Press, Tokyo.

Dambmann, G. (1985), *Japan: Weltmacht als Einzelgänger*, Piper Verlag, Munich.

Dore, R. R. (1988), 'Education and training in Japan and Britain', *Japan Education Journal*, no. 36, Japan Information Centre, London.

Dower, J. (1985), *War Without Mercy: Race and power in the Pacific War*, Faber and Faber, London.

The Economist, (1989), 'The multinationals, eastern-style', 24 June.

Ekusa, A. (1991), 'Students' pick of jobs', *Journal of Japanese Trade and Industry*, September/October.

The Financial Times (1992), 'Fujitsu now faces up to harsh economic realities', 11 August.

Gow, I. (1988), 'Japan', in Handy, C. (ed.), *Making Managers*, Pitman, London.

Hayashi, S. (1991), 'NEC: focus overseas', *Journal of Japanese Trade and Industry*, September/October.

Holden, N. J. (1990a), 'Preparing the ground for organisational learning: graduate training programmes in major Japanese corporations', *Management Education and Development*, vol. 21, part 3.

Holden, N. J. (1990b), 'Language learning in Japanese corporations: the wider sociolinguistic context', *Multilingua*, 9–3.

Holden, N. J. (1991), 'NEC: A case of vision-guided internationalisation', in Barham, K. and Devine, M. (eds), *The Quest for the International Manager: A survey of global human resource strategies*, The Economist Intelligence Unit, London.

Kobayashi, Kaoru (1991), 'Corporate in-house education', *Journal of Japanese Trade and Industry*, September/October.

Kobayashi, Koji (1986), *Computers and Communications: A vision of C & C*, The MIT Press, Cambridge, Mass.

Kobayashi, Koji (1989), *Rising to the Challenge*, Harcourt Brace Jovanovich, Tokyo.

Kobayashi, Koji (1991), *The rise of NEC: How the world's greatest C & C company is managed*, Blackwell, Cambridge, Mass.

Meech-Pekarkik, J. (1986), *The World of the Meiji Print: Impressions of a new civilisation*, John Weatherhill, New York.

Miller, R. A. (1977), 'The Japanese language in contemporary Japan: some sociolinguistic observations', *AEI-Hoover Policy Studies*, 22, American Enterprise Institute for Public Policy, Washington, DC.

Miller, R. A. (1982), *Japan's Modern Myth: The language and beyond*, John Weatherhill, New York.

Morita, A. (1987), *Made in Japan: Akio Morita and Sony*, Collins, London.

Reischauer, E. (1984), *The Japanese*, Charles E. Tuttle Company, Tokyo.

Rohlen, T. (1974), *For Harmony and Strength: Japanese white-collar organisation in anthropological perspective*, University of California Press, Berkeley.

Sasaki, N. (1984), *Management and Industrial Structure in Japan*, Pergamon Press, Oxford.

van Wolferen, K. (1989), *The Enigma of Japanese Power*, Macmillan, London.

CHAPTER 11

Singapore Airlines
Strategic human resource initiatives

LING SING CHEE

Introduction

The study of how human resource initiatives at Singapore Airlines are carried out provides a double bonus. Not only does the exercise provide a behind-the-scenes glimpse as to how a successful airline manages its staff, but because the Group employs 1 out of every 80 workers in Singapore, the reader is automatically introduced to the management practices of Singapore's largest private sector employer. SIA is also Singapore's most well-known multinational, headquartered there but operating offices in more than 40 countries around the globe.

History and background of SIA

Singapore Airlines now enjoys worldwide recognition as a national carrier but its history began in May 1947 under Malayan Airways which flew between Singapore and the peninsula of Malaya. In 1966, the governments of Malaysia and Singapore acquired majority control of the company and renamed it Malaysia–Singapore Airlines Ltd (MSA). But in October 1972 the joint ownership of the airline by the Singapore and Malaysian governments ceased to exist, and in its place two new flag carriers were formed – Singapore Airlines (SIA) and Malaysian Airlines (later Malaysian Airline System, or MAS). At the end of 1972 SIA was a small airline with only 15 aircraft and a route network that linked its home base to 22 cities. The two airlines then embarked on two different strategies: MAS concentrated on domestic services while SIA's interest was in developing long-haul international routes. This outward-looking strategy was inevitable given its small island status. SIA currently flies to 68 destinations in 40 countries around the globe. While SIA itself concentrates on air transportation, its subsidiaries provide related services to the airline industry. As a Group, they employ nearly 23 000 people and contribute 3.7 per cent to the Singapore economy. Even the airline alone employs more than 14 300 people and is Singapore's largest private sector employer; almost 12 000 work in Singapore, while more than 2500 work overseas.

Performance indicators

Over the years, Singapore Airlines has consistently been voted one of the world's top airlines in surveys conducted by different organisations. The highly regarded Intramar (International Travel Market Research) *World Airline Monitor* survey of travel agents has rated SIA highly in its surveys over the years. In 1988–9, it was rated Asia–Pacific's most highly regarded and recommended airline; in 1990–1, it was rated top in three out of seven categories. Other recent accolades came from the December 1991 issue of *Fortune Magazine* which ranked SIA as the twenty-third largest airline in 1990 revenue but the most profitable airline in the world (its Group pre-tax earnings were S$1.11 billion).

Besides gaining recognition for its organisational performance, the quality of SIA's management was also noted when it took first place in a survey commissioned by *Asian Business* to identify Asia's 'most admired companies'. This was no small feat as it beat 244 local, regional and multinational companies in 10 different sectors in the region. Reporting on the survey results, the magazine indicated that top performers in the survey were all notable for their strong, stable, established but visionary teams. SIA is also said to be undergoing a planned transition in senior management at the director level as first generation leaders give way to new blood groomed in SIA's corporate milieu and vision. This vision and competence of SIA's leaders will be tested in what is now turning out to be a turbulent decade.

Environment

The airline industry in the decade of the 1990s is undergoing a period of tumultous change. Deregulation in the United States beginning in the 1970s has speeded changes in routes, prices, players and strategic alliances. In the US deregulation had been rather unsettling for the airlines. Lang and Lockhart's (1990) calculation of the debt ratio, a frequently used indicator of financial dependence, for the American airline industry showed an average increase from 0.576 in 1976 to 0.706 in 1982. The average return on investment for the eight trunk airlines was 0.33 per cent compared with an average ROI of 13.75 per cent for US manufacturing firms! The post-regulation period has also led to increasing uncertainty in the industry. Intense competition and close interdependence among competitors meant that any significant strategic move by a firm will be followed by a wave of moves and countermoves as was seen in the price wars of summer this year. The fare wars launched to bring in more business in the summer months are predicted to result in heavy losses instead.

In the Asian-Pacific region, competition is also becoming increasingly intense. Regional airlines are catching up with SIA and they operate with lower wage costs. This fast-growing region experienced some of the highest growth in passenger and freight traffic but it also attracted new Asian airlines. The presence of so many new airlines competing along roughly the same routes had led to difficulty in ensuring compliance on agreed price ranges. The low fares offered by other airlines to generate cash flow have put pressure on SIA to adjust its own fares and in April 1992 SIA was giving fare discounts of up to 30 per cent to its first and business class passengers for a three-month promotional period.

A new global pattern seems to be emerging. Some industry executives expect only a handful of airlines to emerge as global carriers. The end result could be few but efficient carriers which dominate the airline industry. The transformation now under way in the American airline industry with stronger more competitive airlines replacing the weaker ones is perhaps a precursor of developments elsewhere. One implication at the international level is that if an airline is to compete in a major way in the next decade, it has to be part of the new global alliances now being formed. Airlines form strategic alliances to provide global networks and access. For example, British Airways, which reported a pre-tax profit of £285 million ($882.8 million) during the year ending March 1992 is seeking tie-ups with airlines which will increase its penetration into North America (hence the stake in US Air and potential purchase of TWA assets), Asia (its chief officials are having talks with the Indonesian flag carrier Garuda) and continental Europe. Lord King, BA's then chairman, said that the airline's priority was 'in that order'. SIA has a trilateral alliance with Swissair and Delta Air Lines and has expressed interest (besides a few other parties including BA) in Qantas to reinforce SIA's position in Australia.[1]

Industry analysts are predicting that the smaller airlines will also find it increasingly tough in this market. But they believe that smaller airlines could survive through serving target market niches. What may eventually emerge is a two-tier system in Asia with some airlines forced into becoming more of a regional feeder airline.

Business plan

In an uncertain environment, SIA's official response is a stoical one. The chairman, Mr J. Y. Pillay, writing in its 1991–2 annual report vowed that the SIA Group will be resilient. He pointed to the crucial role that SIA's strategy has played in planning for staff recruitment and training, aircraft and facilities. Pointing to the organisation's strong net cash position and healthy cash flow, he indicated that it could ride out temporary disturbances. Mr Pillay also reiterated that the airline will continue to focus on commercial aviation. He pointed out that the organisation was satisfied with its present size, range of operations and growth rate and had no fashionable objective such as becoming a global mega-carrier.

In marketing, the airline follows a broadly differentiated strategy, targeting a wide range of passengers. It differentiates itself from other airlines through careful projection of both its image and the management of its product. The basic product – a seat on board a plane – remains the same. But successful differentiators are able to convey a message to customers about the uniqueness of the product. SIA has been successful in presenting a consistent image of high-quality service. When it separated from MSA, SIA decided to capitalise on what it had inherited from its predecessor – a reputation for good service. Ian Batey, an Australian, was retained on the SIA advertising account. The result was the highly recognisable sarong-clad 'Singapore girl' who has remained as a symbol, though less conspicuously, of the service-orientation of the airline.

Image is supported by the delivery of the product. SIA is well known for innovation in inflight facilities and services: at different points of time it was the first to provide complimentary headsets and drinks in all three classes, a choice of meals, slumberettes in its B747 lounges, fully reclining snoozers on its B747 upper decks, etcetera. More recently, the airline installed 'Celestel', the world's first commercial global inflight telecommunications system so that passengers can telephone virtually anywhere in the world, send faxes, and link up with computer systems right from the cabin. But the airline admits that marginal rather than quantum leaps in innovation are the order of the day. SIA, recognising the ease with which some of these services may be imitated, also turned its attention to delivering the total product, the aim being to provide an efficient and pleasant experience right from reservation, ticketing through to arrivals handling. The outstanding service-on-the-ground programme was initiated to help the airline strengthen its ground service – part of its strategy to deliver the total product.

Another important way that a superior product or service can be enhanced is through maintaining a modern fleet with the latest in aviation technology. In this way SIA is able to sustain longer journeys that have fewer stops, are faster, more comfortable and are fuel-efficient. Changi airport with its efficient handling and service continues to be a popular hub for other airlines. This is an asset to SIA in negotiations for air rights with other countries.

In an economic environment where passengers have many choices, SIA faces pressure to provide a good-quality product while keeping costs down. Behind SIA's glamorous image is a cost-conscious organisation. Given that the two main cost components are staff and fuel, its efforts at cost control deal with both areas. Fuel efficiency is increased by keeping a young fleet. The airline makes a conscious attempt to renew the fleet and maintain it at an average of 5 years, compared to the industry's average of 11 years. Staff costs are controlled through extensive training in the hope of improving productivity. The airline still records improvements in this respect – the company's staff productivity, measured in different ways, averaged an improvement of 5.9 per cent over the previous year's performance.

Organisation structure

There is an inevitable link between a business strategy which focuses upon service excellence and attention to the people who provide that service. SIA relies upon the commitment of the people to maintain a competitive edge. Among the stated corporate goals is one that refers specifically to human resources: 'To adopt human resource management practices company-wide that attract, develop, motivate and retain employees who contribute to the Company's objectives.' Many of the following details of this case study describe the structure and operation of the human resource function.

The human resource activities in SIA are carried out by four sections: personnel, human resource management, training and industrial relations. All report to the director of personnel who directly reports to the managing director, as do the directors of some other business functions. The managing director places great importance on the human resource aspects of the business. Senior positions in personnel are often stepping stones to other positions; for example, the last director of personnel, Sim Kay Wee became general manager and chief executive of SATS (Airport Services), an important subsidiary, also chairman of Service Quality Centre Pte Ltd and director of Singapore Airport Duty-Free Emporium Pte Ltd.

The overseas units headed by senior vice-presidents are organised on a regional basis, namely, Americas, Europe, North Asia, South East Asia, South West Pacific, and West Asia and Africa. Each unit functions autonomously but reports to the deputy managing director (commercial). Within each region, the organisation structure is as shown in Figure 11.1. The country managers look after all aspects of the company's operations in each country, including airport operations, marketing, finance, administration, personnel and property administration.

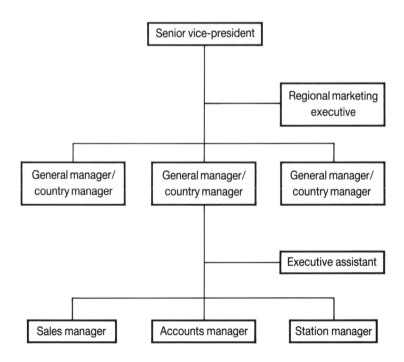

Figure 11.1 Organisation structure of overseas units

Corporate philosophy

SIA's corporate philosophy encourages teamwork and teamplayers rather than star performers. An indication of this orientation is the organisation's reluctance to single out 'the best performer' or 'the best team' in response to the National Productivity Board's appeal for nominations for awards, part of Singapore's productivity drive. SIA's human resource manager said that the organisation does not currently have quality control circles either. Ironical as it may seem, these examples illustrate not so much the organisation's lack of support for the country's manpower plans or campaigns as much as the fact that teamwork already exists. An external consultant, who has close links with the organisation confirmed that teamwork very much characterises its working relationships.

Keeping the entrepreneurial spirit alive in such a large organisation is also very important. SIA realises that to continue its success it needs creative and innovative people with the energy and boldness of entrepreneurs. There is much talk about innovation in their current training courses. One issue is making room for the highly individualistic risk-taker (which some overseas managers are said to be) in a large organisation. The overall plan has been to create the smallest possible unit to carry out required tasks – a structure which enables its management team to be flexible and quick in its decision-making. These smaller units can function autonomously, thus reducing administrative bureaucracy. A recent case in point is the formation of the company's latest subsidiary, SIA Engineering. SIA's managing director Dr Cheong Choong Kong compared its formation to the spawning of a baby with a long prosperous life ahead. 'Such rejuvenations,' he claimed, 'help corporations overcome the ordinary laws of mortality.'

The SIA Engineering Company was formed by a merger between SIA's engineering division and the Singapore Engine Overhaul Centre, itself already a subsidiary. The result is an enlarged subsidiary with an expanded business base for engineering activities. Subjecting subsidiaries to the rigours of the market-place was an indirect way of keeping them competitive rather than complacent. Mr Pillay was reported in the press to have said that the new subsidiary must forge a 'more mature relationship' with SIA:

> The bond, while still informal and friendly, will take on a far more structured or commercial bent . . . While SIA will continue to be the principal customer for the new company, there will be a strong incentive to reach out more forcefully to airlines around the world.

The human resource manager related the unease of the seconded staff to the inevitable trauma of 'cutting the umbilical cord'. While in the initial stages, SIA headquarters may assist in its personnel matters, ultimately, like other subsidiaries before it, the new company will be fully responsible for personnel functions, free also to vary the terms and conditions of appointment. Subsidiaries need not necessarily be small outfits – the restructuring involves some 3400 employees, leaving behind only 400 staff in the airline's engineering division. Other existing subsidiaries were formed in similar fashion, initially starting as operating divisions. They also provide related services while allowing SIA itself to concentrate on the airline business. These subsidiaries include the Singapore Airport Terminal Services Group, and Singapore Properties (Pte) Ltd which undertakes renovation and development projects on behalf of SIA, including a stake in a hotel project in Yogyakarta.

Other schemes jointly encourage creativity and team spirit. For example, 'Staff ideas in action' (S-I-A) is a company-wide productivity scheme which encourages employee suggestions to improve revenue, reduce cost or wastage, increase productivity and efficiency, enhance customer service and improve safety in the workplace.[2] In addition to giving monetary rewards to individuals for ideas that are implemented, the sum of 10 per cent of the award is granted to the award-winner's division, for divisional functions and welfare activities. Response to the scheme has been good. For example, in 1988, of the 1373 ideas evaluated, 15 per cent were accepted for implementation and a total of S$23 767 was awarded for the ideas accepted. However, the S-I-A committee has announced a recent fall in numbers, if not in quality submissions, and organised an exhibition to revive interest in the scheme.

The SIA hierarchy

The human resource function may best be described within the context of the hierarchical structure (see Figure 11.2). The hierarchy may be represented by the following four main grades of employees:

- Divisional directors/senior vice-presidents.
- Managers.
- Administrative staff.
- General staff.

Credit should really be given to senior management for SIA's success. It is generally acknowledged that the organization is managed by a specially competent group. Some of SIA's senior managers have been with the airline since it was founded in 1972. They have been described as people who 'focus on the basics, and do it very well'. It could be this fact that explains why (as shall be seen later) so much care also is given to the selection, identification and development of future senior management. It may be instructive for the reader to refer briefly to Figure 11.3 which specifies the desired attributes of SIA's senior staff as published in the organisation's staff appraisal handbook.

The executive management of the company, comprising the managing director, divisional directors and senior vice-presidents, is responsible to the board of directors. Reporting to the divisional directors are the managers who head the various departments within the divisions. Below the managers are the administrative staff who function as section heads. These personnel either come under the general or the specialist categories and could have been recruited as graduates or promoted from

Figure 11.2 The SIA hierarchy

within the ranks. General staff are employees in first-line supervisory positions, skilled and semi-skilled workers, cabin crew, clerical personnel, computer programmers and licensed aircraft engineers.

For graduates and professionals who join the organisation at the administrative grade, there are three schemes (which may be likened to separate career paths): the generalists, specialists and overseas postings. The generalist scheme provides experience in a wide range of posts in the general administrative areas of the head office with opportunities for overseas postings as country managers. Entry into this scheme requires a good honours degree, or its equivalent, in any discipline. The specialist scheme encompasses careers which require more specialised knowledge such as accountants, engineers, information technology professionals and legal officers. Personnel in the overseas pool are expected to be effective communicators, sensitive to other cultures and to have maturity. Senior positions in overseas postings include that of senior vice-president, general/country manager and state manager. Those in the overseas pool are expected to return to home-based assignments for a few years between overseas assignments.

Organisation of human resource development

The HRD function in SIA is categorised into four main areas: recruitment, appraisal,

The SIA executive of the future

To survive in the environment of the future and to sustain the business of today, there are certain characteristics that an SIA senior staff member ought to display. These characteristics must be based on values that the company wishes to nurture:

Characteristics	Values
1 Strategic orientation	Concern for profitability. Achievement oriented. Long-term outlook. Preparedness for and anticipation of change. Future oriented. Competitive.
2 Concern for service	Service orientation: concern for customer. Customer orientation.
3 Innovative spirit	Imaginative. Creative. Questioning. Entrepreneurial. Prudent risk-taking. Adaptability/Flexibility. Responsive to change.
4 International awareness	Global outlook. Politically sensitive. Willingness to learn from others. Cross-cultural awareness.
5 People-oriented and professional approach	Leadership. Professionalism. Drive. Integrity. Openness. Ethical. Good interpersonal skills. Work discipline. Committed to training & development. Committed to appraisal system. Communicates well.

Figure 11.3   Desirable characteristics for SIA senior staff
(Source: SIA *Head Office Staff Appraisal Handbook*)

career development and rewards. These areas are perceived to be equally important and mutually interdependent (see Figure 11.4).

Recruitment

SIA undertakes extensive recruitment for different levels of employees. While the recruitment process is undertaken with the assistance of the human resource section, the line department's preference is given much weight in making the selection.

The issue of only employing quality personnel appears to be a recurring theme. For example, its recruitment brochure declares 'Singapore Airlines is looking for outstanding graduates and professionals in all disciplines who have the energy, enthusiasm and determination to succeed in a tough commercial world and who have a good record of academic and non-academic achievement'.

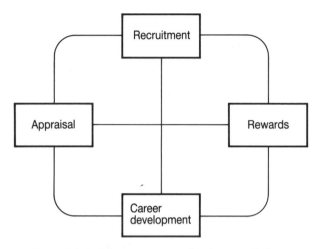

Figure 11.4 Human resource development linkages

The selection procedure for generalists is very strict because of the expectation that the upper echelon of the organisation will come from this category of staff. Generalists are recruited from university graduates with good academic results – the equivalent of an upper second class honours and above. These officers are expected to pass a series of tests. These include tests in writing, English, critical thinking, numerical skills and abstraction. They should clear two rounds of interviews, with the second interview panel comprising top management, including divisional directors. The criteria can be set high given the selection ratio very much in favour of the organisation. From an initial pool of candidates, about 10 per cent are shortlisted and only 2 per cent are selected.

Another source of recruiting staff with very good potential appeared to have been the unexpected result of a scholarship scheme, though it was intended also as part of public service. SIA scholarships tend to attract very bright students in Singapore, who are then sent abroad to good foreign universities, and who return to work for the organisation. The progress of these individuals in the organisation is also monitored.

While the organisation does not specify that Type A personalities be recruited, it does seem that the resulting workforce, especially among senior staff, tend to consist of many Type A individuals. This characteristic is believed to be consistent with the company culture, which is very bottom-line driven, and task and results-oriented.

The tight labour market in Singapore is more acutely felt at the clerical level and in maintaining high standards with the cabin crew. Since the stewardess is a key symbol of the airline's marketing strategy, even senior management is involved in the final selection. While recruiting quality cabin crew is important, comprehensive training is undertaken. Figure 11.5 which describes the training objectives gives an indirect indication of the expectations of the airline's stewardesses.

Singapore Airlines firmly believes the key to maintaining its reputation for superior customer service lies in a thorough and effective staff training programme.

When you start out on your career as a member of SIA's cabin crew, you'll undergo comprehensive training. It's the kind of specialist preparation designed to expose you to all the various situations you may encounter while you're performing your duties. At the end of it, you'll be fully conversant with all aspects of the job – especially important will be your ability to cope with all kinds of minor and major crises – so that you'll always be able to measure up to the exacting standards set by the company.

Here are just a few things you'll learn:

- You'll be more than familiar with all the different types of food served on board, how they are prepared, displayed and served.
- You'll be able to keep a pretty good bar. You'll know how to chill and serve wines, mix and pour drinks, and create alcoholic/non-alcoholic cocktails.
- You'll be a good hostess – gentle and caring. Courses have been specially designed to show you the various ways in which you can help passengers feel at ease and relax fully during the flight.
- You'll learn how to take care of your passengers, including infants and elderly – and how to keep them happy.
- You'll always look your absolute best. Tips on personal grooming are given as part of a series of self-improvement courses specially designed to bring out the best in you. You'll also discover new make-up techniques, while expert advice is on hand to help you improve your own grooming skills.
- You'll also become a better communicator. Great importance is placed on speech training at SIA to enable you to communicate more effectively, whether you're smoothing out the ruffled feathers of a demanding passenger or making in-flight announcements. This area is a crucial part of your job and one which will have a wonderfully positive effect on your self-confidence.

Your training programme concludes with one month's on-the-job training, where you can now demonstrate your newly acquired skills before you are assigned to your regular flying duties.

This comprehensive training programme plays a big role in boosting self-confidence so that recruits will be able to make the transformation to our special 'gentle hostesses in sarong kebayas'.

Figure 11.5 Training expectations for female cabin crew

Performance appraisal system

The organisation operates two co-existing formats for evaluating employee performance – one for evaluating general staff, and another for evaluating senior staff. The general staff appraisal system essentially consists of a written performance appraisal based upon specified dimensions, performance appraisal interviews and guidelines outlining the appraisal procedure. Performance dimensions for general staff include performance factors (quantity and quality), job attitude and behaviour cluster (e.g. dependability, care of property, teamwork and co-operation) and man-management skills (supervision and communication). The assignment of different weights to different job groups allows some flexibility in the use of a standard format for general staff.

For senior staff, the appraisal process is more involved. There are two components, the appraisal of performance, and of potential. Each senior staff member's performance is monitored through a work progress review and his/her potential rating is also evaluated. Both sub-systems will be elaborated in the following section.

The work progress review (WPR) functions much like a management-by-objectives method. The appraisee sets out work plans for the next period, this is reviewed annually, and the information is used to identify specific training requirements. It should be noted that the classification for training and development needs uses a similar system for classifying courses at the Management Development Centre, thus facilitating a close link between training and performance appraisals. The system places the onus of monitoring progress, including the revision of objectives during the period of appraisal, on the appraiser and appraisee. Feedback to the appraisee is expected and provision is also made for staff to indicate that they have seen the comments pertaining to their own appraisal.

While the performance appraisal method described is a standard feature similar to other organisational systems worldwide, SIA permits local adaptations. For instance, the Thai office reported difficulty with the performance appraisal process, namely in writing negative comments (because of religious beliefs about reincarnation)[3] and have adapted the system to accommodate cultural differences.

Besides the standard performance aspects, SIA makes use of potential assessments. Many elements of the potential system in SIA are adapted from Shell International Petroleum Company Ltd. This is no accident, since SIA's chairman, Mr Pillay, led the government team to study Shell's system at its London head office for its applicability to the Singapore civil service. The potential assessment method described below is also currently used in the civil service.

The senior staff members' potential appraisal is derived from two inputs: the staff development report (SDR) and the currently estimated potential (CEP) ranking. Both these reports revolve round the CEP concept. This concept is an assessment of an individual's future capability to do the highest possible job. In practical terms, a person's assessed potential is defined to be an estimation of the highest job level that he or she is capable of performing comfortably and successfully without being overstretched at some time in the future, say, his/her forties. The basic appraisal qualities used in assessment of potential have popularly been referred to by the acronym, HAIR. H stands for 'helicopter' quality, A for 'power of analysis,' I for 'imagination', and R for a 'sense of reality'. The 'helicopter' quality has been described as the ability to look at problems from a higher vantage point without losing simultaneous attention to relevant details. What is unique in this concept is the inclusion of what appears to be diametrically opposing characteristics. The 'helicopter' quality encompasses a capacity for a general orientation without sacrificing the capacity to consider details. Imagination needs to be balanced by another attribute, a sense of reality, otherwise it would be purely visionary. On the other hand, a person lacking in imagination becomes pedestrian.

The staff development report records the assessment of a staff member's potential based on the HAIR qualities, and an additional attribute labelled effective leadership. It also includes proposals for the person's job movement and development plans. The SDR is a very important report as it indicates the type of job the staff member is most suitable for (specialist/generalist/overseas postings), the necessary training and experience required and the next possible jobs. Follow-up action is taken by the personnel and training departments. Perhaps to counter criticisms about what appears to be an elitist system, the staff appraisal handbook reminds its readers that there is no intention of focusing only on the 'high flyers' who have the highest CEP ranking. The argument is that having the profiles of all senior staff enables the organisation to make the right kind of career development plans.

Career development

Even a casual acquaintance with the organisation provides evidence that the corporation values long service, for example, Dr Cheong Choon Kong described those in one 25-year service award ceremony as 'the old heroic breed'. Long-serving staff receive awards of medallions and/or gift vouchers as tokens of appreciation for their loyalty, and the organisation keeps track of numbers of employees by years of service. One executive jokingly described those that remain in the organisation to have been 'stamped with a SIA logo on their foreheads'. The turnover rate is low, around 6 per cent, and around 3 per cent for senior staff, but slightly higher for computer personnel at 7 per cent. Those who do not fit into the organisation usually make career switches within the first three years with the organisation.

It would be useful to refer once again to the hierarchy, now expanded to provide more details (Figure 11.6). Successful graduate applicants to the organisation typically start at administrative officer grade 1. There are four levels of officers within this grade; competition for promotion to the next category 'manager' is stiff. For every manager position, there are seven administrative officer positions. One may, for example, retire at administrative officer grade. Thus while external recruitment provides entry to the organisation, this occurs usually only for the administrative grade (and for the general staff) (see horizontal arrows in the figure). Promotion in the organisation beyond this grade tends to come from within.

Consequently, senior management in SIA tends to be home-grown, with at least 90 per cent staffed internally. Specialists may be recruited for specific posts if these skills are not available internally. The explanation given is that the airline industry is quite unusual and has special characteristics, so that it would take at least 10 years for an exceptionally competent individual to move up into senior management. The promotion rate and career destination of people within the organisation differ. Those

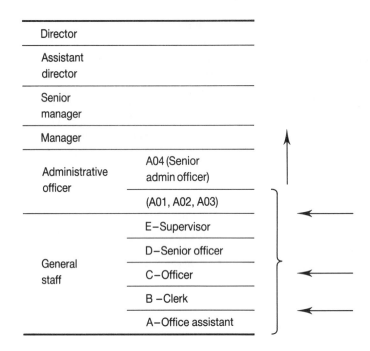

Figure 11.6   The SIA hierarchy (greater detail) to show career entry points

assessed as possessing outstanding abilities quickly progress up the organisation to a very high position; others may level off but still may move laterally in different job functions for wider exposure and job variety. Foreign postings during an individual's career seem to augur well, particularly for those in general management who demonstrate potential for high-level positions.

For those in specialist careers, promotions come with increasing responsibilities but with less diverse job postings. In general, a high degree of job movement within the organisation provides stimulation and exchange of ideas. Most people change their jobs every three to four years, either moving laterally across the organisation or being promoted to jobs with more responsibility. As the human resource manager said: 'The trouble with our organisation chart [which comes equipped with photographs and names of different executives attached] is that every time it gets published, some of the people have already changed their jobs. We move people so fast.'

This movement is not restricted to jobs with SIA itself, with shifts to the subsidiary (and vice versa) also planned for developmental purposes. Staff can also request a change in jobs, which would be granted whenever possible.

Training and development

The training and development function is a cornerstone of the organisation's human resource policy. SIA spent about S$30 million a year on training and development between 1980 and 1988. The figures continue to rise: S$40 million in 1988–9; S$55 million in 1989–90; and around S$83 million last year.

Training in SIA may be categorised under two main types: functional and job-specific versus management and general skills. Functional training is the responsibility of the line management and tends to be decentralised to different training centres. Each training centre focuses upon specific job skills. For example, in early 1974 SIA invested US$1 million in setting up a flight crew training centre; in 1979 this was beefed up by a US$2 million cabin crew training centre which houses three aircraft mock-ups (Figure 11.5 lists some training expectations for female cabin crew). The commercial training centre set up in 1971 conducts a variety of courses in subjects like ticketing. Its engineering training school enables SIA to be not only self-sufficient in engineering capability but also to undertake engineering work for other airlines. The computer training centre conducts computer-related training. Organising training into separate entities enables each division to respond quickly to their specific needs.

However, management and generic skill training was centralised formally under the Management Development Centre in 1987. The centre offers a comprehensive range of courses and talks aimed at the development of managerial, functional and personal skills throughout an individual's career. The courses may be broadly categorised under four groups – core, complementary, optional and specialised. Core programmes are mandatory and sequentially planned – courses which staff have to attend during the various stages of their career with the company. Complementary programmes are skills-based and staff are advised to attend these courses if necessary. Optional programmes are generally self-development pro-grammes to help staff improve themselves in areas such as coping with stress, understanding business protocol, working with personal computers, etcetera. Specialised courses are additional courses identified as being useful to job performance but in specific areas, for example, a specialised insurance course conducted in Montreal.

Other objectives may be more implicit than explicit. An external consultant and trainer to the organisation also sees training as a vehicle for reinforcing company culture. The current human resource manager says that training also enables people to get to know one another – thus emphasising the networking process which is important for such a large organisation. Some courses offered by the MDC are open to other organisations including those from around the region on a cost-sharing basis. Among the reasons cited for opening up the courses in this way is that participants can network with other organisations and benefit from a diversity of opinions in training sessions.

SIA provides an average of 11 man-days of training per year. All courses are conducted in company time and attendance needs the approval of a supervisor. Though the concept of training is encouraged, training is seen as a necessity rather than a reward for good work. Formal university education is another avenue of training for those with proven abilities through the provision of scholarships to study in foreign universities. The group's leadership in the field of training and development was publicly acknowledged in 1990 when the organisation was awarded the National Training Award in the service sector category for its outstanding record in employee training and development.

Compensation rewards

SIA does not claim to be the best paymaster in Singapore. It participates in salary surveys conducted by professional organisations such as the Singapore National Employers' Federation and Hay Associates to compare with market norms. However, in terms of the total compensation packet which includes benefits like medical, travel, loans, insurance coverage, etc., it is one of the best.

Singapore organisations have been exhorted through tripartite mechanisms like the National Wages Council (NWC) to adopt flexible pay schemes whereby in principle people are paid for performance rather than seniority. The NWC recommends smaller service increments which are built into salary scales but a larger component which varies with performance. SIA's service increments were 5 per cent of basic salary or 4 per cent of basic salary plus $15, whichever is the higher, an amount in keeping with the latest (1992) NWC guidelines. It also applies a profit-sharing bonus scheme negotiated with its separate house unions. In the last round of negotiations, it was agreed that only profits from operations be included in the calculations, this resulting in a one-off bonus payoff of S$83 million. Before obtaining a listing on the Stock Exchange – in 1975 – the organisation also offered shares to its staff every year. It was reported in a company publication that the staff of the SIA group have built a stake in the company equal to 20 per cent of its issued share capital. The percentage of share ownership now is, however, difficult to determine.

Conclusion

In an uncertain environment, SIA has continued pursuing a strategy of providing quality products and services, while keeping an eye on cost-control. Over time, it has evolved a management style and system that deliver that strategy. Stringency during recruitment and extensive and continuous training and development make this possible. At the same time, SIA is also interested in maintaining an innovative spirit and an organisational structure and climate in which that spirit may be nurtured. The provision of frequent job rotation within the organisation allows employees to develop a broad range of skills that are useful in other positions; this facilitates informal communication and encourages the cooperative, interdependent behaviour which is necessary for innovation. A performance appraisal system that focuses upon the longer-term and group-based achievements also encourages innovative behaviour. While the organisation may continue to fine-tune its personnel policies, the basic human resource initiatives are well suited to its business strategy. This policy has been vindicated by the company's economic performance.

Notes

1 The Australian government announced in December 1992 that they accepted the bid by British Airways to buy 25 per cent of Qantas for A$665 (S$757 million).
2 The groups which submit ideas for the scheme 'Staff ideas in action' have less of a permanent structure compared with quality circles. These *ad hoc* groups are naturally disbanded when the project is accomplished.
3 There is a general belief in Thailand (a predominantly Buddhist country) that it is not good to highlight the bad points of another person. The Thais believe that how one is reincarnated depends on the amount of good or bad deeds one has done in one's present life.

References

Asian Business (1992), 'A reputation for success', May, pp. 24–36.

Business Times, Singapore.

Lang, J. R. and Lockhart, D. E. (1990), 'Increased environmental uncertainty and changes in broad linkage patterns', *Academy of Management Journal*, vol. 33, no. 1, March, pp. 106–28.

Sikorski, D. J. (1986), 'Singapore Airlines: a case study of public enterprise in international competition', *Research in International Business and International Relations*, vol. 1, pp. 242–74.

Singapore Airlines Publications:
   Annual Reports
   Perspectives
   SIA Head Office Staff Appraisal Handbook
   SIA Orientation Materials
   Outlook

Singapore Broadcasting Corporation:
   Moneymind (1991), 'Silver lining in the clouds', 28 March.
   Friday Background (1992), 'Turbulent skies ahead', 28 August.

Soong, M. (1990), 'Staying on a winning course', *Singapore Business*, August, vol. 14. no. 8, pp. 31–9.

Straits Times, Singapore.

Woods, W. (1991), 'Misery in the air', *Fortune*, 16 December, pp. 54–5.

CHAPTER 12

Rhône Poulenc Agrochemicals
A Franco-American take-over

EVALDE MUTABAZI

Introduction

The business world is more and more marked by the increasing internationalisation of markets and firms. This 'globalisation' of the economy brings into contact business partners from different cultural, national and managerial backgrounds. Each the product of a different culture, of a different historical development and professional experience, they sometimes communicate with each other in a third language and find themselves working together in mergers, take-overs, joint ventures or international alliances.

The inevitable consequence for the firms concerned is that the achievement of the complimentarity necessary at the technological, financial or commercial levels depends to a large extent upon their ability to understand each other and to work in conjunction with the company's systems as well as its strategic and operational management.

When a partnership agreement is signed at the technological, legal or financial levels, the firms concerned are immediately faced with complex problems in the field of human resource management. In practice, while the legal and financial problems are the main concern of those in charge during the initial phases of the operation, the human aspects (organisational, cultural and managerial) become the foremost challenge for managers during the launching stage, when following through all the necessary changes is so important. Making a success of these changes is the only way of obtaining the profits and the competitive advantages sought at the international level in the medium and long term.

An example of these very problems, the Rhône Poulenc Agrochemicals case study described here, deals with the merging of two large international agrochemical corporations: an American one, Union Carbide and a French one, Rhône Poulenc (RP). Based on interviews with leading executives who participated in carrying out

Evalde Mutabazi is a professor in the Department of Human Resource Management in Groupe ESC, Lyons. The case study was prepared under the auspices of the chair of Human Resource Management and Industrial Performance and was sponsored by: Rhône Poulenc, Merlin Gerin and Renault Vehicules Industriels.

this operation, the study shows the challenges facing human resource management teams at the organisational and cultural levels within the group Rhône Poulenc Agrochemicals (RPA) which was set up after the merger.

From the decision to the signing of the agreement

Agrochemicals at the time of the merger

At the end of 1985, agrochemicals throughout the world had been undergoing considerable adjustments for several years. The following are the key features:

- It was noticeable at that time that, due to agrochemicals, the agricultural productivity of developed countries had made remarkable progress.
- This progress was such that these countries did not need all their food production.
- At the same time, the poorest countries did not have the financial means to buy up this surplus.
- In the United States in particular, the area under cultivation and the number of jobs in the agricultural sector had been considerably reduced. This state of affairs had also quickly overtaken certain European countries.
- The discovery of such a large number of active substances meant that most of the corresponding patents ended up on the open market.
- There had been a great deal of infringement of these patents in several countries of the world, including certain developing countries.
- More scientific research had produced a better understanding of the basic behaviours of plant life and its development.
- The increasing application of genetic manipulation techniques and the use of newly developed seeds linked with more sophisticated and more selective active principles, increased world agricultural productivity to an unheard-of degree.

Rhône Poulenc's decision to take over Union Carbide's agrochemical division

All these factors tended to destabilise firms in the agrochemical sector throughout the world. The American market was the most affected, for example: Shell with Du Pont, Stauffer with ICI, Union Carbide with Rhône Poulenc . . . In addition many firms closed down, to the advantage of their more powerful competitors.

Rhône Poulenc was rated sixth in the world, strongly diversified internationally, solidly based in France and had a research potential enabling it to bank on a favourable long-term position. On the other hand, when compared to Ciba-Geigy and Bayer, the two world leaders in agrochemicals, it would have to work hard on its following three main weaknesses:

1 An insufficient range of products in the field of insecticides and growth regulators.
2 A rather limited penetration of the leading world market: that of the United States, in which it occupied only 30 per cent of the total market value.
3 Compared to the two leaders, RP would not have such ready access to the agrochemical technologies of the year 2000 because of the considerable investments involved in R & D.

In view of all these challenges and of the wide and successful experience it had had with mergers and take-overs, RP was looking out for opportunities to strengthen its international position in agrochemicals.

Union Carbide agrochemicals division for sale

Like its 'colleague' Rhône Poulenc, Union Carbide was also trying at that time to increase its international dimension and its market shares.

Union Carbide held seventeenth place in the world rating for agrochemicals, representing 30 per cent of the turnover of RP, 40 per cent of its staffing levels and also held good market shares in the United States, Latin America and the Far East. However, the Bhopal catastrophe meant that the enterprise had to abandon its ambition of becoming a world leader in agrochemicals, and as a result decided to sell its agrochemical division, which represented 4 per cent of its turnover, during the summer of 1986.

The company then circulated to potential buyers an offering memorandum giving relevant information about itself and particularly about the agrochemical division to be sold. Rhône Poulenc was obviously one of the potential buyers for whom this offer represented an unexpected strategic opportunity.

On the basis of the information released, each potential buyer made a non-binding bid. Then, as a third step in the process, Union Carbide shortlisted the candidates and offered further information to the most likely ones to enable them to make a definite firm bid.

As one of the short-listed companies, Rhône Poulenc was anxious to eliminate its competitors and thus realise its ambition to become a world leader in agrochemicals. Finally it was chosen because of the overall positive image it enjoyed throughout the world: and because it was highly thought of by Union Carbide: 'We were considered by our "colleague" as reliable, competent and efficient in our particular field. Our excellent image might well outweigh the rather catastrophic one our colleague now had . . .' said the associate managing director of RPA.

Furthermore, there were very real possibilities of synergy between the two firms as far as products, markets, technologies and worldwide penetration were concerned. Since agrochemicals was one of the main markets depending on synthetic organic chemistry – one of the major fields of activity of the group – Rhône Poulenc now had an excellent opportunity to increase its credibility on the American market and of opening up new perspectives for worldwide development in such areas as advanced organic chemistry.

Thus, Rhône Poulenc negotiated tooth and nail to buy up Union Carbide Agrochemicals.

The negotiation process

In the midst of all this, a negotiation process began which occupied the two partners for six weeks and resulted in RP buying Union Carbide Agrochemicals for a total sum of $575 million.

The negotiation process was characterised not only by the desire on both sides to reach a compromise concerning what was at stake for both parties (which has already been mentioned), but also by a mutual appreciation of each other's experience on international markets. Evidence of this mutual recognition and desire for compromise was seen in the fact that Union Carbide decided to proceed with the sale alone, without having recourse to a trading bank – which is general practice during merger and take-over operations – to organise the negotiation process.

The first stage was, of course, centred on the legal and financial aspects, leaving the human, structural, cultural and managerial aspects until the second phase, even though these latter aspects were fundamental to the accomplishment of any take-over or merger. During this stage, the two parties discussed the complementarity of products and markets, the lessening of financial risks, economies of scale, or the effect of adapting to the international agrochemical market.

However, right from the beginning, the human and cultural aspects proved to be of great importance; indeed, certain meetings were tense and difficult because of problems of mutual understanding, even though all the representatives from both the American and the French firm expressed themselves perfectly well in 'American'. Moreover, the RP representatives felt that the Union Carbide team was composed of too many lawyers and so was not representative of the other specialities of the agrochemical sector. According to a Rhône Poulenc executive: 'With all their lawyers we were worried about not being able to get the merger off the ground quickly enough at the operational, structural and managerial level.'

On the other hand, the American team thought their French counterparts went too quickly and generalised too much in their thinking; they were not rigorous and precise enough in the way they tackled the problems.

However, because of their mutual professional regard and their awareness of what was at stake for both parties, they soon agreed to entrust the running of the negotiation to those, both French and American, who knew the two firms through having worked with them. They also agreed to bring in inside and outside experts to deal with specific points. These experts were to be appointed bilaterally.

Generally speaking, the process should have worked efficiently, and indeed it did, thanks to the realisation on both sides of the importance of constant effort being applied at all times to understanding the respective positions regarding tricky, complex questions. As Rhône Poulenc's associate managing director put it:

> Both sides have committed themselves to doing everything possible to promote mutual comprehension and, above all, to leaving nothing in doubt . . . We did not

want to build on sand . . . That is why some of our meetings lasted until 2 o'clock in the morning . . . To understand certain points, we listened to long and complicated explanations by the experts . . . In some fields, the explanations took from 12 to 24 hours . . . We were not to be frightened or ashamed of looking innocent or ignorant in the eyes of our colleagues by admitting we did not know about certain aspects of a question being discussed.

It was in this spirit of mutual respect, of the desire for mutual comprehension and for achieving common aims that the negotiations took place which ultimately led to the final decision to buy the division on 1 January 1987.

The human and managerial challenge arising from the negotiations

The internationalisation of human resources before the acquisition

Before the acquisition, Rhône Poulenc had 4200 employees and Union Carbide 3600. Of Rhône Poulenc's 4200, 300 worked in the United States, whereas of Union Carbide's 3600, 2500 worked in the USA and only 400 in France, at the Béziers site in particular.

Table 12.1 shows the staffing levels of RP at its Lyons head office between 1983 and 1986, just before the acquisition. The figures show that RP employed some non-French before the acquisition and that between 1983 and 1986 there was a slight increase in the number reflecting the firm's desire even then to develop internationally.

At that time, the posts held by non-French included special missions which were strongly oriented towards the worldwide development of the group. For example, a French executive of international calibre was commissioned to search for foreign enterprises that Rhône Poulenc could take over, or with which they could profitably enter into an international strategic partnership. He was assisted in his task by

Table 12.1 Staffing levels at RP head office 1983–6

Year	Total	French	Non-French	%
1983	870	859	11	1.20
1984	905	894	11	1.23
1985	662	650	12	1.84
1986	695	680	15	2.20

ten other internationally oriented employees, such as five high-flying export executives, one operations executive, two in marketing and two in research. Finally, there was also a non-French member of the group's management committee prior to the acquisition.

Urgent and unavoidable questions to be dealt with

Although it was not possible for a wider range of staff from both firms to be involved in the negotiations, the entire staff of the two concerns, and particularly their senior executives, were automatically involved in the actual setting up of the merger in practical terms. Indeed, in the situation at that time, a mere rumour would have been enough to create a dramatic atmosphere and widespread anxiety about the future – a loss of confidence of the staff in the management of Rhône Poulenc.

Consequently, long before negotiations ended, the following questions concerning strategic and operational management arose in the minds of the principals:

- What attitude should be adopted towards Union Carbide, a partner with its own specific economic, organisational, cultural and managerial characteristics?
- What techniques should be used to bring the staff of the two firms together, spread as they were throughout the world, speaking different languages and with different standards, values, beliefs and expectations?
- How should a consensus about the merger be achieved (as well as a commonly held, favourable image of RP in full expansion)?
- What should be done to counter any resistance to these changes which might emerge among the staff or, in particular, among senior executives?
- What policies should be adopted to increase the overall involvement of the staff in the group's new project?

In the same way the following just such vital questions were being asked by the staff, and particularly by the executives, faced with this new situation:

- What would be the effect of this merger on their jobs, their posts, their career, their pay . . .?
- Would they find themselves 'managed' in a French or in an American way?
- What would be the effects on relationships in the workplace, with one's superiors and with the hierarchy?
- What would the new organisational structures and the new sharing out of responsibilities be? Also, the new work procedures, the assessment of results, of recognition and appreciation of skills and performances?
- How should one behave with superiors, colleagues or subordinates whose nationality or culture is different from one's own?
- What would be the working language used within RPA etc.?

The organisation system adopted after the acquisition

The creation of a common vision and the challenges faced by the group

On 2 January 1987, the day after signing the take-over agreement, the leaders of RPA addressed themselves to these many and complex questions. At that stage, the structural questions seemed both more urgent and more accessible than the cultural aspects, which, though just as important, were naturally, much more complex, considering the number of countries the firm operated in and the corresponding cultural differences between them. And so, because of the determined attitude and the experience and knowledge of those responsible, the merging of the two organisations proceeded methodically and confidently.

To derive the fullest economic and strategic benefit from the acquisition of Union Carbide Agrochemicals, the company had to be successfully integrated into the corresponding activities within Rhône Poulenc. As we have already stated, the aim was to set up economies of scale, to reduce the costs caused by overlapping and to develop synergy within all the areas of potential of the two firms and their personnel. According to a senior executive at that time: 'The first condition for success lay in the teams in both enterprises. It was vital that they felt completely involved in working out the terms of their new programmes of action.'

Before tackling this important operation of developing synergy by means of the reorganisation process, a common vision of the group had to be inculcated in the minds of all the members of the two firms, in order to strengthen their efforts to achieve common goals. This was done on 3 January 1987 by means of a policy speech delivered by the Chairman or President and Managing Director or Chief Executive of RPA, Philippe Desmarescaux, in the presence of all members of the two partner firms (see Appendix 2). His message was also printed and distributed to all the subsidiaries. Senior executives communicated it to their staff and had to record their reactions and suggestions. From this they could obtain operational advice to be given to those responsible for the international management of human resources.

The organisation adopted just after signing the agreement

Without delay, solutions to the problems encountered in the actual day-to-day working out of the merger had to be found so on 15 January 1987 a temporary organisational structure was set up bringing together the ex-Rhône Poulenc and the ex-Union Carbide and embracing all fields of activity (see Appendix 2). Working teams were then set up, watched over by the pilot committee already mentioned by the chairman in his opening address. Their mission was to define the relationship objectives and the corresponding organisational changes concerning all the subsidiaries. 'The new system just had to work and we needed very precise information about the running of each subsidiary and its real potential contribution to the corporation as a whole,' said a senior executive.

In fact, the working teams set about analysing the subsidiaries with a view to proposing to each of them a system of links with the head office, a redistribution of posts and functions and a pilot plan for changes that would facilitate the integration of each subsidiary into RPA (see Appendix 3).

Thus, from 30 April 1987 the first conclusions of the working teams began reaching the pilot committee and six months afterwards practically all of them were included in a plan of action and of the overall reorganisation of the group. In terms of jobs, this plan provided for economies of scale for about 1000 people by the end of 1989 and for a total staffing level of 8300 people. By the end of 1987 600 employees would have left the firm, which represented a potential economy of FFr140 million. The cost of this operation would be FFr90 million. During 1988 restructuring costs would probably reach FFr50 million and would enable FFr210 million to be saved by the year 1989. Finally, in terms of the merger operation, the plan provided for a saving of FFr250 million during a complete year.

On 1 July 1987, the day after the overall ratification of the working teams' results, certain decisions were immediately adopted – such as the setting up of the Rhône Poulenc Agrochemicals Co. in the United States, as well as the progressive establishing of a matrix structure for the whole of the group.

The key principles of the new organisation

To achieve a structural merger, the new organisation was based on the following two key principles:

1 *Give precedence to the international and local levels*
   In this case integration and differentiation had to be applied at the same time:
   - The international level to decide on strategies and policies, as well as to control their application.
   - The local (national) level to see to the day-to-day growth of business within the limits fixed by head office strategies.

2 *Motivate each staff member to increase overall efficiency*
   To motivate every member of all the subsidiaries, important changes were brought about in both the partner firms. These aimed first and foremost at *simplifying the existing structures*. To achieve this it was decided to focus the changes on the following five main points:

   a *Reducing intermediate structures*   To set up the matrix structure, the number of hierarchical levels was reduced overall to strengthen the subsidiaries and enable them to be more autonomous in their management. This autonomy stimulated initiative and motivation at all levels of responsibility.

   b *Improving communication channels around special chemical projects*
      Improving contact between different departments and levels of responsibility within the group and each subsidiary necessitated establishing efficient channels of communication.

To meet this challenge, business teams were set up which brought together the skills and abilities of several departments to function outside the normal hierarchical influence. And so, with the teams working together on common projects, communication was direct, and this led to mutual understanding and the creation of new management techniques and procedures within the group.

Over and above their operational responsibilities, these working teams centred on different specialities (research, marketing, finance, communication, etc.), which are still in existence today, aiming at developing a common cultural basis within the group.

c *Strategic integration of the operations*   The pilot committee of the working teams emphasised the necessity of structuring the different tasks and operations hierarchically according to their strategic importance.

d *Logistical integration*   The functions administrating sales, transport, purchasing, supplies, manufacturing, stocks and customs were grouped on a basis of integrated logistics. This meant that three logistical centres were created, one in France, one in the United States and one in Great Britain. These three centres were coordinated and supervised by the Lyons headquarters to harmonise the commercial and industrial functions at the overall group level.

e *The overall coherence of the management system*   To get the best out of the new organisation, the leaders of the group decided on a system of management control that both respected the autonomy of the subsidiaries and also integrated them within the group (the integrated margin principle). More precisely, with the matrix structure each subsidary could be assessed on the basis of its objectives, and within each subsidiary, each speciality and each department.

With this view of things, production centres (in the industrial sector) were considered as *cost centres*, whose job was to manufacture the quality of goods required by the customer at the most advantageous price. The R & D Centres, from then on known as 'investment centres', were concerned with developing new products and protecting them (patents, etc.) within certain defined budgetary limits. Appendix 5 shows the development of the structures adopted by the group since the acquisition.

Finally, 'profit centres', were set up to manage the commercial activity of the group. Their assessment was based on the trading margins and the running costs.

Two years later, an economic assessment of the merger was carried out. Thanks to the new organisation, the results obtained surpassed expectations and the group strengthened its assets and overcame most of its weaknesses. It launched the products that were lacking in the insecticide and growth regulator ranges, and so improved their complementarity with herbicides and fungicides.

These new advantages pushed RP up to the fourth rank in American agrochemicals.

At the international level, the group moved up from the sixth to the third rank, with an overall volume equal to two-thirds of that of the world leader Bayer.

From the human and cultural point of view, the merger meant that certain executives from Rhône Poulenc moved to the ex-subsidiaries of Union Carbide and vice versa. Within the subsidiaries, only two Frenchmen were sent to the United States, where they did not by any means occupy key positions. RPA's choice was to send young Frenchmen abroad and so give them the chance to develop their potential by working with specialists or managers of a different culture to their own and in a new professional context.

At the same time, as is clearly shown in Table 12.2, there was an increase in the number of non-French at the group's head office in Lyons after the acquisition. The increase in the numbers of non-French members of the head office of the group in France was above all because British and Americans were to be responsible for managing Asia, Africa and the rest of the world except Europe, which was under the control of a French executive, Pierre Belmon. As a result, the human resources department, traditionally very French, now found itself confronted by quite new problems of integration and the motivation of people coming from different cultural and managerial backgrounds.

As in all organisational changes, the new structure met with some resistance, such as the voluntary departure of certain American ex-Union Carbide executives in particular. But as we shall see in the following pages, most of the resistance encountered stemmed from the cultural uncertainties created by the merger of the two firms, French and American.

The effects of the acquisition on human resource management

The uncertainties and conflicting views held the day following the signing of the merger agreement

It is becoming more generally acknowledged today within large groups that the

Table 12.2   Staffing levels at RP head office 1987–91

Year	Total	French	Non-French	%
1987	742	698	44	6.3
1988	733	685	48	7.0
1989	762	718	44	6.1
1990	821	767	54	7.04
1991	831	760	71	9.34

performance of a firm that has a clearly defined formal structure and the efficiency of its members depend largely on the informal structure of the working relationships between the teams and the members within each department.

In the case of RPA, the creating of informal work relationships proved to be more complex following the signing of the merger with Union Carbide. Indeed, the cultures brought together – American and French in particular, but also those of other countries where subsidiaries of the group were set up – were different, even contradictory as far as the standards and values that define work relationships were concerned.

In spite of their wealth of experience gained in mergers and the take-overs of other firms, the leaders of the group could not foresee the behaviour patterns and the attitudes of the ex-Union Carbide members towards the ex-Rhône Poulenc members and vice versa. Group executives had to find answers to the following questions:

- Would the ex-Rhône Poulenc people behave like conquerors and impose their culture on the ex-Union Carbide staff?
- Would they, on the contrary, accept to be influenced by the latter?
- What was the best way to deal with the culture shock between the different management models inculcated into the two groups by their previous professional experience?
- Which management system would turn this cultural and managerial encounter to best advantage?

In the opinion of André Papot, Director of Executive Career Development:

We must remain faithful to the decisions we have taken for carrying out this structural merger. In other words, we should neither impose our own culture, nor allow ourselves to be completely influenced by theirs. We chose to build on a basis of overall complementarity, including the cultural aspects . . .

This statement followed directly on from what M. Desmarescaux, the Chairman and Managing Director of the group said in his address on 2 January 1987: 'It is essential that we benefit fully from the skills of the men and women from the two organisations . . .' (see Appendix 2). In other words, contrary to the traditional procedures adopted by firms going international: there was no question of adopting a universalist approach, the aim of which would be to standardise the different cultures existing in the two firms.

As the plant manager at Villefrance explained, the leaders of the group were perfectly aware of the fact that the members of the two firms did not have the same concept either of their original firm or of the future of RPA: 'Straight after the merger, there was no common vision of the group nor of its future development. Besides, certain American ex-Union Carbide executives were to leave us very promptly . . . They knew nothing of France nor of Rhône Poulenc.' And the marketing manager went on to speak of the American colleagues: 'In the eyes of certain of them, France was an underdeveloped, agricultural country, close to Chernobyl . . . It was as if they had been taken over by Turks or Africans.'

In another vein, the head of global communication, said: 'for certain French executives, Union Carbide was a nightmare . . . In taking it over, the Directors of RPA completely jeopardised their firm, its credibility and its image in the eyes of the world at large.' For other ex-Rhône Poulenc members 'taking over Union Carbide could mean being dominated by the American partner which might take over the leadership of the group and impose its language, its culture, its standards and management procedures.'

According to the associate general manager of the group:

> these fears are quite understandable in the case of those who have had no international experience. At a more general level, these fears can be explained by the fact that, on the one hand, there was the young, fragile culture of Rhône Poulenc Agrochemicals, still unsure of itself because of previous acquisitions, and on the other hand, the confident, older, more dominant culture of Union Carbide . . . Our less mature culture was less resistant, more vulnerable than our partner's, represented by a team of older managers more conditioned by a certain style of management and a set of procedures that claimed, as it were, to be universal . . .

To promote a cultural merger and the successful running of the system the leaders of the group tried to take account of all these elements, linked with cultural specificities and with the reciprocal conceptions held by members of the two firms. Therefore, the merging of all the staff members, particularly at executive level, was to take place in *a spirit of mutual acceptation and of respect for the cultural specificities of the various countries* that the group was set up in. This ethical choice was later to guide the development of a cultural fusion within the daily functioning of the enterprise and so lead to staff motivation and a feeling of complementarity between subsidiaries and between individuals. In management terms, the group was to count more and more on this ethical choice *to develop an international culture* by means of new global communication policies and by their management of the international executives.

Aiming specifically for development and dealing with human resource management in intercultural situations

We have already pointed out that fusions within product lines and in R & D in particular took off so fast that they produced economic results which surpassed the forecasts. On the other hand, the assessment of the new management system pointed to a certain degree of malfunctioning (duplication of posts and functions, for example) involving unforeseen structural costs. Furthermore, 'hidden costs' were revealed; these were associated to a large extent with the co-existence of different cultures and management models. All this became apparent in difficult work relationships, difficult communication or co-operation between ex-members of the two merged firms. Again, in the opinion of the director of executive career development:

Our former experience in human resource management and expatriate executives was sadly lacking when faced with the new demands made by the internationalisation of the personnel . . . We found ourselves forced to innovate and to think no longer in terms of simple expatriation, but of exchanging our executives.

The existence of this exchange mobility of executives (expatriation–repatriation) triggered off an important reflex within the management team. They felt the need to develop a new culture within the group, focused on open-mindedness and mutual respect. This seemed to them to be essential for inculcating loyalty in staff members for the company project. It was also necessary to facilitate communication and work relationships, to derive full advantage from all that was complementary and to ensure the ongoing mutual enrichment of staff members in the subsidiaries.

Closely allied to the overall project of Rhône Poulenc, this internationalisation of the staff, and of executives in particular, was to be based on the policy of *geographical and professional mobility of efficient executives*, whatever their subsidiary, their nationality, their speciality or their original culture. To apply this new policy, the leaders agreed to all the conditions necessary for a real sharing of power, of know-how and of willingness among the executives regardless of their origin. The only criteria that would influence an executive's career development within the group in the future would be his or her *competence and personal motivation*. In the words of one senior manager: 'When dealing with highly qualified and very demanding executives, this is the only approach that could reconcile each one's personal satisfaction and the international development of the group while respecting the cultural specificities of those concerned.'

At the very beginning, this approach was strongly upheld by the former human resource manager, a Frenchman who had an intimate knowledge of American culture and the managerial practices resulting from it. In the words of one of his senior colleagues:

His sincerity and the personal dedication in launching this new group culture were as much appreciated by the ex-Union Carbide staff as by those who came from Rhône Poulenc. With the general management team behind him, his multicultural approach to problems helped greatly in the integration of the first waves of foreign executives coming into France and vice versa.

To give only a few examples, the American head of the former subsidiary of RPA in the United States became head of the group in the USA after the merger, whereas the former sales manager of Union Carbide in the USA held the same territorial post and was a member of the decisions committee at the level of the agrochemicals sector.

These same principles were used within subsidiaries and industrial sites to effect the change-over to the new system of human resource management from the former management style. Thus, at the Béziers factory which previously belonged to Union Carbide, Rhône Poulenc built upon the former experience of that factory, particularly its excellent handling of shop-floor safety problems. Certain management processes were retained without any modification. The former production manager became the plant manager and very successfully saw through the numerous changes that followed from the take-over – for example, the cutting down of certain business activities, the reduction in staffing levels and so on. These examples illustrate how the group will share power, responsibility and know-how.

This same line of thought is still held today in terms of the strategic management of human resources and concerns all high-ranking executives and the development of their careers within the group. An operational structure was put in place at the end of 1988 to develop to the fullest the international management of executive careers. The purpose of this structure was to identify and pinpoint available skills and relate them to existing or anticipated posts, and then to work out an overall plan of international mobility for executives based on the needs of the subsidiaries and in conformity with the worldwide development strategy of the group.

To date, in the opinion of one senior executive, this operational structure has not yet completely attained its objective:

> Our procedures are not yet precise enough. We often act in the heat of the moment . . . We are not yet in sufficient control of the problems posed by mobility and the replacing of executives that this involves. And we are even less able to deal with the problems arising from cultural shock and the differences in management models . . . We still spend too much time identifying the particular skills we often urgently need somewhere in the group. . .

A BREEDING GROUND FOR YOUNG INTERNATIONAL EXECUTIVES
Realising that 'the industrial project meant nothing without the personal commitment of each member of the staff', about six years ago the group set up its own school for training young international executives.

It saw in this an important strategic means of meeting the human and cultural challenges arising from its long-term international development. The underlying idea was to identify young executives who were gifted in a particular field (the high fliers) in their country of origin, to attract them and train them in the spirit of the group while developing their international dimension and inculcating into them the group's working methods. After this, they would have an international career within the group.

These young people were recruited from prestigious schools and universities throughout the world (Tokyo, Stanford, Wharton, Bocconi, Esade, Insead, etc.) to follow a five-month induction seminar in France. During the seminar they worked with senior executives of the group and made several visits to subsidiaries in France and abroad. Each participant thus enriched his or her knowledge in his or her own special field while experiencing the realities and down-to-earth problems of the group.

At the end of the seminar the young executives were posted to a subsidiary of the group in France for five years. They then set out on their second mission to a foreign country, again for five years, before finally returning to their country of origin.

The purpose of this 'breeding ground' for RPA, as well as for the group as a whole, was to increase the number of international executives and also to build up their company loyalty by having them within the firm itself for 10 to 15 years. So, by 1990 19 young international executives had already been recruited into the firm, 9 from the 1988 intake, and 10 from the second intake in 1989. The latter was made up of 4 Americans, 2 Germans, 2 Brazilians, 1 Belgian and 1 Dutchman, with as many women as men.

In 1990, the group considered these experiments as great successes, since the young executives, each highly qualified, developed very well on the intercultural level and adapted perfectly to their professional context within the group no matter where they were sent.

This was not always the case in other firms where 'breeding-grounds' of the same type had been created but for Rhône Poulenc, as for the young executives themselves, the experiment turned out to be positive in all respects. The following is a comment made by a young Japanese executive from the 1988 intake:

> The desire to follow an international career is not at all approved of in Japan. Personally, that is just what I wanted and I am sure I have taken the right decision for my career. Thanks to the seminar I participated in at the Training Centre at Cergy, I was able to improve my knowledge of the French language and above all of life in a firm in an international group. If I return to Japan, I shall certainly have acquired a wealth of experience unusual for that country.

In the light of the results of the first two intakes of executives, the group decided to pursue this strategy of recruiting, integrating and generating company loyalty and planned to take up to 15 young executives per year, in order to fulfil the subsidiaries' different needs and to develop a strong sense of the importance of international culture in the minds of the high-ranking executives within the group and all its subsidiaries.

THE INTERNATIONAL MOBILITY OF EXPERIENCED EXECUTIVES
Within Rhône Poulenc, it was essential that executives should have a highly developed international dimension to assure cohesion throughout the firm, to consolidate the feeling of belonging and to encourage attitudes of solidarity and commitment within the subsidiaries as well as between individuals, whatever their nationality and their professional culture.

The basic values of this culture should underlie the group's development project and shine through it at all levels, for example:

- To be reliable providers to our customers.
- To be an efficient international group, respecting the countries that host us.
- To acknowledge and to appraise everyone according to their contribution and skills.
- To be mobile and to promote the internationalisation of careers.

With regard to the international mobility of internally recruited, experienced executives, the present practices can be summed up in the following main points:

1 Executives should be chosen according to their technical and linguistic skills, with extra training in the host country's language if necessary.

2 Each candidate should be interviewed to define his or her potential for development and adaptation in a different cultural context. However, as a senior executive warned, 'our detection and selection criteria are not yet sufficiently worked out. They will have to be more subtle if we are to get the best out of our recruitment methods for international executives.'

3 The executive and his or her spouse are then offered an exploratory visit of one week to the host country. This enables them to get on-the-spot impressions of the legislative, professional and living conditions as well as general information, and above all, the possibilities for cultural adaptation.

4 After this trip, the executive and his or her superiors within the group decide about a posting abroad. The executive can then benefit from the facilities available within the group for preparing for this mission and for improving the language he or she will use once there. The spouse can also participate in this linguistic and preparatory training.

Usually, this preparation takes place very rapidly since the urgency of the situations that arise quite often prevents longer and more thorough preparation periods from being organised.

Indeed, until 1990 only executives going to Japan underwent a thorough preparation covering linguistic, cultural and managerial aspects. This training period was organised by the EC for European executives and businesspeople. It took place in Japan and consisted of three months of total immersion in the Japanese cultural and professional context.

Even though there are other countries that are just as important strategically as Japan for the group, no other such intensive training programmes exist to prepare executives for their operational, managerial and strategic role in these countries. One top executive advised:

An intensive preparation for such target countries as Latin America, the countries of Eastern and Northern Europe, so different in their cultural and managerial specificities would certainly increase the efficiency of our executives. In the future, we must be better organised and select them three months before their departure. They should be taken out of their operational sphere and they should concentrate on preparing their successor.

The success of this kind of system depends upon the details of executive mobility and replacement being well prepared in advance, thus enabling follow-up problems and difficulties arising from the return of international executives to be dealt with. Besides, different people from executive career management departments have high-lighted the importance of follow-up as far as international executives are concerned which should involve more than the simple administrative, legal and financial aspects:

While working in a foreign country, one picks up more than just professional experience. One can acquire strategic information that could be of great importance to the group. First-hand knowledge of the local market, competitors' strategies, the attitudes of partners and local political leaders, the local workforce, etc., can be picked up . . . We are not yet sufficiently well organised to benefit fully from this strategic information.

THE NEW DEMANDS MADE BY COMMUNICATION

Apart from arranging the exchanges of international executives, RPA is seeking to consolidate its international culture by means of internal and external communication policies. These policies are the concern of the participative management section.

Since 1975, and above all from 1986 onwards, Rhône Poulenc has worked on original methods for developing communication and participative management. This undertaking has affected about 80 per cent of the staff involved in the expression groups and direct participation groups such as the groups for internal work (GIW) and for quality improvement (GQI) or for safety improvement (GSI).

In parallel progression with the communication and participation projects in France, the group has created structures to promote direct communication between subsidiaries and associated business sectors throughout the world. The basic aim of these structures is to develop within all staff members the feeling of belonging to the group.

Also, run along collegiate decision-making lines, an executive committee of six members was set up to oversee the overall cohesion of all the members of Rhône Poulenc and to develop the fusion of and solidarity between business sectors and management teams. This committee relies on a panel of 50 top executives of whom 20 per cent are non-French. This panel meets every two months to discuss questions of strategy and their feasibility within every business sector and subsidiary of the group. Such direct communication does not stop at the top of the pyramid. It spreads out to 600 executives throughout the world who meet twice a year to review the financial results of the preceding half year and the development plans for the following three years.

In the same vein as these large meetings, the group has adopted, over the last four years, a rather unusual practice: over a weekly dinner, a dozen top executives talk with a member of the executive committee to get a better understanding of how the strategic choices made by the board are reflected in the daily operations within the different units of the group. This style of direct communication, like the ripples caused by a stone thrown into a pond, has been set up in each subsidiary and unit of the group.

The merger of Union Carbide with Rhône Poulenc has increased the need to develop an international culture as well as new methods of communication. To refer solely to the experiences of Rhône Poulenc does not develop a real feeling of belonging and an urge to work together in the minds of the members of both merged firms. 'Some time after the merger, we realised the limitations of our former communication techniques which were characterised by rather indirect exchanges of technical information or urgent messages between our subsidiaries,' said one employee.

In the light of this realisation, four years ago RPA created a 'Service of global communication' with the aim of improving their 'traditional' communication, both internal and external, and also of developing an international culture within the group. In the Human Resource Management Department, five people now work on harmonising internal and external communication and on developing a feeling of belonging in staff members of the subsidiaries set up in 80 different countries.

The challenge facing this department is threefold as follows:

- How can messages be understood in the same way by all the subsidiaries?
- How can one surpass the information stage and create a common cultural identity and strengthen synergies?
- How does one create a community of international executives?

Creating a common cultural and managerial basis

In answer to these questions, two complementary approaches were developed from 1990 onwards.

THE 'ACTION' DOSSIERS

The communication service produced an information letter for the agrochemicals sector in the form of an 'Action' dossier. This dynamic, realistic title was chosen to give the executives of all countries concerned the latest relevant, coherent information regarding the development strategy of the group. Published today in French and in English, this letter will probably later be translated into a minimum of four other languages to reach a greater number of executives and create a dynamic interchange between subsidiaries.

The content of the message aims at the following:

1 Involving the staff, by way of the executives, in the strategic vision of the general management of the group. This means keeping everyone informed of the results, the current situation and the progress made by the RPA on the world market. Special numbers are devoted to new commercial triumphs of the group, joint ventures, acquisitions, etc.

2 Creating a common cultural basis within the group by imparting to all its members the international dimension of its activities, as well as the corresponding challenges and values at stake.

The key information is presented and commented on in a clear, precise way so as to increase the feeling of belonging to the group and of commitment to its international development strategy.

CREATING INTERCULTURAL SYNERGY

As a result of the information letter, the communication service, keenly supported by the general management, accepted the major challenge of trying to create a community of international executives within RPA. Basing their efforts on the key principles of complementarity and respect for cultural differences laid down by the general management, this department sought to develop interactive dynamics based on experiences derived from communication and work done in multicultural teams.

This idea was sparked off by the discovery by executives of Global Communication that there was a certain cultural resistance from members during multicultural operational meetings when they had to use a foreign language. To the concern of general management, it was discovered that using English is a serious problem for most non-English-speaking executives and having to use French or any other language poses the same problem for English speakers. And what is more serious, is that this reluctance to use a foreign language shows up in behaviour as well: 'They blame each other for not learning the other language and do all they can to avoid trying to use a foreign language.'

As a member of the Communication Department and the plant manager at Villefrance explained:

> For certain American executives in particular, English is a universal language which will spread throughout the Common Market in 1993. So why should they give themselves headaches learning French?

> French-speaking executives consider that using English is a sort of American imperialism. To them, it is as if they had been taken over by Union Carbide and not the reverse, since English is being imposed on them!

Although these two extreme positions do not involve a majority of the executives of the group, general management is anxious about one of the possible consequences of this attitude: the forming of clans, the English-speaking clan and the French-speaking clan. This tendency could of course lead to a division forming between senior and international executives, who speak several languages including English and the rest of the members of the group. This would run counter to the desired effects of complementarity. Besides, the relationships arising from communication and work done in multicultural teams have clearly shown the limitations of using only English as a common language.

It was noticed during certain meetings at head office that the executives could speak the same language without really understanding their different respective positions. 'We understand each other easily as long as it is technical or statistical information . . . and almost not at all when management procedures and human resource management are concerned,' stated an American executive in the Executive Career Management Department.

In other words, this one means of communication is not sufficient to create complementary relationships. The overall efficiency of the group also relies on intuitive exchange, the unexpressed, the implied, the non-quantifiable elements which are strongly influenced by specific national cultures. 'We have noticed, for example, that he found it difficult to get his idea across when the meeting was chaired by a Frenchman, and considerably easier when it was being led by American colleagues.'

Realising this, since 1988 the communication service has undertaken to set up multicultural experiments enabling executives to work together and, above all, to get to know each other more fully outside the professional and formal limits. To help them to integrate their respective cultural specificities and to adapt to each other, these experiments were based on direct contact and communication, face-to-face intercultural relationships.

Fully convinced of the efficacy of this approach and of its positive effects on the development of the group and the consolidating of synergies between the subsidiaries and individuals, the general management encouraged the organising of an integration seminar for executives. This seminar brought together 80 executives representing the group's subsidiaries for two days in Monaco in June 1989. The programme included a presentation of the group's strategies (its project) and exchanging and developing ideas in groups. In addition there were games organised by Global Communication.

It was due to the pragmatic approach of this seminar that the strategic vision of the group project could be adjusted, since it was submitted by general management to the top executives of the subsidiaries. This is what one participant had to say on this subject:

> It appeared to us that the thinking of the executives was focused not so much on the strategic levels of the project, but rather on the human, cultural and managerial aspects, such as security procedures, appraisal of performances, team management, ethical principles and practices enabling the development objectives of each sector as well as the personal fulfilment of each individual to be catered for.

Since the first integration seminar was considered a great success by all involved, general management instructed the communication service to prepare a summer seminar in 1990 to continue thinking along the lines of the group project. Further seminars were organised in 1991 and 1992 to encourage international executives to get to know each other and to help each of them to feel more personally concerned with the international development of the group.

As well as these seminars, the Human Resource Management Department set up meetings between the different departments and between executives and their opposite numbers from different countries and subsidiaries. 'It is a very rewarding experience as it enables us to compare our methods and work out procedures together between colleagues and opposite numbers in the same professional specialities but in different subsidiaries,' reported one executive.

At the present moment the group has not had enough time to be able to assess the result of these meetings before planning to extend them to other levels of responsibility. It should nevertheless be pointed out, that everyone has proved to be in favour of developing these multicultural experiments further and believes in the positive effects they will have on the group's international performance in the medium term.

When it is decided to enlarge the scope of these experiments to other staff categories, the executives responsible will be able to draw on a thorough knowledge of the group's human resources. They will probably take into account the present degree of international awareness of each department, of each speciality, age and training. For instance, marketing and R & D executives are generally speaking more mobile and internationally minded because of their professional experience. These features are less highly developed in the case of industrialists and administrators who are comparatively less involved in intercultural relationships in the workplace and in working abroad.

As one executive remarked, these intercultural actions involving communication and the individual as a whole must be continued with the participation of people from all cultural and professional origins:

> If this is not done, our international culture and our group project will remain divided into three levels: efficient and thoroughly integrated at the top management level, very weak at the executive level and almost non-existent at the technician, supervisor, white and blue collar worker level.

And another added:

> In developing these intercultural work experiments, we are certainly acting differently to our competitors. In the world market, we will have a solid common cultural basis to rely on, a central force that will enable us to bring together in active cooperation all our subsidiaries, professional categories and specialities in the group development project.

The main results of the operation

The main results are as follows:

- At the present moment, this operation has had several types of positive results. Indeed, it is true that executive and specialist mobility involves fairly heavy expenses for international management of human resources: not including salaries in 1991–2, these costs were estimated at between FFr300,000 and 500,000 a year for a Frenchman going abroad; from FFr300,000 to 600,000 during the first year and from FFr200,000 to 400,000 the second year for a foreigner coming to France.
- With the gradual opening up and easier circulation of people within the Common Market, mobility within this zone will be considered more and more as a simple transfer. This is the case for certain British, Belgians and Dutch working in the group, for whom mobility costs between FFr200,000 and 300,000 the first year, then falls away to under FFr 10,000 the following year.
- In spite of these cost differences accounted for by moving, accommodation, children's schooling, time off and linguistic training for international executives, the results of the operation had already surpassed forecast profits by 1990.
- As is shown in Table 12.3, the financial expenditure continues to increase.
- Realising its success, the group considers these social costs today as investments in brain power, which is more than ever necessary with the internationalisation of markets.

Table 12.3 Development of financial results

(in FFr million)

		83	84	85	86	87	88	89	90	91	92
Operating assumption	Turnover	4.680	5.615	6.505	6.530	6.250	6.750	7.150	7.850	8.150	8.620
Without Union Carbide	OM	420	550	660	615	345	460	560	640	690	770
	OM Turnover	8,9	8,9	10,1	7,8	5,5	6,8	7,8	8,2	8,5	8,9
Actual Outturn	Turnover					8.410	9.043	9.700	10.600	11.150	11.800
	OM					490	705	850	950	1.070	1.155
	OM Turnover %					5,8	7,8	8,8	9,3	9,6	9,8

Profitability of the acquisition:

Internal rates of return	20 to 22%
Expected pay-back (10%)	6 to 8 years
Effective pay-back (September 1990)	5 years 3 months

N.B. OM: operational margin

- In another sense, due to this successful experiment, the group has noticeably increased its know-how and, in particular, has developed its ability to turn cultural and managerial differences to great advantage.
- In terms of international management of human resources, the group has learnt to manage the exchange mobility of executives both at head office and between subsidiaries.
- Furthermore, at its head office in Lyons the ratio of foreign to French staff has been completely reversed: from 11/15 before the merger it developed to 71/35 in 1991.
- Profiting from this experience, the group today banks on the differences and the complementarity within its staff as a whole and continues to grow towards the goal it has set itself: to become the leader in the international agrochemicals sector.

Appendix 1
RPA and UCA – a complementary partnership

An address given by Jean-René Fourtou, Chairman of the Executive Committee of Rhône Poulenc Agrochemicals, 14 November 1986 in Paris. (An extract from *Agrochemical Courrier*, no. 81, November 1986)

> It is with great pleasure that I announce to you that yesterday we signed an agreement, which commits us mutually and definitively, Union Carbide and Rhône Poulenc, to the takeover by RP of the agrochemical division of Union Carbide. This decision will take effect from 1st January 1987.

It was in these terms that the chairman, Jean-René Fourtou launched his press conference in Paris on 14 November. He then went on to say:

> I must add straight away that in this agreement India is not mentioned at all, and so the factory at Bhopal is not included in our acquisition ... The aim of the group is simple: we must reinforce our strategic activities and agrochemicals is one of them ... The structures within the chemistry sector are changing and, as there are opportunities for restructuring, we must take part in this, and so assure long-term opportunities for the Rhône Poulenc group.

The chairman having thus set the scene, it was Philippe Desmarescaux's turn to supply the necessary details about this acquisition, which raises RPA to the number three position in the world, below Bayer and Ciba-Geigy.

The amount paid in the transaction was in the $540 to 580 million bracket (about FFr3.5 to 4 billion). It will be definitively established before the end of the year, after various necessary evaluations have been made (that state of the stocks, etc.). This buyout will be financed by both self-financing and loans, in France and in the United States. Mr Desmarescaux emphasised that due time would be taken to define the future structure, and that the two organisations would continue in parallel until 1 September 1987 at the latest. But is it not of primary importance to know exactly what this purchase includes: the activities, the products, the personnel and, finally, what it is all going to bring to Rhône Poulenc Agrochemicals in the short and medium terms? We will give you this information now.

The future

There is a high degree of complementarity between the two firms, both on the geographical as well as the product level. Commercially speaking, RPA now occupies an important position in the American market, which alone represents a third of the world market. RPA holds fifth place in the world market, with about 6 per cent of the market share. But RPA will also be set up in Canada and in Brazil and, in Asia, it will occupy a strong position in Indonesia, in the Philippines and in Thailand. Overall, RPA is moving up to third place in the world market, with more than 8 per cent of the market share.

It is at the level of product range that the complementarity is seen best: RPA was strong in herbicides and fungicides; it is now becoming a force to be reckoned with in insecticides and regulators. Triangle Park Research Center, inaugurated in 1981, has rapidly become the world leader in carbamate insecticide chemicals. A new nematicide, aldoxycarb, is being launched under the name of Standak. For several years the Triangle Park Center has been involved in research into the growth of insects and is in the process of completing an evaluation of a new generation insecticide which has an effect on the development of the larvae and on the eggs, preventing the insects, particularly the doryphore, from developing into adults. This product could be commercialised in the agricultural and animal health markets around the year 1990.

At the strategic level, the Triangle Park Research Center, situated in a very convenient scientific and university environment, is directly complementary to our centres in La Dargoire and Ongar. All this means that we can expect a high degree of synergy in research themes. The four new American experimental stations will be an invaluable support for evaluating and developing new products in common.

Finally, we must remember that the RPA strategy is to have research centres available in the countries where the environment for creation is the most promising. It remains for a research centre to be set up in Japan. Let us undertake to do this as quickly as possible!

The business activities

The merger concerns the international agrochemicals business sector of Union Carbide, which had a turnover in 1986 of close to $450 million (about FFr3 billion), of which almost half was made in the United States. It includes:

IN THE UNITED STATES

Union Carbide Agricultural Products (UCAPCO) whose head office is at Triangle Park, near Raleigh, North Carolina, has a large commercial network in the USA: 3 production units for active substances at Woodbine (Georgia), Ambler (Pennsylvania) and Institute (West Virginia) and 14 formulation factories throughout the world, of which 5 are in the USA at Clinton (Iowa), Saint-Joseph and Saint-Louis (Missouri). It is intended that the factory at Institute, where most of the product range of Union Carbide are manufactured should keep their production workshops in plastic materials which will be run by Rhône Poulenc in the interests and under the responsibility of Union Carbide.

The Agrochemical Research Center is likewise sited at Triangle Park; it employs 160 people of whom 90 are executives. The main areas of research are carbamate and organophosphorous insecticides, growth regulators of insects of the acylurous family, the anilides as well as herbicides and growth regulators for plants. Experimental sites are situated at Clayton (North Carolina), Newton (Iowa), Greenville and Menteca (Mississippi).

OUTSIDE THE UNITED STATES

- La Littorale, in France, whose head office is at Béziers (Hérault), has a factory for agrochemical products and a sales network in France. Altogether there is a staff of about 330 people. In 1986, La Littorale had a turnover close to FFr200 million.
- Ucapcan, in Canada, has a unit at Calgary (Alberta) employing 60 people.
- UC Do Brazil, in Brazil, employs 180 people.
- PT Agrocarb, in Indonesia, employs 200 people.
- Unicar in Guatemala.
- UC Agrichem, an American subsidiary for sales in North Africa and the Middle East.
- Production units in Argentina, Columbia, the Philippines, Thailand, England, South Africa.
- Two coordination centres, one in Geneva for Europe and the other in Hong Kong for Asia, and different offices with an activity that cuts across the divisions and whose agrochemical section could be transferred into the Rhône Poulenc structures. In all, the agrochemical business employs about 3200 people.

The products

The whole of Union Carbide's agrochemical product range has been transferred to Rhône Poulenc Agrochemicals. It is based essentially on insecticides, but it also includes herbicides and a growth regulator.

INSECTICIDES

Aldicarb is the active matter in Temik, a well-known insecticide and nematicide, 50 to 60 per cent of which is sold in the United States. Although it has been banned on the open market for several years. Temik can now expect to develop. Aldicarb is produced at Institute and its formulation is done at Woodbine in the USA, at Cubaotao (UC Do Brazil) and at Béziers (La Littorale, France). Temik is used on a number of crops, the main ones being cotton, soya, corn, potatoes, beetroot, etc.

Carbaryl, also produced at Institute, is the active element in Sevin, an insecticide of the carbamate family, used for almost 30 years throughout the world on a hundred or so very varied crops and in household gardens. This product seems to have reached maturity and should maintain its position on the markets.

Methomyl, sold in the USA under the tradenames of Methavin by UCAPCO and Nudrin by Shell and in the rest of the world under the name of Lannate by Dupont is manufactured at Institute. Although it is sold by other firms, its production will be continued as in the past. This insecticide of the carbamate family is used on cotton crops, corn, fruit trees and market gardens.

Thiodicarb is a relatively new insecticide, authorised for sale in the United States in 1982, and now found in 20 or so countries. It is commercialised under the trade-names of Larvin, Semevin and Secure. Almost 70 per cent is sold outside the USA, notably in Egypt, Turkey, Brazil, etc. It is used on cotton and soya, and should develop considerably because of its fine selectivity and of its respect for the environment. All this should encourage its wider use and make it much more competitive compared with the pyrethroids.

Trimethacarb, or Broot, is being launched in the United States. It is produced in a pilot factory at Institute and should develop rapidly throughout the world. It could also find important outlets in the fight against mosquitoes and termites.

HERBICIDES
The firm Amchem which co-discovered 2.4-D in 1943 was taken over by Union Carbide in 1976. It brought with it a range of herbicides, fairly ordinary kinds of products, like MCPA and 2.4-D, produced at Saint-Joseph (Missouri) under the marks Weedone and Weedar. The HBNs that also came over with Amchem are already part of the Rhône Poulenc Agrochemicals range. These products are ioxynil and bromoxynil, and the brands Certrol and Brominal belong to UCAPCO.

Chloramben, better known under the name of Amiben is the main herbicide in the UCAPCO range. It is mainly commercialised in North America, and is used alone or mixed with other products on soya, corn, peas, beans, etc.

REGULATOR
Ethephon, commercialised under the brands Ethrel, Pep, Cerone, is used to encourage flowering and the maturing of certain fruit, such as pears and apples, but also oranges, sugar cane, etc. It improves the yield of cotton and resinous trees and it can still be developed on rice, corn, etc.

The Union Carbide range is a good complement to the Rhône Poulenc Agrochemicals range. Union Carbide products pose no problems of toxicity and do not threaten the environment. Temik at the moment is undergoing special tests by the EPA (The Environmental Protection Agency) for its possible polluting of underground water. A full report has already been submitted, and it seems likely that Temik will continue to be sold but with certain restrictions being imposed on its use.

Appendix 2
The Message from Philippe Desmarescaux, Chairman or President and Managing Director or Chief Executive of the international agrochemical sector of Rhône Poulenc

(An extract from *Agrochemical Courrier*, no. 83, January 1987)

The merger of the two companies, Rhône Poulenc and Union Carbide will enable their combined assets to be used to the full; this will be our main priority in 1987, along with achieving our budget objectives. That is why we mean to study the key elements of the two respective organisations as quickly as possible. The merger procedure we have worked out will require the full co-operation of all staff members of Rhône Poulenc and of UCAPCO (the ex-Union Carbide Agrochemicals Division) at every level of the two organisations. By means of this letter, I should like to share with you our plans for the temporary organisation of the general management level of UCAPCO, of the organisation of the international agrochemical sector of Rhône Poulenc and of the merging procedure itself.

The temporary organisation of the general management level of UCAPCO

A temporary organisation has been set up to manage UCAPCO. I shall take over the functions of chairman and managing director, assisted by two key figures: Jean Lefebvre, Vice-chairman and Associate Managing Director for Operational and Administrative Services, and Phil Nelson, Vice-chairman and Associate Managing Director for Commercial Activities. Figure 12.1 shows the basic hierarchical relationships within the temporary organisation of UCAPCO. For all employees other than those answering to Mr Lefebvre and Mr Nelson, the usual hierarchical channels remain unchanged.

Gene Boros, the former chairman of UCAPCO, will assume the temporary function of consultant to the management committee of the international agrochemical sector of RP, so that we may all benefit from his skill and his great knowledge of UCAPCO during the international merging process. He will come and spend a few weeks in Lyons. Once this mission is complete, he will take up other functions within Union Carbide.

The international agrochemical sector of RP

The new organisation of the international agrochemical sector of RP will include the following functions: strategy and economy; R & D; international marketing; manufacturing; human resource management.

Based on the strategies and policies defined by these functions, three large, geographically structured operational entities have been created. They are: the agrochemicals division of May & Baker, covering Great Britain and the countries of the Commonwealth; the agrochemicals division of Rhône Poulenc Inc., in the United States, and Rhône Poulenc Agrochemicals SA for Europe and the other countries

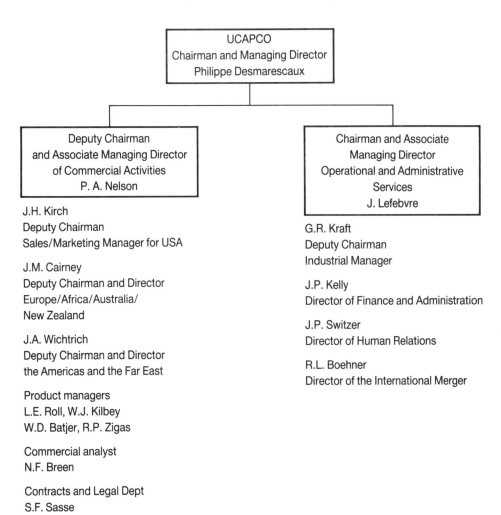

Figure 12.1 The basic hierarchy within UCAPCO

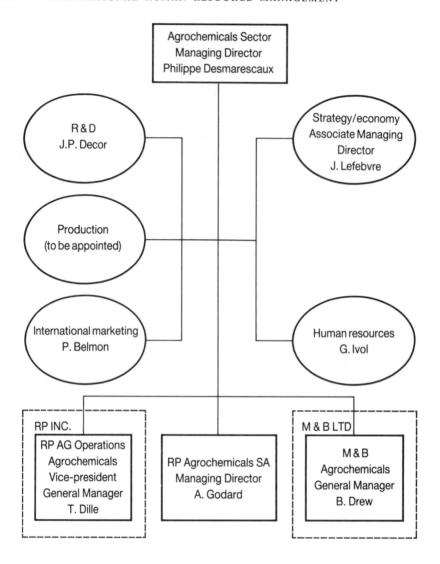

Figure 12.1   Continued

of the world. The present organisation of UCAPCO will be integrated into these three
entities when the merger is completed (see Figure 12.1).

The merger procedure

'Pilot committees' will be set up for two centralised activities: R & D and marketing.
They will also be set up in each of the three large operational entities.

The function of these pilot committees will be based on the following principles:

- New structures and the schedule for the corresponding staff movements will be proposed by the pilot committees and then confirmed by the management committee of the international agrochemicals sector of RP.
- Once the management committee have approved, the people will be chosen from the appropriate hierarchical levels, based on the following criteria:
  competence and experience;
  potential and development;
  flexibility, including geographical mobility.
  Actually being a member of an organisation must not be the principal criterion of choice. Individual desiderata and difficulties will be taken into consideration as much as possible, along with the needs of the organisations.
- All the questions concerning transfer contracts with UCAPCO will be centralised. J. Lefebvre and R. Boehner will decide on the action to be taken as the restructuring continues.

The different pilot committees are made up of people from RP and UCAPCO. It is their responsibility to organise, to manage and to assess the results of different working teams which will study the basic facts in terms of resources and will prepare a series of propositions to be submitted to the pilot committees. In this context, different members of staff from UCAPCO and from RPA can be interviewed.

The pilot committees and the working teams of May & Baker, RP Inc. in the United States and RPA SA are given in detail in Figure 12.2. The pilot committees for marketing international and R & D will be published separately [and are not shown here].

Marc Polaud was appointed director in charge of the merger procedure in the United States; he is responsible to Tom Dille and is a member of the American pilot committee. R. Boehner is now the director in charge of the merger procedure at the international level; he is answerable to Jean Lefebvre. Mr Polaud and Mr Boehner will be responsible for the co-ordination of all the processes concerned with the merger. They must also see to it that every application from competent people is properly examined at an international level; both in the agrochemicals sector and in other sectors of RP.

The pilot committee in the United States and the corresponding working teams will be helped by an outside consultant who has a wide experience in this type of project. Marc Polaud and John Switzer will co-ordinate all this activity.

We are beginning the merger procedure immediately. The structure of the new organisation resulting from the merger will be set up gradually and we think that all should be in place by mid-1987. We shall keep you informed of the progress of this merger operation, fully realising that day-to-day business activities must have first priority.

I am convinced that this merger will provide us with the necessary growth we are looking for. It is of the utmost importance for us to use the skills of all staff members of both organisations to the fullest advantage, so that we may reach the position of market leader in the new generation of agrochemical firms. [. . .]

Rhône Poulenc Agrochemicals

Pilot committee   *UCAPO* E. Boros/J. Wichtrich/J. Cairney, *RPA* A.Godard/G. Ivol/J. Mace

Work groups	*Supervisor*	*Team*
France	M. Paupy *RPA*	T. Bourgeron *RPA*, Ruiz *UCAPCO*
Spain	M. de Bourmont *RPA*	J. Ville *RPA*, J. Cairney *UCAPCO* A local *UCAPCO*
Greece	M. de Bourmont *RPA*	G. Doublet *RPA*, J. Cairney *UCAPCO* A local *UCAPCO*
Italy/West Germany/Benelux	M. de Bourmont *RPA*	E. de Bruin *RPA*, B. Meheut *RPA* M. Stephenson *UCAPCO* R. Benwell *UCAPCO*
Central and Latin America Columbia + other countries of Latin America	A. Abreu *RPA*	J.N. Bridon, a local *UCAPCO* (designate)
Argentina	M. Maupu *RPA*	A local *RP*, a local *UCAPCO* (designate)
Central America	J. Yvon *RPA*	A local *RP*, a local *UCAPCO* (designate)
Brazil	G. Lutz *RPA*	M. Maupu *RPA*, 2 local *UCAPCO* (designate)
Other countries/Europe/Africa	J. Yvon *RPA*	G. Brau *RPA*, M. Stephenson *UCAPCO*
Asia		R. Benwell *UCAPCO*
Indonesia	E. de Bruin	G. Thierry *RPA*, 2 local *UCAPCO* (designate)
The Philippines	D. Caron	J.P. Rouffet *RPA*, 2 local *UCAPCO* (designate)
Finance/Administration	J. Bandon *RPA*	F. Ouin *RPA*, J. Robertson *UCAPCO*
Industrial	J.C. Choulet *RPA*	J.L. Genin *RPA*, Brian *UCAPCO*, Guiot *UCAPCO*

May & Baker

Pilot committee   *UCAPCO* E. Boros/J. Cairney/J. Wichtrich, *M & B AG* B. Drew/P. Sargent/B. Booth

Work groups	*Supervisor*	*Team*
UK Agrochem	B. Booth *M & B*	T. Lynch *M & B*, J. Drinkwater *M & B* D. Gilby *UCAPCO*, B. Joyce *UCAPCO* + *UCAPCO* Manager
UK Hostin Farmery	P. Sargent *M & B*	Peter Moring *M & B*, G. Bruge *RPA* J. Atkinson *UCAPCO*, W. Kilbey *UCAPCO* + *UCAPCO* Manager

Figure 12.2   The new agrochemicals sector of Rhône Poulenc

Work groups	Supervisor	Team
Canada	B. Philip *M & B*	D. Havers *M & B*, P. Cook *M & B* R. Reep *UCAPCO*, B. Foley *UCAPCO* + *UCAPCO* manager
South Africa	S. Anderson *M & B*	L. Halowitz *M & B*, V. Vogel *M & B* A. Rhodes *UCAPCO*, P. Bennett *UCAPCO* + *UCAPCO* Manager
Thailand	B. Hughes *M & B*	C. Cowper *M & B*, Pradt *M & B* Charoonsack *UCAPCO*, J. So *UCAPCO* + *UCAPCO* Manager

Rhône Poulenc Inc

Pilot committee   *UCAPO* J.M. Kirch/G.R. Kraft/P.A. Nelson/J.P. Switzer, *R.P. Inc* T.M. Dille/
M. Polaud/M.S. Leo

Work groups	Supervisor	Team
Human resources	M. Polaud *RP* J. Switzer *UCAPCO*	R. Johns *UCAPCO*, E. McKanna *RP* D. Rotunno *RP*
Marketing/Sales	T. Dille *RP*	C. Jongeward *RP*, R. Iphman *RP* P. Nelson *UCAPCO*, J. Weeks *UCAPCO* R. Baughman *UCAPCO*
Biological sciences product development	J. Kirch *UCAPCO*	N. Abdalla *UCAPCO*, R. Berner *RP* R. Holm *RP*, D. Olson *RP* E. Ouattlebaum *UCAPCO*
Industrial purchases/ scheduling	G. Kraft *UCAPCO*	R. Briggs *RP*, C. Debard *RP* T. Labue *RP*, H. Johnson *UCAPCO* B. Mollchen *UCAPCO*
Finance/administration	J. Lefebvre/M. Leo *RP*	J. Chichocki *UCAPCO*, P. Kelly *UCAPCO* P. Langlois *RP*, B. Phillips *RP* C. Anderson *UCAPCO*
Patents/legal and government affairs	M. Leo *RP*	C. Brachotte *RP*, H. Himmelman *RP* A. Rady *RP*

Figure 12.2   Continued

Appendix 3
With the merger underway –
piloting the working teams

(An extract from *Agrochemical Courrier*, no. 85, January 1987)

As we announced in issue no. 83 of *Courrier*, the pilot committees and working teams for R & D and for marketing international have been set up or are in the process of being set up. To avoid any loss of time, we shall now give all the details.

Marketing international

The pilot committee, supervised by P. Belmon is made up as follows: A. Chalandon/ D. Simon/W. Kibley/W. Batjer.
Three working-teams will be set up on the following subjects:

- Herbicides.
- Insecticides.
- Methods, means and liaisons with other management centres within the enterprise. This group will be made up of several sub-groups.

The members of these groups will be appointed at the beginning of February. At the end of March the conclusions of most of the groups will be submitted to the pilot committee. Only those sub-groups connected with the running of the other management centres and in liaison with them will be granted extra time.

R & D

Nine groups have been made up under the direction of a pilot committee led by J. P. Decor, which is constituted as follows: J. Lefebvre/G. Marechal/J. Kirch/P. Woodrow/ B. Savory/B. Holm.

The objective of this committee is to define a new strategy for R & D in the agrochemicals sector, and to integrate the research centre at Triangle Park and the development team at UCAPCO.

The working teams

(The names of the supervisors are in italic.)

1 Synthesis of new molecules
   G. Santini
   E.W. Parnell/J.A. Durden/A. Kurtz

2 Biological evaluation
   J.C. Debourge
   R. Hewett/K.A. Kukurowski/R.M. See

3 New approaches: growth regulators, biochemistry, biotechnologies
   A.R. Cooke
   D.F. Bushey/C. Anding/G. Freyssinet/B. Thomas

4 Formulation and processing
   J.D. Stuck
   A.K. Taori/A. Bertrand/L. Spicer
      J. Varagnat
      C. Debard/E.A. Rick/K.W. Young

5 Experimentation and development
   G. Marechal
   E.C. Quattelbaum/B. Holm/A.R. Cooke/R. Berner/D. Bony

6 Patents – innovation
   C. Brachotte
   J.A. Durden

7 Homologation
   N.A. Abdalla/B. Savory
   R.L. Baron/G. Simons/A. Pelfrene
   S.L. Harrison/A. Guardigu/J. Unsworth
   W.M. Casey/D. Olson/D. Demozay

8 Defence of commercial products
   E.C. Quattelbaum
   N.A. Abdalla/D. Olson/D. Demozay

9 Human resources and R & D
   J.C. Debourge
   P.T. Woodrow/B. Savory

The conclusions reached by the working teams will be drawn up under the direction of:
   J.C. Debourge for groups 1, 2, 9
   J. Varagnat for groups 3, 4
   E.C. Quattelbaum for group 5
   C. Brachotte for group 6
   N.A. Abdalla for groups 7, 8
and they will present them to the pilot committee.

Appendix 4
General facts about
Rhône Poulenc Agrochemicals

RP group's sales turnover: FFr83.8 billion

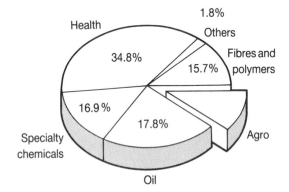

The agro sector,
Integrated plant protection

The agro sector's crop protection activity provides world agriculture with herbicides, insecticides, fungicides and growth regulators to protect and improve plant production.

It is our concern in this business to constantly develop products, formulations, packaging and application systems which increasingly respect the environment.

In-depth research into seeds (genetics and protection) will be decisive as part of an integrated plant protection approach for field crops.

The garden and amenity care activity markets products for the upkeep of gardens, house plants and amenity areas for use by the general public and local authorities.

Figure 12.3   The agrochemicals sector within the RP group, 1991

Sales turnover

FFr11.1 billion

Distribution by activity

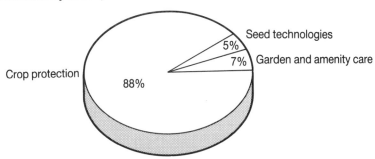

Seed technologies 5%

Garden and amenity care 7%

Crop protection 88%

Distribution for each geographical area

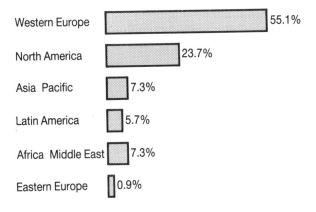

Western Europe 55.1%

North America 23.7%

Asia Pacific 7.3%

Latin America 5.7%

Africa Middle East 7.3%

Eastern Europe 0.9%

Distribution for each product family

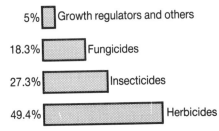

5% Growth regulators and others

18.3% Fungicides

27.3% Insecticides

49.4% Herbicides

Figure 12.3   Continued

Worldwide market share

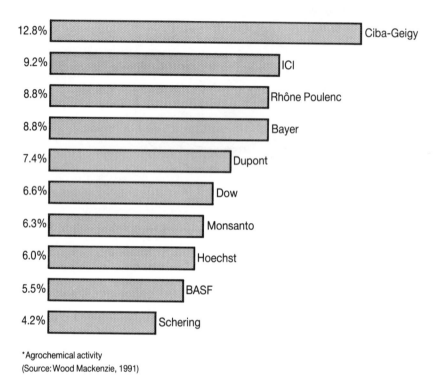

12.8%	Ciba-Geigy
9.2%	ICI
8.8%	Rhône Poulenc
8.8%	Bayer
7.4%	Dupont
6.6%	Dow
6.3%	Monsanto
6.0%	Hoechst
5.5%	BASF
4.2%	Schering

*Agrochemical activity
(Source: Wood Mackenzie, 1991)

An active research

7.3% of the sales turnover (FFr812 million)

1200 people spread among 5 specialised research centres: La Dargoire and Sophia Antiopolis in France, Ongar in the United Kingdom, Research Triangle Park in the USA, Tsukuba in Japan

15 research farms on 5 continents and representative of all climates and all crops

Figure 12.4 Products and market share

Main products

Herbicides
- Acifluorfen (TACKLE®)
- Aclonifen (CHALLENGE®, BANDUR®)
- Asulam (ASULOX®, CANDEX®, TARGET®)
- Bifenox (FOXPRO®, FOXTAR®, MODOWN®)
- Bromoxynil (PARDNER®, BUCTRIL®)
- Carbetamide (PRADONE®, LEGURAME®, CARBETAMEX®)
- Diflufenican (IONIZ®, QUARTZ®, COUGAR®, JAVELIN®)
- Ionyxil (ACTRIL®, OXYTRIL®, FOXTRIL®, TOTRIL®)
- Isoproturon (IP 50®, IP FLO®, TOLKAN®, PRODIX®, BELGRAN®)
- Oxadiazon (RONSTAR®, DELCUT®)
- 3,4 DCA/3,4 DCPI/DIURON

Fungicides
- Iprodione (ROVRAL®, KIDAN®, CALIDAN®, CHIPCO 26019®)
- Phosethyl-AL/Fosetyl-AL (ALIETTE®, MIKAL®, RHODAX®, VALIANT®)
- Bromuconazole (GRANIT®, GRANIT® TR)

Insecticides
- Aldicarb (TEMIK®)
- Carbaryl (SEVIN®)
- Ethion (RHODOCIDE®)
- Ethoprophos (MOCAP®)
- Lindane (LINDAFOR®, ICA FLO®, LINDAMUL®)
- Monocrothophos
- Phosalone (ZOLONE®, RUBITOX®)
- Thiodicarb (LARVIN®, SKIPPER®, SEMEVIN®)
- Thiofanox (DACAMOX®)
- Vamidothion (KILVAL®)

Plant growth regulators
- Ethephon (ETHREL®, CERONE®, PREP®)

Figure 12.4   Continued

Appendix 5
The development of the structures adopted by Rhône Poulenc Agrochemicals

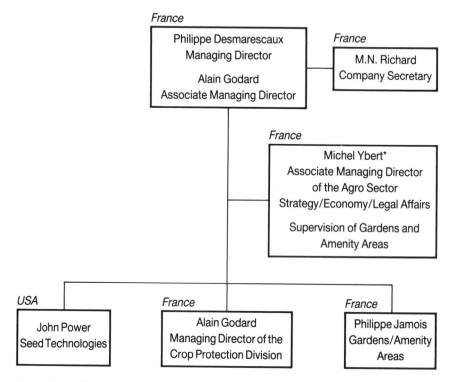

*Bruce Drew, Managing Director of RPAL, with responsibility at the strategic level

This organizational chart under no circumstances represents hierarchical positions.

Figure 12.5 The RPA agrochemicals sector, 1992

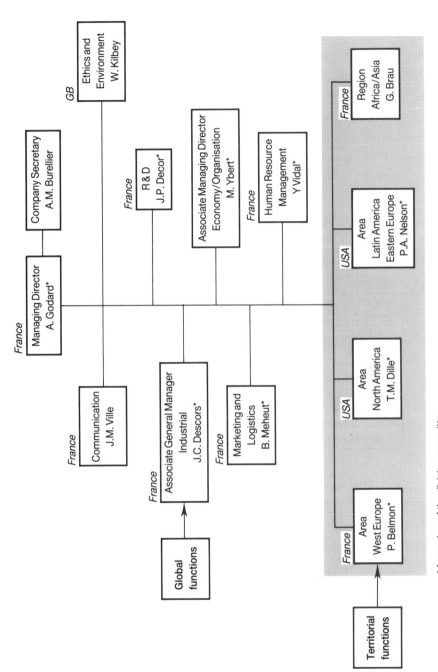

* A member of the division committee.

This organisation chart under no circumstances represents hierarchical positions.

Figure 12.6 The RPA crop protection division, 1992 continued

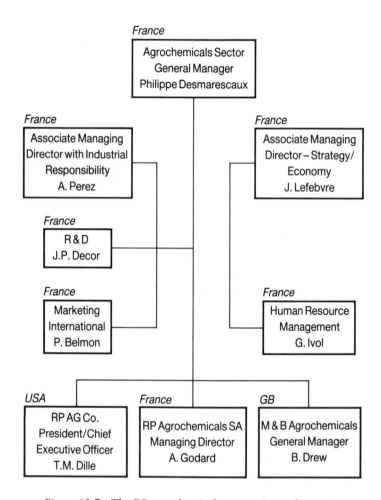

Figure 12.7   The RP agrochemicals sector, September 1987

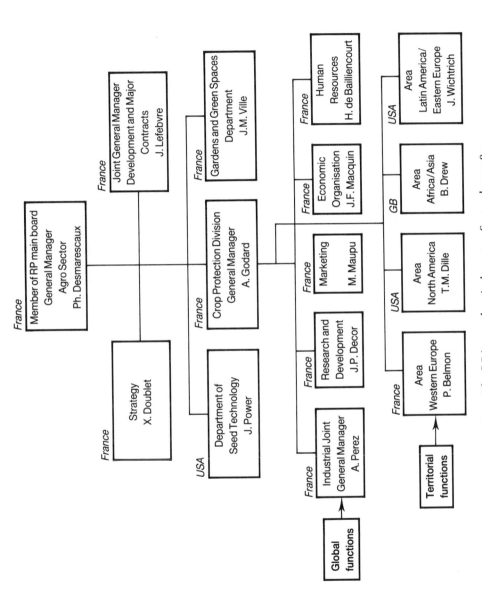

Figure 12.8 The RPA agrochemicals sector, September 1987

The development of a global human resource management approach in ZENECA Pharmaceuticals

REG CARR

Introduction

ICI plc is the fourth largest chemical company in the world and is often described as the company with the widest geographic spread, selling in over 150 countries, manufacturing in 40 countries, with more than 600 locations worldwide and over 100 000 direct customers. It continues to be an enormous challenge to lead and direct such a complex business and engender the worldwide teamworking necessary to achieve the required competitive advantage. Since its formation in 1926 ICI has had many organisation structures and has shown itself skilful at adjusting the organisation to suit the needs of the prevailing economic scene. It was, until recently, organised around seven international businesses, each of which was responsible for P/L and the delivery of the appropriate management strategies including human resource management strategies. ICI was a very integrated company as far as research and manufacturing functions are concerned, but increasingly, variations in policy and practice have developed as each business has responded to its particular competitive market environment. ICI plc has now decided to split itself into two completely separate public companies, namely ZENECA plc and ICI plc.

ZENECA Pharmaceuticals grew steadily from the 1960s within the ICI Group when its traditional markets were the United Kingdom and what is described as the 'Old Commonwealth' countries. Today there are more than 3000 employees engaged in international medical research and development in three centres in the United States, France and the UK, and 90 per cent of the current sales derive from products of the company's own research. On the basis of 1991 sales ZENECA is ranked ninth among the world's leading pharmaceutical companies, employing just under 35 000 employees worldwide. ZENECA comprises the Pharmaceuticals, Agrochemicals, Seeds and Specialities Businesses. Pharmaceuticals employs just under 13 000 employees worldwide.

Particularly strong growth has been achieved since the early 1970s based on three major products discovered in the business's research laboratories. 'Inderal' and 'Tenormin', both cardiovascular beta-blocker drugs, were the result of highly innovative research ultimately resulting in the award of the Nobel Prize to Sir James Black, and 'Nolvadex', a treatment for various stages of breast cancer. In many territories markets were extended by acquisition of a local company into which the business put increased resources as the sales performance improved. There was extremely rapid growth in the United Kingdom and the major continental European territories throughout the 1970s following the UK's entry into the European Community. The philosophy has always been to staff the local Pharma companies, whenever possible, with nationals of that territory as the business believes better links are possible with governmental agencies and there is a better understanding of the culture, both national and medical, and consequently of the market. The emphasis in human resource management (HRM) in this period of development was upon management development to ensure there were sufficient succession candidates to replace key managers and to staff the expanding sales and marketing organisations. In the 1970s the local companies remained primarily sales and marketing operations and were closely managed from the business headquarters in the UK. The research, development and regulatory approval processes were controlled tightly from headquarters and a large amount of marketing support was also provided to the Pharma companies.

By 1980 the business had become fully international and significant investment was taking place in the United States and Japan to support the launch of 'Tenormin', which was destined to become a top-10 compound. In the United States the sales forces and marketing teams were more than doubled to bring the business more into line with its competitors and this placed a tremendous load on the HRM function. In Japan a joint venture with Sumitomo Chemicals was maturing and significant business growth was occurring with a concurrent expansion of the sales teams. Throughout the 1980s the major Pharmas developed their organisations and became fully resourced and relatively independent with their own sales, marketing, medical, development, finance and administrative and human resource management functions, and in some also a manufacturing function. These operations were supported by the business headquarters in the United Kingdom and major research and development groups in the UK and USA. Today the major markets for ZENECA Pharmaceuticals are the USA, Japan and Western Europe. New compounds are being developed to replace the successful products which have fuelled the growth of the last two decades and the business is well established in the major markets and expects significant growth to be sustained throughout the 1990s.

The challenge of the late 1980s was to develop the management structures and processes to reflect the new business circumstances and the expertise which now existed in the company's local business units. Particularly important was: the need to begin to ease many of the central controls applied by the business in favour of local operational freedom; to recognise the need to integrate what had become largely independent Pharma units into an international team capable of meeting the challenges posed by competitors; and to establish international teams among the key research and development groups. In other words, management style evolved from the 'international' model towards the 'transnational' model, as described by Bartlett and Ghoshal (1989) in their book *Managing Across Borders: The transnational solution*. People development and international experience were seen as key strategies and international human resource management was recognised by senior management as having a significant influence on ZENECA Pharmaceuticals' ability to sustain competitive advantage in the future.

In 1989 the headquarters personnel function had reorganised to reflect the growing international relationships and two personnel manager roles were established reporting to the business personnel manager with responsibility for UK and international personnel policy and procedures respectively. The International Personnel and Training Group (IPTG) was deliberately set up as a small unit whose key task was to facilitate the development and delivery of key human resource (HR) activities across the business and provide measured support and assistance directly to local Pharmas on key issues. Major Pharmas have their own personnel managers and smaller units either rely on a ZENECA personnel manager for support, if the territory has one, or will seek the support of IPTG or a local adviser. It was important, and remains so, that the members of IPTG were professionally credible and also able to act in a culturally sensitive manner with any part of the business. The key competences for staff working in this area are considered to be:

Conceptual thinking	Concern for standards
Strategic thinking	Concern for impact
Adaptability (cultural)	Strategic influencing
Flexibility	Results orientation
	Development orientation

IPTG is responsible for working with the key business managers both in the headquarters and the Pharma units to deliver the HR strategies agreed by the executive. This is a relatively simple matter for those Pharmas which are fully independent companies and have their own personnel resources; it was less so when the Pharma was essentially a 'department' of a national ICI company whose personnel manager had his own views on how personnel policies should develop as HR attempted to match the differing requirements of a number of international businesses. The setting up of ZENECA on 1 January 1993 removed some of these difficulties as the HR resources were all located in business units. Successful development of HR management in ZENECA Pharmaceuticals worldwide is a direct result of clear strategy reviews which link HR strategy to business strategy, and the articulation of that HR strategy in a form which provides clarity and direction but allows flexibility to meet local cultural and business needs.

The integrated human resource strategy for the 1990s

The way the business was being managed in the 1980s was largely determined by the history of its evolution through acquisition of national companies, and the headquarters philosophy which was to recognise cultural diversity in some areas of business strategy such as HR management and development. In these areas there was a recognition that there may be more than one way of achieving a given objective and there was usually a fuller commitment to a locally developed approach. However, there is a difficult balance to achieve between the headquarters need for 'control' and the business unit's need for autonomy and many more managers needed to develop the necessary skills and experience of international teamworking. Quite difficult issues arose from time to time because of attempts to over-manage or to manage too closely many of the Pharmas and it was clear the headquarters approach was often too prescriptive and 'Anglo-Saxon' in outlook. By 1988 it was obvious to senior HR management that the growth and complexity of the organisation had generated issues, which unless addressed, would significantly inhibit successful business development in the next decade.

In 1988 the Pharmaceutical Council, the executive committee of ZENECA Pharmaceuticals, conducted a review of the culture and organisation of the business, with the assistance of the HR function, and concluded that:

- Business strategy and values were not fully shared across the business.
- The processes by which the business was managed were not as valued as the completion of the tasks themselves.
- The organisation design was often over-complex and compartmentalised.

Attention was therefore focused on organisation capability and the development of an improvement culture, the success of which would come from the following developments:

- A widely shared vision of the future.
- A set of values and beliefs for the business.
- A set of targets readily understood throughout the organisation.
- An open culture trusting in the competency and potential of people.
- A culture valuing the management of people alongside professional skills.
- A performance-improvement culture challenging employees to match self-development with business objectives.
- 'Looseness/tightness' – devolved management but central control on core values/targets.

The outcome of this review was a strategic initiative early in 1989 entitled 'Towards a healthy future' which described the new mission statement and the three strategic objectives for the business (Appendix 1). This was introduced by an integrated communication process worldwide to ensure all employees understood fully the new business emphasis both in the United Kingdom and all the Pharmas. Subsequently, all the Pharmas have reworked their own mission statements and re-established the strategic objectives for their business operation taking account of local cultures.

The chief executive of ZENECA Pharmaceuticals has been personally highly committed to this development and simultaneously introduced a series of meetings in headquarters departments and Pharmas. He has committed a considerable amount of time to the discussion of business strategy and performance with a cross-section of employees, listening to their views and ideas for new business opportunities. Eight of the major Pharma units, the USA and the UK were covered during 1989–91 and a regular pattern of return visits has been established. The chief executive is supported at these meetings by the business's organisation development consultant who provides the link back to the business personnel manager and the personnel manager (international). This approach has been welcomed by staff and has led to a better understanding across the business of the strategic imperatives for the 1990s.

The initiative was supported by a quarterly communication process led by senior managers in every unit and department using business information provided by headquarters to which is added local information. ZENECA Ltd and ZENECA Pharmaceuticals' business performance statistics are provided and discussed in some detail along with major business initiatives or HR strategies. This communication process has been operating since 1989 and has become established as an essential vehicle for providing the information necessary to allow staff to operate effectively within the international business context.

However, the business was certain that talking about issues and sharing information alone would not lead to the required culture change and a series of other steps were planned to develop the organisation and HR management processes.

Organisation

Previously the Pharmaceutical Council met quarterly. Because of the complexity of the business and the need to have an international perspective on many more issues the Council decided to meet every month and for its appointments committee to meet every two months. The appointments committee confirms senior appointments and the HR strategy for the business. The Pharmaceutical Council establishes and steers business strategy and regularly involves senior managers from Pharmas in its deliberations. These strategy workshops are held twice a year and involve the CEO, directors of the business and general managers of the four major Pharmas.

In the research and development area it was recognised that greater clarity was required concerning the roles and remits of groups involved in the drug development process so that lengthy development timescales could be cut to equal or better the best level in the pharmaceutical industry. The vision towards which the R & D function is working is a clear timetabled pathway for each new compound with each responsible group, wherever they are located in the world, knowing exactly what they have to achieve and by when, so the whole group operates as an international team dedicated to the fastest possible registration for sale of that compound. To achieve the objective local Pharmas are becoming responsible for quality control of the clinical data which is then submitted to headquarters who will only audit for quality assurance purposes. The aim is for headquarters and the major Pharmas to operate as equal partners in this activity, which is a major tangible example of the business's intention to operate transnationally. It was important that the actions spoke as loudly as the words.

This is a major cultural shift on the part of the headquarters, first, to manage less closely and second, to allow local operations freedom to decide how to provide the required data within the target time-scales. Progress continues to be made as international teamworking experience develops and more examples of cultural sensitivity are being reported. Further work in this area, which is mentioned later in the chapter, is being planned to ensure the desired long-term culture shift is sustained.

The expansion of the Pharmas over the last 10 years has been matched by concurrent changes in the headquarters commercial function. The management of the Pharmas is overseen by the territorial director now working through two new departments, set up from January 1992 and responsible for supporting the business units worldwide. The first is the Business Management Department, which works closely with the major Pharmas and reviews business performance periodically through the business review committee meetings for each unit. Each Pharma general manager is responsible for delivery of the budgeted local profit and has considerable freedom as to how to use the resources allocated to him or her, provided he or she achieves the targets agreed each year. Headquarters business managers act as facilitators and as a resource to the Pharma when there are specific difficulties.

The second department responsible for Pharmas is Pharma International. This operates as a self-standing Pharma company which is responsible for the management of the smaller Pharmas and the provision of support services to them. In addition, it handles the joint venture operations and other trading relations in a more direct way than would be appropriate with the major Pharmas. Territorial support services tend to be smaller in these territories.

IPTG works closely both with the Business Management Department and Pharma International to ensure that the HR strategy is being delivered in each business unit in the most appropriate way.

The international marketing department, Product Strategy, will in future concentrate solely on providing high-level strategic marketing leadership to the principal Pharmas, each of whom are fully capable of developing this strategy in the most appropriate way for their market. The headquarters focus will be upon understanding the rapidly changing international environment through debate with Pharmas and ensuring that products are developed with sustained competitive advantage.

These organisation changes are designed to assist the move towards the trans-national business management structure, where broad strategy is set by headquarters taking account of global trends as reported by the major Pharmas. The Pharmas are well resourced and have the freedom to manage the strategic development and day-to-day operations in their territory with the aim of achieving the business targets set by headquarters. The HR function in the business has been fully involved in these developments both at the conceptual and implementation phases and such activity is a vital part of the role and is highly valued by business managers.

Human resource organisation

It was decided in the mid-1980s that flexible HRM approaches were very important as the business was made up of staff working in many national cultures. The concept was a global HR strategy comprising a framework of policies and practices to allow Pharmas the maximum flexibility to adopt the approach that suited them best. Expansion during this period required an emphasis on management succession and development to ensure sufficient key managers with the necessary breadth of skills to manage the expansion. By 1989 it was clear that the emphasis must change as the growth of the business and its increasing complexity meant many more staff required development to equip them to contribute more in their current jobs as well as to prepare them for future job opportunities. Much more emphasis was therefore placed on broad people-development approaches, although management succession and development remained a priority activity.

The overall philosophy flowed from two of the strategic objectives, related to improving business performance and people development and the main theme was continuous improvement in every activity. Improving business performance was seen as vital to sustained business success and it was recognised that this would largely be achieved through people. The setting of clear group objectives and individual targets, both regularly monitored by managers in a supportive way, was seen as crucial. Integrated with this was personal development planning for all members of staff and this process came to be described as performance management (Figure 13.1). This linkage has been appreciated by staff who value the commitment to develop everyone to help them do their existing job better and to prepare them for future job opportunities. The overall emphasis is continuous improvement and the business believes that through improved business performance and people development it will maintain and extend its competitive advantage. The key elements which have been brought together into an integrated global HR approach are:

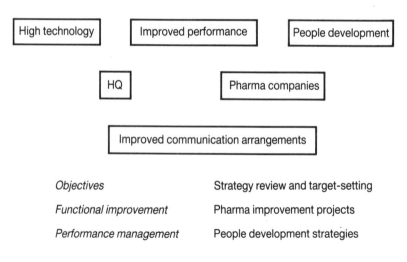

Figure 13.1 International HRM approach 1990

- Performance management.
- People development strategy.
- Management succession and development.
- International experience.
- Training.
- Leading change in the international business.
- Managing diversity.
- Remuneration and benefits development.

HR APPROACHES

In 1989 as part of the culture and organisation development initiative the policy on people development was restated and re-emphasised (Appendix 2). IPTG began to consider how best to promote the importance of the policy in Pharmas taking account of the fact that the rate of change and pressures on the units precluded the launching of a new HR initiative. The people development and improving business performance elements were brought together into an integrated approach known as 'HR approaches'. The purpose was to achieve a strategic focusing of existing HRM resources on a number of key areas which were judged to have the most impact on business performance and would encourage the development of a continuous improvement culture across the business. 'HR approaches' was launched by the territorial director in April 1990. The five key areas for development initially were:

1 Performance management.
2 Training for the current role.
3 Personal development planning.
4 Business communications processes.
5 Remuneration and benefits development.

Key headquarters managers still have difficulty accepting that there is more than one way of achieving the same objective. There has also been an unwillingness to involve key managers from the major Pharmas at the earliest design stage and to train and coach managers on how to lead change in international situations and to make them more culturally aware.

Of the other elements of the global HR approach, management succession and development and 'leading change' processes were already well established and headquarters were considering the best approaches for international awareness and managing diversity.

For each key area the principle and a set of minimum standards were laid down. These were very broad in scope as the business remained convinced that business units must be free to develop approaches which were most appropriate for their organisation. The establishing of minimum standards allowed the business managers and IPTG periodically to monitor progress across the business without inhibiting flexibility.

The plan expects progress in all key areas over the next five to six years. Each

Pharma is expected to review its current business strategy and agree, in conjunction with the headquarters business manager who liaises with them, the HR strategy to be adopted for the forthcoming year. The achievements would then be monitored annually and new targets set for the following year.

In September 1990 a presentation was made to the annual Pharma General Managers' Conference on the 'HR approaches' strategy to reinforce the messages and gain commitment. This was followed by a workshop reviewing the need for people-development activities and the result was a confirmation by all present that people development was a vital activity for the business and a clear commitment to the 'HR approaches' strategy. Following this conference Pharmas prepared their 1991 HR strategy and discussed it with business management and IPTG. The HR targets were included in the company targets for the unit and were monitored in the annual review process at the end of 1991. At the same time new targets were set for the next year (Appendix 3).

'HR approaches' has been received very well by the Pharmas, who see it as providing clear strategic leadership and guidance without inhibiting them from developing the best approach for their national and Pharma culture. The approach adopted takes account of the fact that Pharmas range in size from over 2700 in the United States to 600–800 in France, Germany and Italy and to less than 80 in Sweden, Holland and Portugal. Many of these operations have no dedicated HR resource to support their activities so it is important the HR approaches developed by headquarters are clear and simple and sufficiently flexible to meet the varying needs. Pharma general managers also need ongoing support if progress is to be sustained. IPTG has developed a 'People development guide' covering all the key aspects of HR management and development for the company's Pharma general managers and the HR management which supports them. This follows the same format as the 'HR approaches': establishes the principle for each activity, sets down minimum standards and also has guidance notes on applications and approaches which may be considered. Headquarters business managers have been fully trained in the content of the guide and use it as part of their regular HR reviews. The business thus has line-led HR management and is engendering a continuous improvement philosophy in every unit, although it is not intended to bring everyone up to the same standard. Rather, sustained, year-on-year progress in HR management is expected.

Pharma Italy is a good example of how a national Pharma has used this strategic guidance to develop its own culturally acceptable approach. They have taken the performance management principle and minimum standards and worked with IPTG and business management to develop a performance management model acceptable to Italy (Figure 13.2). They are now introducing the model on a phased basis starting with senior and middle management and then the sales force. They have developed modular training for managers covering group objectives/target setting, coaching and personal development planning and are currently reviewing and translating the ZENECA 'Pharmaceuticals management competency framework' so it can be used to support the performance management process. They are committed to this because first, they see it as beneficial to the business strategy established for Italy and second,

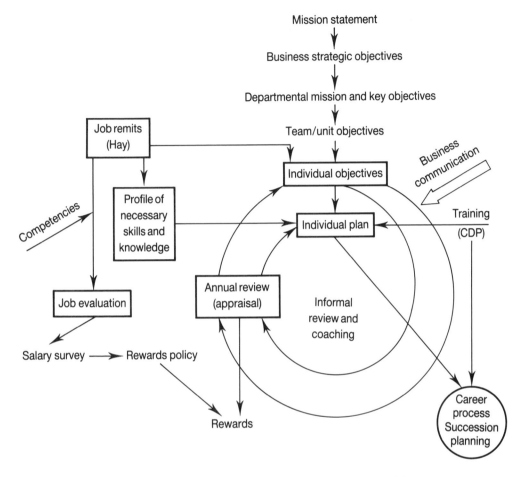

Figure 13.2 Performance management reference model

because it has been capable of local adaptation. In Japan, on the other hand, a very different model has evolved to suit the local culture but which incorporates similar underlying principles.

INTERNATIONAL UNDERSTANDING
As a business begins to operate globally and to recognise the need to integrate its management processes it usually finds that international teamworking becomes a critical factor. The conclusion from the literature is that the business which can make international teamworking a success will gain competitive advantage in the global market-place. ZENECA Pharmaceuticals has recognised for some considerable time that senior managers should have international experience before they are appointed general manager of a Pharma or to the headquarters executive. In the past this was

usually via a two- to three-year assignment in another territory. Over the last few years we have come to recognise that as the business becomes transnational many more employees require some education and understanding of cultural difference and international teamworking since international interaction now occurs more frequently at junior levels. The strategy adopted to broaden international experience is as follows:

- Internationalise the headquarters staff to a greater extent through secondments and transfers.
- Extend the use of international secondments.
- Extend the use of short-term international assignments (6–12 months).
- Make greater use of extended business visits (1–2 months).
- Identify and use international co-ordination roles across the business.
- Make greater use of cultural awareness/business briefings/language training.

Currently the headquarters group is all British, although 8 of the 14 members have had international secondments during their career and the same situation applies at middle management levels. The business wishes to increase the number of non-British managers so that prevailing attitudes are challenged and decisions are taken from a truly transnational point of view. Work is progressing to address this issue which may result in a larger international presence in HQ achieved through a mix of secondments, permanent international transfers and short assignments. Permanent transfers may be difficult to manage and therefore limited in number.

Secondments are very costly, both financially and through the disruption caused in departments, and probably are not the best way of providing international experience for most staff. Therefore greater use is being made of short-term international assignments, extended business visits and international project team involvement. The latter can be a very rich international experience if the project is well structured and group working, project management and cultural awareness training is provided at the outset. The project teams will also make a major contribution to business performance. The HR function has developed a key actions check-list and basic rules for those setting up international project teams so the maximum benefit may be obtained from these activities.

In 1990 IPTG recognised the need for an education programme to improve the cultural awareness of staff. A. Laurent, F. Bartholemy and Canning Associates were used to brief managerial groups and a link was established with Fons Trompenaars of the Centre for International Business Studies to explore the cultural differences within ZENECA Pharmaceuticals. Cultural awareness seminars have been developed, initially focusing on European business cultures, and were highly regarded by both business and functional managers. A module derived from this course will be used as part of project team training in the future.

REMUNERATION AND BENEFITS DEVELOPMENT
IPTG monitors the remuneration and benefits competitiveness of our Pharma units worldwide and provides leadership and advice on the policy being adopted. In many

territories remuneration and benefits have followed the ICI Group approach very closely. The Group monitors its competitiveness against a target group of chemical industry competitors but unfortunately being competitive with this group does not mean competitiveness with major pharmaceutical companies. Since 1986 the business has been steadily improving the monitoring of pharmaceutical remuneration and benefits competitiveness across the world and developing new approaches designed to support the key business strategies. As performance management processes have been introduced so have performance pay systems, and incentive compensation was introduced based on the annual performance of the unit and the achievement of personal objectives. From the beginning of 1992 Pharmas were encouraged to introduce local incentive bonuses for their senior managers.

As with other aspects of HR management it is the business's intention to develop a framework of approaches from which Pharmas will choose the most appropriate for their culture. We now judge our competitiveness in terms of total remuneration not basic pay and would expect, in many cultures, a significant component of performance-related pay.

The future

Since the mid-1980s ZENECA Pharmaceuticals has been steadily evolving from an international to a transnational organisation. International HR management has made a major contribution because it has been intimately involved in the development of the business strategy, and the HR strategy developed has been highly consistent with and supportive of the overall business strategy. The development of the culture

Figure 13.3   Development of the culture and organisation

and organisation is progressing to plan, but this is a long-term project and it is likely to be quite some time before the business is able to say it operates in a truly transnational manner. Figure 13.3 summarises the concept and the business is now moving towards Stage 3. The overall success of the culture and organisation shift project will depend on continued coherence and consistency between business and HR strategy and the key part played by HR managers to ensure an integrated global HR management approach for ZENECA Pharmaceuticals is sustained. Whilst it is important to get specific aspects correct, it is the overall balance of the global HR approach which in the longer term will have the greatest impact on competitive advantage.

Developing and improving the business means developing and improving people, teams and organisations: people development is at the heart of transnational HRM philosophy, and HRM must be at the heart of business strategy.

Appendix 1
Mission statement and strategic objectives 'Towards a healthy future'

Our mission

To contribute to human health by providing worthwhile products which enable our business to grow and the people within it to prosper and lead fulfilling lives; to rise up the world's pharmaceutical league table over the next ten years by:

1 Being a leader in cardiovascular and oncological medicines.
2 Broadening the therapeutic base into other areas of important medical need.

Strategic objectives

For each of us to participate in working towards a healthy future, the first step must be to produce a clearly defined strategic plan. The key aspects of our strategic objectives can be described as:

1 To focus on high technology – leading to the introduction and supply of products that make a worthwhile contribution to human health.
2 To improve business performance – matching in all important aspects that of the best companies in the pharmaceutical industry and achieving year-on-year profit growth.
3 To ensure a well-motivated organisation in which people are respected, enjoy their jobs and obtain fulfilment.

Appendix 2
People development

People development is a fundamental activity for our business. It is not a single activity: there are many components, one or more of which may be used in any given circumstance. This section describes the overall people development strategy for our business and the minimum standard which should be achieved for the key components of this strategy.

People development strategy

1 The Pharmaceuticals business believes that its employees are its single most important asset and has therefore set the third strategic business objective as:
    'To ensure a well-motivated organisation in which people are respected, enjoy their jobs and obtain fulfilment.'
   This policy relates to all employees, not just to managers or people of high potential. It relates to the continuing development of ability and contribution in each person's current job and, if considered to have the potential to progress further, towards subsequent jobs.

2 People development strategies are vital to the well-being of the business but it is important that they support the key business strategies. The appropriate resources must be available to meet the key priorities for people development. Expenditure on appropriate education, training and development is regarded as a necessary and calculated investment yielding considerable pay-off in terms of enhanced business performance.

3 Managers have a clear responsibility to develop their subordinates. Performance management, which is a key management process that brings together the setting of personal work targets and development plans, is the preferred integrated approach by which employees' learning and development are managed continually in relation to all work activities.

4 All employees must have a personal development plan jointly agreed with their managers and this plan must be progressed and regularly reviewed and updated. This should be derived from the accountabilities of the job holder and the personal targets for the coming period, plus any anticipated future needs. This plan should cover on-job and off-the-job training and experience in the areas of induction/business/individual and team skills/professional and management skills.

5 All employees are to be encouraged to continually develop their skills and experience both for their own benefit and that of the business through the improved contribution which will result, thus maintaining and extending the business's competitive advantage.

6 Career planning will be a joint activity between the individual and the manager, with employees having a major responsibility for their own career management, including personal development.

7 The development of individuals must take into account that ZENECA Pharmaceuticals is a complex, globally managed business. Particular emphasis should be placed on the need for good business understanding and teamwork across the business worldwide. The nature of the business requires special attention in the areas of organisation development activities, team building, project management and cross-cultural management skills.

8 People development activities will regularly be audited to ensure that appropriate, cost-effective investment is made in all parts of the organisation to support current business priorities.

Appendix 3
Performance management

Principle

Goal setting, training and development, performance review and reward should form part of a management process which encourages motivated performance towards business goals.

'Performance management' is the description currently in wide use with ZENECA Pharmaceuticals, and more widely in ICI, for this integrated management process. The guidelines below were set out in April 1990 by the territorial director in communication with general managers of Pharma companies on the subject of 'Human resources'.

Minimum standard

1 A job description setting out the purpose and accountabilities of the job plus key activities. (Initially this may be the job description used for Hay job evaluation purposes, although ideally a more detailed specification should be prepared.)

2 An objective-setting process carried out at least once a year which sets individual targets linked to team and business objectives.

3 A periodic informal review of performance against objectives between manager and individual between formal performance discussions.

4 At least once a year, a performance discussion between manager and individual with the aim of maintaining and improving motivated performance in the current job.

5 Linked to the performance review process, a plan for the development of employee performance in the current job and, depending on potential, for future jobs.

6 Development of performance against the plan by on-job coaching by the manager and others, plus appropriate off-job training.

7 An opportunity for the employee to discuss career aims and receive counselling.
8 Business communication processes designed to give all employees appropriate information on business performance to enable them to align their contribution to business goals and to maintain interest and motivation in the progress of ZENECA Pharmaceuticals.

Reference

Bartlett, C. A. and Ghoshal, S. (1989), *Managing Across Borders: The transnational solution*, Random House, London.

CHAPTER 14

How Shell's organisation and HR practices help it to be both global and local

CYNTHIA HADDOCK AND BASIL SOUTH

Shell* is a truly international business. It operates in more than a hundred countries, and 5500 of its 135 000 staff representing 64 nationalities are working outside their own country at any one time. It is engaged in a wide variety of activities across six business sectors. As well as being the largest player in the world oil industry it has substantial interests in gas, chemicals, coal and metals, and is involved in more than a thousand joint ventures. Together these businesses represent net assets of some $50 billion, sales of $110 billion per annum and annual investments of around $10 billion. Like other complex businesses in a global setting it has to make choices about the degree to which it centralises or decentralises its organisation. Although these choices are largely influenced by the nature of the company's products and markets, history and culture also have a part to play. Shell is generally regarded as a successful company. It is a regular member of the $5 billion plus net profit club, at the very top of the *Fortune* 500 list.

It sees the nature of its organisation as contributing to that success and, because it is unique, as a source of competitive advantage. Shell has concluded over the years that a basically decentralised organisation within an agreed business framework suits it best. How does it achieve this while at the same time reaping the advantages and meeting today's challenges of being an international business competing in global markets?

The required co-ordination and cohesion is provided through a variety of methods which avoid the need for central control of operational decisions. The most important of these are the structure and roles of the central offices and the Group's key business processes; communications and experience exchange; the Group's values which underpin its culture; and the deployment and development of its professional and management staff together with supporting HR policies. All these approaches combine to develop in Shell's managers the capacity to 'think globally and act locally' and gives to its staff the advantages of identifying with relatively small units of

---

* Shell companies have their own separate identities but in this publication the collective expressions 'Shell' and 'Group' and 'Royal Dutch/Shell Group of Companies' may sometimes be used for convenience in contexts where reference is made to the companies of the Royal Dutch/Shell Group in general. Those expressions are also used where no useful purpose is served by identifying the particular company or companies.

operation while enjoying the benefits (and obligations!) of belonging to a worldwide family. This chapter will describe these co-ordinating methods against the background of an understanding of Shell's decentralised business philosophy and the need to provide cohesion for a diverse and diversified group of companies.

The organisation of Shell's business

Decentralised management is achieved through an organisational structure which has as its basic business unit the local operating company whose management team has full accountability for its operations. These local companies are based on nation states, although groupings of countries are evolving to reflect developments, for example, in the EC and the ASEAN region. The philosophy of decentralised management within geographical units, however, remains the same.

As can be seen in Figure 14.1 the activities of the Group's central offices (comprising the service companies) largely take the form of advice and services to operating companies. The shareholder rights of the holding companies, however, are exercised in practice through regional organisations which are also part of the service companies. Whereas both local chief executive officers and the relevant regional organisation have responsibility for ensuring that appropriate advice is sought and received, ultimately it is the chief executive who decides whether to act on it. These arrangements apply throughout the Royal Dutch/Shell Group of Companies except to Shell Oil Company in the United States and Shell Canada which have different relationships with their holding company.

Why has Shell followed this decentralised management approach? As indicated earlier, there are a number of reasons, including the Group's history. The founding companies of the Group, the Royal Dutch Petroleum Company and the 'Shell' Transport and Trading Company both operated far away from their home base. Neither began business by operating in their home country, developing overseas through exports, which is a more traditional route to internationalisation. When they merged nearly a hundred years ago, communications did not allow for day-to-day interference in the business and there was no choice but to give local management a high degree of autonomy. Any instruction from the London or The Hague headquarters would have taken three months to reach its destination and receive a response. What started as necessity became a valued approach to management as the Group learned that the best information on which to make decisions is that available to local management in a local environment. It ensures a high level of responsiveness and speedy decision-taking and implementation. Having local autonomy also meant that the managers in these countries gained wide experience, and it became natural to select from them many top managers for the Group. Thus were laid the foundations of the Group's management development system.

Underpinning this experience is a strong belief that the position of a Shell company in its community must be one of long-term mutual advantage. Any investment must be good for Shell and for the country and a nation's legal and political systems,

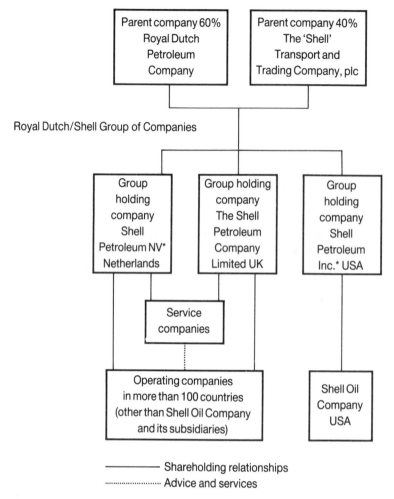

Figure 14.1 The Royal Dutch/Shell Group of Companies

cultures, economics, history and traditions must all be taken into account. This belief in responsible citizenship is particularly important because of Shell's prominence in any community due to the nature of its product and its size. It is often the number one company or in the top grouping of companies in each country in which it operates.

Decentralised management is also valued as it allows the Group to evolve to meet changing circumstances. Local managements have the duty and motivation to adapt their organisations in order to remain competitive in their own environments. This encourages radical experiments locally leading to revolutionary change when necessary. It enables the Group as a whole to adopt an evolutionary approach to change, maintaining the appropriate balance between change and continuity. As local companies also put pressure on the service companies to be efficient and give value for money they pay fees for general and specific services.

Shell has long recognised however that to be a global player requires co-ordination and cohesion within the Group to complement local management of operations. First, there is a business requirement for both operational and strategic reasons. Operationally there is a need to integrate activities which are international in nature such as the diversity of trading and supply networks. In some areas, for example chemicals, it is essential to mirror the needs of global customers and suppliers. Decisions to explore in new areas of the world can only be centrally initiated. More generally there is a need for strategic control to ensure the effective use of Group funds and resources and in a globally competitive environment there is a need to watch and monitor developments worldwide, and provide insight to the operating companies. Second, there is a need to ensure that the Group harvests the benefits of being international, to remain competitive. There is a need to share technology, to leverage worldwide experience and have access to global technical resources. This international capability makes us an attractive joint venture partner, thereby substantially increasing our business opportunities. A third requirement stems from the fact that modern communications has turned the world into a global village. There is a recognition that actions in any part of the world can rapidly impact on Shell's reputation.

The role of the central offices matrix structure and Group processes in global co-ordination and integration

The central offices structure and processes

The central offices of the Group outside the United States (plural because they have dual locations in London and The Hague) are organised in a three-dimensional matrix structure of regions, business sectors and functions (all called co-ordinations) (see Figure 14.2). The shareholder rights of the holding companies are exercised by the regions through well-structured Group-wide planning and appraisal processes. They agree operating company strategies and plans, approve major capital expenditure, acquisition and divestments, and appraise business performance. They are responsible for the appointment, personal appraisal and rewards of the chief executives.

The business sector co-ordinations do not, as might be expected, have bottom-line responsibility for business sector results, as chief executives are accountable for the results of all business sectors active within their local company. The sectors are responsible for forming an overview of business sector strategy, for selection of

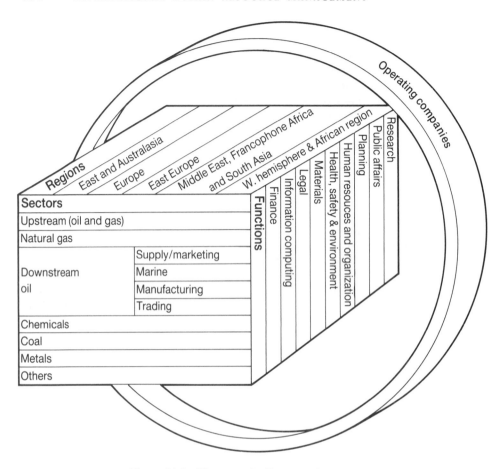

Figure 14.2 The central offices matrix structure

research programmes and development of new technology. They are required to advise the regions on the soundness of investment proposals and plans in the light of overall sector strategy, and to assess them in the appraisal of the performance of particular businesses within an operating company. They support local companies by examining the global implications of various businesses and developing insight into the commercial global environment in which they operate. They have an important role in co-ordinating and stimulating the recruitment and development of people for their business sectors on a worldwide basis.

One role of the functional co-ordinations is to keep abreast of professional and technical knowledge and best practice both externally and within Shell, and to disseminate it throughout the Group. Another role is concerned with the development of standards, guidelines and professional audits. Like the business sectors, functions have a responsibility for ensuring adequate skill pools of staff for the Group and for the selection and development of the management cadres for their functions.

Each part of the matrix is, therefore, concerned with different aspects of global co-ordination and integration. Notwithstanding this, it is important to note that whatever amount of advice and service the operating company chooses to request, or however important the global overview, nothing is allowed to detract from the basic principle of local accountability. Within Europe some management structures are emerging which are cross-company, and involve cross-border, multilocation teams. These organisations are federal in nature requiring 'double hatting' of chief executives who carry dual accountabilities, locally as individuals and centrally collectively for different aspects of the business.

Like all matrix organisations, the central offices matrix requires regular health checks and housekeeping to keep it functioning effectively, ensuring the parts keep in appropriate relationship and balance to each other and to the operating companies. The central HR and organisation co-ordination has a key role in this. It acts as 'guardian' of the matrix on behalf of the shareholders and is required to give its opinions on any proposed change in role or role relationships of any part of it. On request it also provides consultancy advice to the co-ordinations in reviewing their organisations or the interfaces between them. It may carry out a formal review of the matrix from time to time at the request of the Group managing directors who may then make adjustments to the respective roles. The job evaluation system is also used as a means of being alerted to creeping changes in relative accountabilities and overlaps and gaps in advice and services provided.

The role of the central HR and organisation co-ordination

Consistent with a decentralised management structure, the nature of human resource management and the diversity of the Group, human resource management practices and policies are primarily the responsibility of operating companies. However, the central HR co-ordination fosters cohesion by engaging in similar activities to other functions. It has a responsibility for identifying Group-wide human resource issues and the development of strategies to support these which then provide a framework for operating companies. The prime example is its shareholder responsibility to promote the long-term continuity of the Group through the deployment and development of its management and professional staff. About 80 per cent of the co-ordination staff are engaged in this important role (see p. 227). In parallel with other functions, it also stimulates and co-ordinates the recruitment and development of HR professional staff across the Group. It provides a template for HR competence development and a suite of central HR training programmes.

The central HR function advises the regional co-ordinations on the quality of the HR and organisation aspects of operating company business strategies and plans. It also assists the regions in appraising local company performance in human resource management. Very few rigid standards are appropriate in the human resource arena and where they exist, for example, in relation to drugs and alcohol, they take the form of principles laid down by Group managing directors supplemented by information and advice to help companies adapt them to their local culture. The HR co-ordination is responsible, however, for the formulation of guidelines and best practice in all areas of human resource management and organisation, encouraging and supporting their adoption by operating companies and reviewing performance against them on behalf of the regions. Formulation of guidelines is done in consultation with operating companies and the regional and business sector organisations.

Development of best practice involves keeping in touch with both external and internal developments. It is recognised that Group best practice may originate in any part of the Group and that many operating companies both large and small are at the leading edge of human resource management in a number of areas. Adoption is encouraged and supported by dissemination and communication through publications and conferences where experience is exchanged, by developing tools and new technologies which are transferred through training courses and workshops, and by the provision of consultancy advice. The central co-ordination audits implementation by conducting periodic HR reviews either at the request or with the agreement of the local company, subsequently offering guidance. This cycle of formulation of guidelines and best practice, followed by implementation, review and improvement, leading to further formulation is seen as a continuous improvement cycle.

Another role of the HR co-ordination is to provide a small number of operational services to operating companies on their behalf for cohesion and efficiency reasons. These include administration of expatriate terms and conditions, graduate recruitment for some operating companies and early technical and professional training. It also provides specialised consultancy in the fields of recruitment, remuneration, training, organisation and change management to operating companies at their request and for which they pay special fees. Organisation effectiveness and change management competences are regarded as part of the core HR skills.

It must be emphasised that none of the activities of the central co-ordination detract from the responsibility of the local management team for all aspects of HR management and for developing appropriate local HR policies. The local personnel director is a member of the management team and reports to the chief executive of the local company. The chief executives are responsible for ensuring that their companies are capable of capturing and retaining the talent necessary to meet their own requirements, and for ensuring that adequate local talent is available through time for succession to management team positions. They are expected actively to participate in cross-company exchange schemes both inward and outward, as well as maximising development positions within their companies. They are required to report to the regions on all these aspects.

The role of communication in facilitating business co-ordination and leveraging the advantages of being international

There are two rather different requirements for information-sharing across the Group. The first stems from the need to support business co-ordination, both operationally and strategically. Information exchange plays a key role in operating specific cross-border activities such as oil trading and in technology transfer. Co-ordinated information for strategic reasons is also required. For example, the Group needs to assess whether it has sufficient resources to meet the demands arising from all the local operating company business plans, each of which may be reasonable when considered individually but which together could overstretch the Group's resources.

The second requirement is concerned with gaining maximum benefit from Shell's international diversity by tapping into local experience, facilitating experience exchange and disseminating best practice over a whole range of activities. These processes encourage organisational learning and develop the Group's capacity to respond to change globally as well as locally.

Both information technology and human networks are used extensively to promote open communications and HR professionals have a role in supporting them. The development of an international telecommunications network is well advanced. Because the technology is organisationally neutral it can be used in ways which potentially lead to a centralising 'drift' or it can be used to facilitate communications between local companies rather than to and from the central offices. HR staff have assisted the development of norms for its use which support the decentralised but networked organisation. The ease and speed of informal communications technologies such as electronic mail and computer conferencing foster cohesion by lowering organisational barriers and lessening internal competition, thereby reinforcing a culture of collaboration through shared experience. This is particularly true in an international company where traditional forms of informal communication such as the telephone are hampered by widely differing time zones. The HR function has helped to promote the behavioural and cultural potential of these new technologies.

Shell relies heavily on its human networks, both formal and informal, to function effectively and provide cohesion. These are reinforced by formally bringing people together from time to time (a practice sometimes known as 'flocking'). Many professional and management staff belong to a number of such networks with different purposes and interests and will attend conferences and workshops, meeting colleagues from across the Group. The careful design and facilitation of such meetings can ensure open and transparent communication between people of many nationalities and cultures and can achieve an atmosphere which will sustain communication and collaboration long after the specific meeting has been forgotten. HR professionals such as organisation development specialists and learning consultants have a key role in planning and supporting these meetings. The development and maintenance of human networks are also seen as essential to obtaining maximum benefit from the information technology network.

The role of values in providing Group cohesion, identity and common culture

A major pillar of Group cohesion is a strong Shell identity and culture, based on a common set of values. These are derived from the Group's age and sense of history, its brand, its set of business principles and above all from its people.

The oldest of the operating companies in the Shell Group have just celebrated a hundred years in business. There are few industrial companies in the world that have lasted longer and this in itself provides a strong sense of identity and demonstrates a core value, namely that Shell takes a long-term perspective of its business activities. The Group's reputation is symbolised through its famous brand. The Shell emblem (pecten) represents a strict worldwide adherence to the highest operational safety, environmental and product quality standards and the professionalism of its people. To belong to this 'club' or family carries obligations and limitations to freedom as well as advantages.

Shell believes an important source of cohesion in such a diverse Group is its standards of behaviour, its norms and values. These were publicly set out in 1976 in a statement of business principles which are reviewed from time to time. In common with the overall decentralised approach these were not imposed from the top but were a codification of already accepted behaviour and therefore were readily adopted by Shell operating companies. Bearing in mind the variation in ethical values around the world Shell believes it is vital that some form of code of conduct is agreed and communicated both internally and externally. The business principles are a set of beliefs which say what the Shell Group stands for and covers in general terms its responsibilities to its principal stakeholders, its shareholders, employees, customers and society. They are concerned with economic principles, business integrity, political activities, the environment, the community and availability of information. Policy guidelines on health, safety and the environment are elaborated further in a separate document. Shell places great importance on these business principles, demonstrated by its policy to promote their adoption in any joint venture and implement them in acquisitions through introducing standards, processes, systems and training. Acceptance of this policy is a determining factor in entering partnerships which are an important proportion of the Group's total business activities. Indeed, Shell has withdrawn from joint ventures and even countries where the business principles have not been honoured.

The principles are supported through an active communications policy where difficult issues are debated and proper conduct reinforced. They are embedded in the business appraisal process where how things are done is examined as well as bottom-line performance. They are reinforced through Group training programmes and exposure to senior management. For example, all chief executives understand that if there is a fatal accident in the operations for which they are responsible they will be on the next available flight to London or The Hague to account to one of the Group's managing directors for what has happened. A prime focus of the Group's system of integrating internal auditing is to assure proper business and management controls. Other means of assessing performance against these standards include employee attitude surveys and customer surveys.

Perhaps the most important factor in promoting a common set of values in the Group, however, are Shell's people, sometimes called its 'values on legs'. The regular flow of people around the world is an important mechanism for the transfer of values and standards. People provide the real corporate 'glue' in the decentralised structure.

Shell is proud of the fact that a Shell company anywhere can be recognised for the quality of its products, its operations and its people. It implies that while local companies are responsive to their environments, they have an obligation to be mindful of the wider Group business context in which they operate. Their senior managers are indeed required to 'think globally and act locally'. How are they developed to do this?

The role of the people, their deployment and development

Professional and management staff are developed in ways which enable them to see the big picture but act in response to local conditions. They are moved between operating companies, between those companies and the central offices, and within central offices between different parts of the matrix. In this way senior managers develop global insight and breadth. They develop a sensitive interest in world affairs. Many of them also become personally acquainted in this process, which is a source of great cohesion allowing many problems to be solved quickly and amicably. Most people in Shell are there for careers rather than jobs and this long-term view gives them a sense of common purpose. The movement of people across the Group structure, shared experience through communications, and common values provide an appreciation of the overall company objectives and approach far deeper than could ever be provided by a stream of central office instructions. People come to understand what is expected of them without being told and they have the freedom for local action. They also understand how such a complex and diverse business system works. There are a number of specific strategies which underpin the simultaneous development of global and local perspectives in Shell's managers and support the co-ordination of the Group through its people.

First, there are strategies which are the direct responsibility of the central HR co-ordination, as follows:

1 A central staff resourcing and career planning activity, unique in that it engages 75 people full-time moving between 2000 and 2500 people each year.

2 International management succession guidelines which state that all members of a local management team should have had at least one assignment outside the country and that at all times at least one member of the team should be on assignment from another country.
3 Recruitment to the central skill pool of international staff is co-ordinated by the central HR function thereby ensuring common standards of selection.
4 Professional development structures have been created for each business sector and function which provide common standards of competence requirements, training and experience pathways.
5 A Group-wide template for management and interfunctional training has been developed. In-house middle and senior management training is provided centrally. This helps to develop a common language and shared values and fosters experience exchange and networking as well as skill development and education.

Another strategy designed to support Group cohesion and a simultaneous global and local perspective is the dual role of the chief executive in operating companies. He is both the representative of the shareholders in that country, charged with guarding the long-term interest of the Group, and the chief operating officer of the local business. His senior management belongs to the local company but is at the same time regarded as a Group resource of which he is given temporary stewardship. Chief executives have to report centrally all promotions to senior management, allowing the quality of the Group's senior management cadre to be monitored. Chief executives are themselves appointed, appraised and rewarded centrally. Even though staff may see themselves as a Group resource they are encouraged to identify with their local company and community and expatriates are encouraged to learn the local language, to help integration and develop sensitivity to the local culture.

Shell is famous for its global scenarios which are developed every two years. These are actively used to develop global perspectives among its senior managers. They are disseminated not only through publications and videos, but are discussed in workshops specially designed for operating company management teams. The team is presented with the new scenarios which deliberately polarise the possibilities for change in the world and describe a range of possible responses. They cover global economic, political and social scenarios as well as possibilities for the future of energy. The team is invited to develop local scenarios based on these and to test their business strategies against them. The managers' mind-sets are challenged by this intake of new thinking so that it has become an important development activity not just for them as individuals but for the whole team. Business sector and functional management teams are also given this opportunity.

It is obvious that Shell puts a huge investment of HR support, money and senior management attention into the deployment and development of its people, evidence of the value placed on them as one of its greatest assets.

The role of common Group personnel policies which support the deployment and development strategies

Although personnel policies are local to support decentralised operations there are a number of Group-wide policies which support international management development and the movement of staff generally, as follows:

1 Specified information is required centrally on the performance assessment of all professional staff of a certain seniority or potential, and for all current or potential expatriates. They are seen as Group resources, their progress is actively monitored and activities are planned to develop them.

2 A common approach to development assessment including criteria, methods for assessing potential, and even a common form is used for all staff seen as a Group resource. This allows comparisons to be made on the quality of staff based on their currently estimated potential, and enables succession plans to be developed.

3 A system of 'parenting' which identifies where the ownership for an individual lies within Shell and who has the ultimate responsibility for the career of that individual even if they work for long periods away from that base country or function. This provides the individual with some sense of identity continuity and security, and thereby encourages mobility.

4 A Group-wide system of job evaluation, based on the Hay system, allows comparisons to be made of the relative value of jobs across countries and very diverse business activities. This allows resourcing managers to gauge the experience of potential candidates, and candidates to assess the job challenge in terms of personal development. It also helps to determine remuneration and establish equitable treatment and transparency, both necessary lubricants to staff mobility.

5 All aspects of expatriate personnel policy are centrally determined to enable Shell to have an internally equitable system and to ensure it is externally competitive, important when expatriates are so critical to the operation of the business. Personnel policies for expatriates cover education, housing, insurance and relocation as well as remuneration. The remuneration system is uniform for all expatriates, and is capable of responding to changing local circumstances and exchange rate fluctuations. It retains a base country link while minimising nationality differentials through a common currency base and a uniform incentive structure. However, it also has flexibility for developing non-standard solutions within the system. All these policies are designed to ensure the smooth transfer of staff from one country to another.

There is never any one policy or strategy which determines whether a multinational company can operate effectively both globally and locally. The Shell approach consists of a collection of organisation and HR practices which are combined together in a reinforcing system which distinguishes the company from its competitors in the various international businesses in which it operates. This system is subject to many pressure points due to economic realities, political upheavals and changes in societal norms and values. The management challenge for Shell is whether it can continue to adapt individual policies and practices sufficiently and still keep the existing system functioning effectively, or whether it will need radically to review the system itself.

CHAPTER 15

Generale de Service Informatique (GSI)

HEATHER LUSSEY

Background to the company

GSI is a service company in information technology. Its services are built around working with clients to find solutions to the problems they face in developing and using computer services best suited to their individual needs. 'Its special offer in the computer world is neither hardware nor software, but . . . solware, that is to say, solutions that it finds for specific activities' (Crozier, 1989).

GSI was originally founded in early 1971 under the banner of the giant French conglomerate CGE, now Alcatel Alstrom. However, when CGE was privatised in 1987, the directors of GSI decided to take GSI out of the group. What followed was a highly successful management buyout; the value of GSI multiplied sevenfold in the following four years. Sixty-six per cent of the holding capital is now in the hands of its employees. The majority of the borrowed capital to finance the buyout was repaid two years ahead of schedule in 1991.

GSI is a successful international company, making consistent headway in terms of growth and profitability in an industrial climate which is undergoing accelerating radical change and is often far from supplier friendly. How does it continue to succeed even in times of recession whilst so much of the information technology (IT) industry is seeing dramatic falls in profits and undergoing radical restructuring?

Perhaps the key lies in the approach which it takes to handling its human resources. It is a company which, from its foundation, has sought to build an internal culture which values its people as its greatest asset. Unlike many IT companies it has always maintained a shallow hierarchy and encourages its people to be flexible, creative and customer-driven. Both its own employees and clients who take part in its customer surveys talk in terms of a company with a different, open, honest and 'friendly feel'.

Laudable as this is in itself, it seems that the benefits of GSI's cultural norms may not only make GSI a pleasant organisation to work for, but may also have a profound, positive effect on its ability to compete. GSI's cultural values empower its people to respond rapidly and effectively to the changing demands of their customers and of their technical and commercial environments.

Structure, size and geographic spread

From the earliest days the intention of the founding directors was to build an international company. Within the first eight years GSI had acquired subsidiary companies in Italy, Switzerland, Germany, the United Kingdom, the United States, Belgium and Spain. The organisational structure at the beginning was by geographic profit centre, with a country manager co-ordinating each of the territories outside France.

Although GSI is now a sizeable company with net sales of over £280 million in 1992, its business is spread across 11 countries and 6 different operating divisions. Most of GSI's basic growth throughout its early history came through a series of what are openly acknowledged to have been opportunist and often unrelated acquisitions. The nature of the growth rather dictated the nature of the organisational problems which followed. GSI became something of a mishmash of different units with different backgrounds, in different locations with different specialist markets; a complex portfolio of IT-related subsidiaries, products and services.

Central management at that time operated a characteristically hands-off approach with their acquired management teams – in particular with their rising stars. 'If it ain't broke don't fix it' was a policy which paid them handsome dividends in terms of revenue and profit. Indeed, one of the early problems of central management in the 1970s was an embarrassment of cash. GSI found itself with plenty of money to invest in potential new business, but a lack of clear criteria to decide which of their own horses to back. However, for a small company in a booming market, this sort of problem need not be fatal.

The early 1980s, however, were quite different from the boom years of the 1970s. There followed a number of very difficult years for the computer industry in general and for GSI in particular. Markets changed and the dynamics of the business shifted more and more towards a view of computing as a core function in many businesses and the development of their capacity to process their computing in-house. At the same time hardware suppliers were themselves locked in a fierce competitive battle, and also looked to exclude as many small new players as possible from entering or doing well in their arena.

European information technology was to see a shake-out of many of its major players with a spate of mergers and acquisitions across the industry. These included in France, for example, the partial collapse of the hardware giant Bull and the recent takeover of the leading French software house Cap Sogeti by a subsidiary of the German giant Daimler Benz. In England ICL were taken over by Fujitsu and subsequently bought out Nokia Data from Finland. Weaker companies across the industry were being swallowed up daily in an effort by the larger players to globalise and reduce competition in their chosen sectors of activity.

It was clear that in such dangerous times, means were needed by which to decide strategically what were GSI's real potential advantages in the market and to concentrate efforts in those areas. GSI chose at that stage to bring in specialist consultants in portfolio management: the Boston Consulting Group (BCG) were invited to produce a report outlining the changes necessary in order to build on the company's strengths and help it to maintain independence.

The BCG report

BCG recommended the grouping together of associated business units based on the core business of their potential clients; for example, motor trade clients, banking clients. The advantages lay in enabling GSI's people to differentiate their offer based on a profound understanding of the nature of their clients' business. This allowed them to develop what they described as a 'double expertise'; they 'lived the metier' of their clients, but also added detailed knowledge of a broad range of potential technical computing solutions to enhance their business processes.

This new strategy meant that geographic boundaries were no longer a reasonable definition for the organisation. For example, banking or motor trade clients existed in each of the countries, and larger clients and potential clients were themselves operating across the national boundaries. The strategy had two immediate effects on the existing human resource structure.

First, GSI's management team decided to break down its existing geographic structure and replace it with one which better reflected the markets in which they sought to prosper. To this end they established divisions with a director at the head of each specialist client-based organisation. However, the removal of national boundary distinctions, which had provided the basis of the original organisation, impacted upon each of the newly created divisions very differently. Two of them at the time had no clients or staff outside France. Two others immediately acquired responsibility for small operational units in more than six countries. It also meant that efforts had to be made inside the new divisions to develop synergy by building multinational management and product development teams within GSI to work on solutions for individual and shared clients. Until then profit centres in each country had been largely free to develop individual customised solutions locally. Very little work on development had been done cross-nationally or cross-divisionally.

At the same time, organisational, language and cultural differences were acknowledged which suggested that these changes could not be put into immediate effect without endangering local client relations. GSI decided that for an interim period their country management structure needed to be supported rather than replaced by a divisional structure.

A matrix organisation was subsequently established which meant that managers were reporting to both a senior manager by country at local meetings and to another divisional head in France. As usual in a situation where a person is being asked to please two different people simultaneously, conflicts occurred. Indeed, implementation of this strategy did not run smoothly in many areas. Pockets of local power were maintained and indeed supported, particularly in the more successful subsidiaries such as the advanced technology division in Germany. Here the German operation was running with considerably more success than its French counterpart. In such a situation it becomes very difficult indeed to justify alignment with a common French system.

The original head of the Spanish organisation separately and for different reasons argued forcibly and successfully for the maintenance of the existing geographic structure in Spain. As the only member of the all-French board who speaks fluent Spanish, he continues to maintain a pivotal role in all communication with the largely monolingual Spanish management team.

More generally, however, the divisional structure did increasingly assert itself, effectively eroding the positions of the country managers. Although this did help in focusing international teams and co-ordinating development, decision-making itself then focused increasingly on the central French heads of divisions. This had several disadvantages, in particular, it was contrary to GSI's decentralisation efforts. A second disadvantage of this new divisional structure which becomes more apparent over time lies in overfocusing the attention and interest of managers and others inside the divisions to the potential detriment of the organisation as a whole.

Both of these effects seemed likely, if left unchallenged, to lead GSI, which had in any case always been a diversified, decentralised organisation, towards a process of splintering. GSI's answer was to bend. Where overriding economic or geographic logic, or even perhaps force of character prevailed, they flexed the sytem. This makes for very untidy organisation charts. However, as GSI actively discourage the use of such tools, steering away at every opportunity from the rigidity that such charts may engender, that did not especially trouble them.

The management team's approach remains essentially pragmatic. They maintain that real and meaningful change takes time. Time lost fighting internal battles is time lost serving customers and running the business. Steady pressure through sustained argument is seen as the most legitimate and in the long term the most effective lever for change. This approach frustrates the purists at GSI, but earns the management team a great deal of respect.

How does the central management team affect the strategy and culture of GSI?

The role of the central management team and of head office functions has been quite deliberately restricted at GSI. The head offices are smart but small and relatively modest. For example, no distinct human resource department has ever existed; indeed these responsibilities are held to be at the core of each manager's role.

Most key spending and operational decisions have always been made at the level of the operating businesses on the basis that those people closest to the market are in the best position to respond to it. However, the board operates as the key directional and co-ordinating force behind the ultimate strategic choices thrust forward from the operating units. The board, and in particular the president, Jacques Raiman, and the managing director, Jacques Bentz, have consistently played a pivotal role as leaders in changing the overall nature and directions of the organisation.

It is critical to understand their leadership role primarily in defining shared values and strategies which can successfully support and unify such a diverse operation. At the same time it is necessary to recognise that these developing strategies must be seen to support the founding principles of GSI – participation, decentralisation, empowerment. GSI make money by letting their people do their jobs. Clearly, this board has not set itself an easy task – selling the benefits of order and unity whilst upholding the value of autonomy.

Liberalism and autonomy as core values at GSI

From the conception of the company in 1971, GSI's leadership have followed precepts of management which they believed to be both durable and potentially universal; core values capable of translation into many languages and operating environments. In particular it has focused on the development and maintenance of a human resource management approach based on participation and autonomy for all its people. Under the leadership of their president, Jacques Raiman, management has developed an extremely open, liberalist view of leadership. Bureaucracy in GSI is seen as the enemy of economic success. Many companies may believe this, they may even say it, but at GSI they live it.

For example, as was mentioned earlier, organisation charts and also job descriptions are actively discouraged on the grounds that in practice what they usually do is limit and restrict the potential output and development of the organisation and the job holder. GSI encourages its managers to recruit the best people to work in a given area and then let them define, by negotiation with their boss, how they can best add value to the organisation. This involves allowing those people the time and resources up front to get to learn about the organisation without being entirely clear themselves how they can fit in.

In an article in *Le Figaro* magazine in June 1991 they were described as 'GSI: a strange free tribe'. GSI were described both as one of the most brilliant enterprises in the European market and as one of the most original.

Central to this approach is a belief by the leaders that it is not what they alone do that counts for economic success, but what all of the 3600 people of GSI do each day: themselves included, that will determine results. Leadership is characterised as the art of putting people into a situation where they are able to do their job to the best of their abilities. Jacques Raiman maintains, 'It is freedom within the organisation which guarantees economic success.' This freedom has always been maintained at the expense of many of the more detailed bureaucratic procedures developed early and beloved in so many other organisations. GSI adopt rules and procedures with extreme caution and limit standardisation to a minimum. Red-taping is typically characterised as an excellent way of sidetracking people and encouraging them to hide from the central issues of doing their job well and helping the company to succeed. Entrepreneurial spirit is nurtured at all levels.

If you ask senior managers if this apparent lack of rigour can lead to wasted resources, they will tell you quite honestly, of course it does; but compared to the staggering amount of time wasted on bureaucracy and departmental in-fighting in so many companies GSI win all the time. Self-discipline and responsibility are personal issues; individuals are all encouraged to see the proper allocation of the resources which they control as a natural part of their job.

Communication channels

The close relationships with bosses and colleagues reinforce a focus on honesty and openness. The system focuses on individual honesty in other ways too. One of the core leadership messages is never to punish someone who freely admits a mistake, but to encourage openness, that in its turn encourages creativity and the will to improve performance. Teaching people to hide their mistakes is bad management practice.

One-to-one communication with bosses and leaders is the driving force of GSI's communication policy. In the words of Jacques Raiman, 'The key is decentralisation. Each participant has the right to know all about the company. Their direct boss should tell them everything.'

Developing shared values across the international organisation

From its origins, the philosophy and development strategy of GSI was built on the shared knowledge and values of a small nucleus of highly mobile and dedicated managers who participated in the foundation of the company. These managers form the basis of today's senior management team. Since the beginning they have met regularly, shared information verbally, and felt and acted as a team.

This is not to say that they are similar, or that they agree personally on most issues. However, what they have in common is an agreement on how things should proceed. In the past all of the big decisions and many of the smaller ones were debated, argued, amended and eventually dropped or followed through. Experience has reinforced the belief of top management in the efficiency of verbal communication. It has always been done that way and it worked.

When the company first started, the impact of the founders' values was direct and personal. They operated internationally, travelling, at various stages acting as heads of operations in various countries, and selecting and developing staff. However, GSI's early pattern of opportunist acquisition meant that the direct influence of the managers themselves was simply not sufficient to tie together such a diverse group.

The practical outcome of this was apparent as the group tried to implement the cross-divisional strategies suggested by the BCG. Without sufficient understanding among the middle management team of what were areas of common interest and understanding, it proved inordinately difficult to action the implementation of shared strategies. Each profit centre was interested in the ways that sharing could benefit them but no one wanted to give anything up. Without a clear vision of superordinate goals beyond their operating unit, managers effectively sabotaged vague, common objectives in favour of more tangible local benefits.

GSI's senior management decided that the only way to build a common strategy was to start by developing a solid common foundation of cultural norms and values across the organisation. At this time they met and became interested in the work of the Centre de Perfectionnement Culturel des Entreprises (CPCE). The CPCE were able to offer a systematic programme of seminars which supported and advanced precisely those values of participation and autonomy which had marked GSI from the start.

Since 1980 personnel across GSI have attended over three hundred seminars since given by Yves Tillard representing CPCE. These seminars bring together people from differing roles and at different hierarchical levels within a particular operating unit. They are then encouraged to reflect and comment freely on the operating norms and values of their own unit. The trainers talk in terms of shared symbols and values which can help to build effective teams by recognising the value of all the players.

Many of the values are underlined by visual imagery such as:

> *The hammer and the nail* – give people the appropriate resources they need to do their job – and then let them do it!

If you give someone the job of putting a nail into the wall, you must logically offer that person the tools needed for the job. The hammer chosen should be proportionate in size to the nail. The best placed person to decide how big the hammer needs to be is the closest one to the job. At the same time, if you expect someone to put a nail in the wall for you, but you insist that they hold the nail while you keep the hammer, someone is going to get crushed fingers!

The organisational consequence of this is that once you give someone responsibility to complete a task you must respect their views on how best to complete it and what the necessary resources are likely to be – otherwise do the job yourself!

> *A staircase is swept from the top* – lead by example.

Managers and employees at all levels must recognise that the way they conduct their own relationships with colleagues and subordinates is critical in developing and supporting shared values; actions speak louder than words.

The key cultural norms underlined in the seminars are as follows:

- Respect for the individual's responsibility and operating space.
- Respect for the hierarchy as a channel of communication.
- Respect for individuality and creativity in finding a response to new and difficult problems.
- A breaking down of the traditional barriers between clients and suppliers, bosses and subordinates, developer and end-user.

- Giving people all the means they need to complete tasks which are their responsibility.
- Encouraging participation at all levels in decisions which affect people.

Together these values and behaviours form the 'règles de vie' which translates literally, but rather poorly, as the 'rules of life', rule is rather too solid and cool in English to carry the real intent here. Perhaps the 'life blood' of the company carries a closer meaning.

The practical effects of these cultural norms have been described thus:

When you first come to the company you expect to be told exactly what to do . . . but nobody does . . . you are left with a lot of space to decide how you want to do your job. This is very difficult to accept at first. I'm the kind of person who doesn't like to make too many mistakes – I think this wastes my time and everybody else's. When I explained this to my boss he said he was quite sure that I would make mistakes at first, he was counting on it. However, after a time you get used to it and you get lots of freedom to do things the way you want to do them . . . it's funny when you look back, now I wonder if I could work any other way. (Credit controller – Paris)

When you have worked elsewhere you expect your boss to tell you exactly how to do your job and what he expects. Here, your boss will never tell you not to do something. Instead, he will simply give you his opinion but immediately after he will say 'but I will measure you by what you achieve – it's you who must take the decision – and you who will be measured against it'. (Operational manager – Lyons)

The internationalisation of the 'rules of life' at GSI

The problem with Tillard's methods seem to be that except among those people with closest contact to the board, the 'rules of life' have spread only with difficulty outside France. The explanations given in the other countries revolve around the difficulties not only of literal translation of the messages involved, but most importantly of their particular Gallic qualities of these particular seminars as viewed from outside.

Tillard himself is a very cultured, urbane man, and the seminars are peppered with humour, parody and reference to literature and politics. He also uses references from other notable large organisations; references which mean a great deal to an understanding audience. He uses external references to bring the seminars alive. Unfortunately, for a non-French audience it is almost impossible for him to add the equivalent stories relevant to their culture. The very things that give his delivery its power and richness in French are therefore largely missing in translation. Therefore outside France it is felt that whilst the Tillard seminars are good in principle, and the content clearly valuable, so much is lost in translation as to render them of marginal interest and benefit outside France.

Quite apart from this, in simply practical terms you cannot rely on the strength of one national-based individual or small group of individuals to support the underpinning of vital cultural messages across an expanding organisation. No one can be everywhere, or be equally accepted everywhere. This has been a real barrier to the overall international integration of the values of the group.

When looking for a method to underline and build on common values, it is vital not only to review the content of the messages but also a way of communicating them which can be readily adapted to all the various countries and languages which you are trying to co-ordinate. It is critical to see external help as what is – merely a support to the real work which must be done by the operational people themselves. Unless the spread of cultural norms is one of the responsibilities of each member of the organisation, it will not be owned by them. Internal people are able to adapt global messages to differing needs and situations and draw out their full potential value in action.

Important messages such as these must filter through the people themselves. People need to see and hear about values such as devolved responsibility, trust and empowerment as they apply to live situations in the organisation for them to have real impact and credibility. What we do speaks volumes compared to what we say in terms of 'rules of life'. At the same time the Tillard seminars and the values which they support have nonetheless achieved a limited amount of influence internationally for several reasons. First, they have had a great deal of significant impact on the values and operational realities of the parent French company. French people form contacts internationally which directly affect the work of the wider organisation. The closer and more frequently individuals from other countries work with the French company, the more likely they are to understand and support the key values of the parent organisation.

Second, the senior managers in the other countries are normally selected by, and report directly to, senior French managers. At the senior levels leadership values can be encouraged through regular contact, which promotes participation and respect for people in their immediate charge. What the other countries lack is the additional support to the system which comes in France through Tillard. In France the messages do not simply pass via senior managers but are discussed at seminars which include people at all operating levels and from all job areas. Everyone hears the same story. This sets checks into the system as everyone in the hierarchy hears objectively 'how we do things around here'. The seminars give an organised forum in which to discuss positively how to close the gap between 'how it is' and 'how it should be'.

What does not seem to be challenged in GSI internationally are the 'how it should be' values of GSI. As indeed with 'quality' in organisations, everyone supports the principle of how it should be. Far less evident is how they can close the gap with 'how it is'. Adherence to the cultural norms is largely unchecked and therefore at the discretion of the local management. Of course, as a result the reality varies widely from country to country and from manager to manager.

The challenge of international management

Internationalisation of business generally received a particular boost during the 1980s. A great deal of organisational change came as companies sought to be proactive to the real or imagined implications of 'Europe 1992'.

Companies modelled a variety of scenarios most of which led inevitably to the decision to 'have a go' in Europe. 'Europe' being for them a vision which was largely dependent on their original nationality, their potential client base and the scale of the market changes which their modelling predicted. Adapting successfully is difficult. In particular since two things are actually changing simultaneously, but not necessarily in unison. Organisations are having to change themselves and at the same time they are being asked to service the changing needs of potential and actual clients. Their organisations may increasingly seek business solutions which help them to operate successfully across borders.

The continuing acquisition activity and globalisation of many spheres of industry also lead to sudden and often traumatic changes following the announcement of the acquisition of a foreign company. Integrating foreign staff and servicing foreign customers is a major challenge for human resource deployment, particularly given the short timeframes in which such integration often has to take place. The best employees and the best customers are likely to be the first to disappear if international expansion is not organised properly, particularly from the point of view of handling people and understanding what they value. When you are trying to make these judgements in a foreign country you are usually working at a disadvantage. The cultural norms and values which have served to underpin successful decisions in the past may honestly not be enough to help you make sense of the new environment. If you want to succeed then you may have to seek help in understanding and acting within cultural norms which vary from those in which you are used to succeeding.

Another issue is the objective view of your company which may be taken by international clients who work with your organisation in different and varied places. Increasingly your customers are likely to bump into people representing your operation in a number of different locations and countries. Suddenly this means that many organisations are faced with the grim reality of examining just how similar their operations are in different locations. Do your own divisions portray themselves and the company in a unified, compatible way? Do managers from one division or country know enough about other internal operations to put a lucid, credible story to a potential client who is simply not interested in your own internal structuring but wants to know what sort of global offer you can make to solve his/her diverse problems?

Despite lack of relevant experience companies appear to be moving into new countries and new markets driven by a pioneering spirit, which they fortify by logical arguments about the changing needs of their customers and activities of their competitors. Often there also seems to be a fear that whatever the difficulties they simply cannot afford to be left out of the race.

At GSI it is openly recognised that right from the outset the founders had always intended to build an international company; and not simply because of pure business rationale. Equally, they themselves were travelled people who wanted to enjoy the benefits of an international context which allowed them to expand the range of operation both of the company and themselves. Running an international group well is a complex task. In order to implement a common strategy it is necessary to take into account, as we have already seen, not only a desired organisational culture, but to overlay this with an understanding of the impact of a variety of national cultures and the overall increased complexity of long-distance communication.

Choice of languages inside international companies

Increasingly English has become the key language of business communication. This throws up a particular difficulty for companies such as GSI whose native majority speak French. The process of internationalisation has not historically been based on having to use secondary languages. With notable exceptions such as the Dutch and the Scandinavians, most Europeans have adapted badly to the use of each other's languages, often using them under sufferance or for personal amusement.

Companies who adopt the line that everyone will speak the native tongue of the parent company face far less of a challenge when it comes to tying together their own operations in various countries. To a large extent this has been the pattern of British and American corporations such as British Aerospace and IBM and echoes a colonial approach to expansionism – simply rolling out the dominant values and language of the organisation into new territories. However, European unity presents us with a more sophisticated problem or rather with the need for more sophisticated solutions. Few Europeans are naive enough to expect that their cultural norms are automatically going to carry equal value in all of their partner countries. At the same time, we are also widely aware of the language differences of even our immediate neighbours.

The history of European development and two wars fought this century alone should suffice to sensitise European managers to the need to find common ground rather than to try to dominate the values of others. The European Community underlines this political, economic and social message at state level. Companies are tackling the same basic problems of readjustment at organisational level. Managers are doing so at the sharp end: on a personal level.

Common language as a key to effective communication

Although approximately 65 per cent of the people in GSI are native French speakers, the company's official language from the outset has been English rather than French, a strategic choice. This largely reflects the dominance of key players, e.g. Americans and Japanese, within the industry, who use English as their working language, and the use of English in technical communication across the information processing industry. However, in practice, the use of English still represents the best possible compromise rather than an ideal solution.

GSI currently employ only 9 per cent of their people in either the United Kingdom or the United States, which implies that a figure of loosely the same percentage have the advantage of using English as their first language. For GSI's management team this implies that more than 90 per cent of their staff are at best using English as a second language with varying levels of competency.

What frequently happens in practice is that senior management meetings still take place in French where the overall majority of participants have French as their first language. Many of the senior managers are so competent in English and often in a third or fourth language that for them using English is not really a problem, however at all levels of management there are notable exceptions. These exceptions occur because organisations are imperfect worlds coloured by history and bias. When a manager continues to do an excellent job over many years without speaking a second language it seems wrong to focus only on this omission when considering his or her promotion; on the other hand, a person may speak half a dozen languages and never make a decent manager. These two things tie very imperfectly together.

It would not be possible for a non-French-speaking manager to take part at strategy level within GSI and exert an equivalent influence to a French manager. This does not reflect the policy of GSI, but the practice. In an international company with a verbal tradition, the greater your strength in different languages, the greater your potential range of contact and influence.

The reality seems to be that even in international companies multilingual managers are a finite resource at any given time, and most companies also seek other skills in their employees which often have to take precedence over language ability. The outcome is that a limited number of multilingual people may be expected to play a pivotal role in the communication process between what will otherwise often be monolingual operations in various countries. A great deal may have to ride on the personal and language skills of these professionals.

Looking to the future at GSI

GSI's international activity continues to strengthen. All the major acquisitions of the past three years have been made outside France, particularly in Germany and the Netherlands. Input from local managers has always provided the company with the majority of ideas for strategic development but ultimately the strategic resource decisions have been made at board level.

Until very recently, however, the real influence of all non-French managers was limited to dialogue with senior French managers about their relevant national organisation. Last year GSI appointed the first non-French national onto the board. This senior German manager now shares the post as head of an operating division.

Clearly this represents a significant step towards a broader cultural input to the decision-making process.

Recent strategic change at GSI has focused very much on the development of all the businesses outside France. This applies not only to current and planned acquisitions and growth of existing business, but also to a real attempt to tackle the disparities which exist between the operations in the different countries and across divisions.

Communication within the company, including the annual report, is shifting emphasis increasingly towards global concepts such as customer service and quality. The messages are about synergy and uncovering common ground across the organisation as a whole. This approach emphasises the importance of internal shared resources such as the European network services offered by GSI's Telematics service. Increasingly the divisions are finding ways in which people involved in this area can help individual divisional businesses to share common hardware solutions with other areas of the company. By combining their hardware capacities through a multi-centred, tele-connected network they are therefore able to offer enormous and very cost-effective processing capacity to individual clients.

Telematics as an operation has been perhaps 5 to 10 years ahead of most of the rest of the company in developing a fully international operation. Its people commonly move between centres to deal with specialised technical problems. Indeed its development serves as a useful model for the rest of the organisation. The former head of this service has moved across to add his expertise to GSI's recently formed platform for software development.

A small nucleus of experts has been drawn together from different divisions and different countries to provide common support for the development of large packages required by any of the divisions. The logic is clear. GSI continues to grow and maintain steady profitability. It has now reached a stage where its senior managers just cannot knowingly continue to allow diversity in all areas at the cost of major potential gains in terms of shared competence and economy.

GSI is in a position to capitalise on its experience of international development, recognising both its strengths and very importantly its historic errors. No company can expand, especially abroad, without making mistakes. GSI may recognise that they have made a host of poor moves in the past, but also that they have made even more good ones. They are in the happy position that they have experience and data to prove what works and what does not work for them. They are also able to generalise from modest successes and build solid reasoned strategies for the future.

International training

Simultaneously with the decision to harmonise the software development within the company came the decision to start an international training programme which GSI refers to as its internal university. These decisions are not taken lightly at GSI. As is the way with all major shifts of this kind, more than a year was spent in the development of the project. Opinions were enlisted from all geographic and operational areas of the organisation. The current author was personally involved in interviewing 70 people from all countries to enlist their opinions on what sort of training organisation could be most useful to GSI as a whole.

Across the information technology industry generally, developing a university project has helped companies to further their strategic human resource goals in a number of ways. Rapid changes in technology and the growth of new fields of business have led to widespread organisational change. Trying to grow and develop within radically changing markets has meant that IT companies constantly need to reflect on their own strategies for change. For example, over the past five years ICL have invested millions of pounds in a joint research project with Massachusetts Institute of Technology to predict and prepare for change in the IT market.

Courses are held to help prepare staff for forthcoming developments in terms of new products, services or even roles. In particular, such projects are often expected to professionalize the induction of new recruits to the company; to help to assimilate them into their working environment quickly, efficiently and with a minimum of stress. It also provides an opportunity to give an introduction to the company's strategies and culture.

In particular at GSI, courses are an opportunity for people from all geographic locations to mix together and to build contacts beyond their own sphere of operations. At the general presentation of the company, 'Getting to know GSI', they hear contributions on the company as a whole along with sections prepared and given by individual divisions. Each of these sessions closes with a section in which participants directly question one of the most senior company managers about any aspect of the organisation. Frequently these sessions focus centrally on strategic intent. They help both the questioners and the senior managers to focus on which aspects of the organisation's behaviour are contentious or unclear. In this way the session serves as a very useful flag to senior management. A very senior manager has to commit one afternoon per month to participate in such a session. Even so, the commitment has been consistently maintained throughout the operation of the course over two years.

GSI as a company are highly committed to quality, and with this in mind they have recently undertaken two huge development programmes, the training and support for which will be delivered internationally right from the outset. Both are actually being delivered initially through American consultant companies. The first is certainly the most extensive undertaking which many modern companies, including GSI, are likely to undertake over the next five years; a full programme of training and implementation of the 'Total quality management' (TQM) process. GSI have chosen this difficult path both as a progression of their existing policies and as a potentially fully international response to the needs of their customers and their own people. Initial responses seem to show that interest and enthusiasm for the project are widespread.

TQM is grounded in global 'common-sense' values such as respect for people and market-driven improvement. Perhaps it is precisely the appeal of universal values such as these which will be capable of overcoming important national cultural differences. TQM also offers a systematic methodology of problem-solving process which also appears to be effective in translation. Its great strength lies in the tying together of these two elements – both the content of the GSI value messages and the means for putting them into action appear to be effective in different languages and cultures.

The second training initiative which ties in closely with TQM is a package of technical training modules which specifically supports software development. Advancing GSI's own technical development is seen as a key survival factor in a fierce competitive environment. In this context investment in training can be seen as one strand of a human resource development strategy aimed at allowing staff to adapt with the changing environment, and develop quality products and services in a highly turbulent market.

Conclusion

Like all organisations in the information industry GSI is operating in a constantly changing market environment characterised by fierce and highly professional competitors. It is a market in which only the best-run companies will survive.

Since its conception, GSI has passed through a number of developmental phases which have led to significant restructuring of its operations. At all times, however, the leadership have fostered an approach to human resourcing which holds managing the needs and expectations of their staff as a central responsibility of each of its managers. The organisation does not devolve responsibility for any of the aspects of recruitment, advancement or welfare to a central function such as a personnel department. The decentralised international nature of their operations has, however, led them to seek ways in which the individuals who make up the organisation can be linked together coherently, whilst at the same time avoiding centralisation. Common strategies alone were not found to be sufficient in forming this link.

The effort to implement shared strategies and goals has been actively reinforced in recent years by the conscious spreading of values supporting participation, individual freedom, responsibility, and creativity. A common understanding of and belief in shared values and ground rules can allow even the most decentralised organisation to pursue a measure of joint development, without threatening the autonomy of its individual managers. The management style that GSI has consciously adopted has not made life easy, but it has helped to create a company which is perhaps unique in its efforts to create an open, honest working environment, providing its people with the tools they need to find the best solutions for their clients' rapidly changing needs.

Despite a recession period across industry, GSI are continuing to look for growth, and to work on long-term plans for the future by investing heavily in their greatest asset – the people. In doing so they have encouraged the application of universal values such as ethical operation, respect for the individual and respect for creativity and entrepreneurial flair at all levels of the organisation. These values extend to the treatment of employees, colleagues, customers and suppliers alike. They are committed to building a company which 'feels' different and aims to succeed through the success and growth of each of its individual participants.

What must be underlined is that GSI are not a new company. They have been operating under the same principles of management for 21 years. During that time they have, various directors will tell you, made every mistake in the book. Yet they continue to learn and they continue to be successful. Perhaps two books which are close to the heart of GSI give some clues to their culture. The first, GSI's bible which they have recently had reprinted under their own label, is Robert Townsend's *Up the Organisation* (1970). The second, co-authored by the marketing and communications director, Jean Brousse, is a highly successful short book of cartoons and anecdotes entitled *Management by Smiling Around* . . . (published in house).

References

Crozier, M. (1989), *L'Entreprise à l'écoute: apprendre le management post-industriel*, InterEditions, Paris.

Townsend, R. (1970), *Up the Organisation*, Michael Joseph, London.

CHAPTER 16

IHRM: where next?

DEREK TORRINGTON

This has been a particularly difficult book to write, because a discrete area of work that can be identified as IHRM, *and which is generally found in international companies*, has been hard to pin down. In any personnel or HRM text written during the last 50 years, there have been inescapable common themes, such as recruitment and selection, training and development, motivation and job design, industrial relations and employment law, and payment administration. The titles vary over time and between the nationality of the writers, but the themes are always there. Other themes are often there, but not always: human resource planning, organisation design and development, leadership, equal rights and performance management being some of the more recent arrivals.

The themes have always been addressed from one particular cultural perspective within a particular legal framework. This book is largely exploratory, in search of how a form of human resource management can be identified and described that cuts across cultural, political and legal boundaries. What else do we need to consider?

Regionalism

There may be an intermediate stage between national HRM and international HRM, and that is a form of HRM that is generally applicable in one of the main regions of the globe. The great majority of international companies are originally either North American, West European or Japanese. In 1985 Kenichi Ohmae described this as the Triad, three regions with 600 million residents:

> whose academic backgrounds, income levels, life style, use of leisure time and aspirations are quite similar. In these democratic countries, the national infrastructure, in terms of highways, telephone systems, sewage disposal, power transmission, and governmental systems, is also very similar. (Ohmae, 1985, p. 37)

Despite the similarities, we have seen how marked are the differences in matters affecting HRM. Also the decade since the remarks were made has seen the inexorable rise of the South East Asian countries.

Canada, Mexico and the United States are making moves to harmonise the nature of their employment legislation, there are moves towards harmonisation among the ASEAN countries and the development of the European Community is slowly continuing.

In Britain most of the writing about *international* management is in fact about management across Europe, and the evolution of Community legislation is gradually bringing together the legal framework within which employment is managed. In the ASEAN countries there is a similar degree of common features, despite the marked difference in economic health of the constituent countries. These common features derive from the legacy of nineteenth-/twentieth-century colonialism, the high level of unemployment and illegal migration between member countries, the prominent role of trade unions in achieving political independence, and the fact that many of the workers are illiterate and therefore require a great degree of protection from unscrupulous employers (Torrington and Tan Chwee Huat, 1994, chapter 21).

With this type of economic and social co-operation, there may be a stage at which it is possible to recognise regional HRM as a stage of management activity lying between national and international, with national HRM gradually being superseded by its regional version.

Industrial relations

By the 1960s trade unions had become a feature of almost every industrial country of the world and personnel managers always had the industrial relations portfolio as a key part of their role. Trade unions, however, varied greatly between different countries in their ways of operating. In some they were the vehicle of fundamental political change, especially in the overthrow of colonial rule. In some they were the vehicle for the intended achievement of a communist government; in others they became a part of the mainstream political movements. They grew in power and influence, but then the tide turned against them in the West.

Unions in the United States lost popularity because of allegations of corruption and a disenchantment with their methods. The elected leaders of the new post-colonial powers felt that unions were useful when in opposition, but an encumbrance when in government. The Communist Party failed to achieve government in the countries of Western Europe and one of the most popular stories of the decline of communism in Eastern Europe was the rise of Lech Waleswa and the trade union Solidarity to bring about the collapse of a communist government under the inspiration of the Roman Catholic Church. By 1985 the percentage of employees who were trade union members had sunk to 17 per cent in both France and the United States, 29 per cent in Japan and 52 per cent in the United Kingdom (Dowling and Schuler, 1990, p. 142).

In the age of HRM industrial relations and trade union negotiation has nothing like the prominence it had, and practice is extremely varied;

> industrial relations phenomena are a very faithful expression of the society in
> which they operate, of its characteristic features and of the power relations between

different interest groups. Industrial relations cannot be understood without an understanding . . . of the society concerned. (Schregle, 1981, p. 27)

These variations are often solidified in a legal framework that was elaborately constructed at a time when governments saw unions as a threat to social stability.

This diversity means that there is little scope for a co-ordinated global industrial relations strategy for any business. There may be a strong case for a regional strategy.

Social responsibility

In the United States, and to a lesser extent in Europe, topics like business ethics, social responsibility and corporate governance have been appearing on the roster of courses taught in business schools.

In 1976 there was a leakage of dioxin at the Hoffman-LaRoche chemical plant in Seveso, Italy. It caused serious environmental pollution in a wide area around the plant. In 1986 there was a fire at the Sandox plant in Schweizerhalle, Switzerland, resulting in a chemical spill into the river Rhine. In the same year began a bribery scandal concerning the Japanese company Recruit that caused the prime minister and several other members of the cabinet to resign.

These are just a few of the better known examples of commercial organisations being held accountable for business actions which produce social or environmental damage. The issues of ethics and socially responsible action by managements grow constantly more diverse and complex. Who was to blame for the Recruit scandal or the Exxon Valdez oil spill in Alaska? Are we more concerned to identify the culprits than to avoid repetitions? Do we need scapegoats while resigning ourselves to the impossibility of finding solutions? Are we conditioned to the idea that blame must be pushed as far 'up' as possible, so taking away reasonable responsibility from the rest of us?

The particular point of interest here is the international dimension of these issues. During the last half of 1992 several powerful Western countries suffered serious economic problems because of speculation against their currencies and much of this was at the hands of major banks. Logging operations in South America are ravaging the rain forests, which are essential to life continuing on the planet. Error, or neglect, in the management of manufacturing processes can produce a tragedy like that of Bhopal in India, Chernobyl in Russia or the various discharges of crude oil that have occurred all over the world. Since the first formal warning by the American surgeon general about the risks of smoking, tobacco consumption has been falling in Western countries, so the tobacco companies have increased their marketing in less developed countries.

Ethical standards vary. In the aftermath of the Recruit affair, there was much American criticism of Japanese business practices and a flurry of righteous indignation in Western newspapers about the need to use 'slush funds' in various countries to obtain business. Becker and Fritzsche (1987) carried out a study of different ethical perceptions among American, French and German executives. Thirty-nine per cent of the Americans said that paying money for business favours was unethical; only 12 per cent of the French and none of the Germans agreed. In the United States Japanese companies have been accused of avoiding the employment of ethnic minority groups by the careful location of their factories (Cole and Deskins, 1988, pp. 17–19). On the other hand, Japanese standards on employee health and safety are as high as anywhere in the world (Wokutch, 1990). In South East Asia the contrast in prosperity between countries like Malaysia and Singapore on the one hand, and Indonesia and the Philippines on the other, means that there are ethical questions about the employment of illegal immigrants that do not occur in other parts of the world (Torrington and Tan Chwee Huat, 1994, chapter 3). There is apartheid in South Africa, very low wages and long working hours in China, and in Europe, Britain refuses to accept the social chapter of the Maastricht Treaty harmonising employment conditions across the European Community.

This disparate nature of ethical standards between countries will be one of the key issues to be addressed by HRM specialists operating in the international arena in the future. There will gradually be a growing together of national practice on working hours, but it will take a lot longer for rates of pay to harmonise. One can visualise common standards on health and safety developing much more quickly than equality of opportunity between the sexes and across ethnic divisions. Some people regard these as issues requiring the attention of government to introduce appropriate legislation, regulation or other types of political initiative; or requiring corporate response to public protest. Is this adequate? Is it possible? The legitimacy of corporations is based on their effectiveness in achieving economic goals which require companies to be successful in commercial terms in discharging their responsibility to shareholders. How can social responsibility be made consistent with corporate growth and profitability? How readily will consumers in country A pay more for their goods in order to improve the quality of life for workers in country B?

Probably the biggest stimulus to social responsibility recently has been the intense interest in green issues. Consumer power is being mobilised to press companies to 'green' their products and their processes (Corson *et al.*, 1989). Management response has been positive: the Institute of Directors reported that 43 per cent of UK companies had adopted specific environmental policies and 21 per cent had appointed managers specifically concerned with greening the company (*The Guardian*, 23 July 1990). At an international level there seem to be games being played between governments and multinational companies:

> Corporations in the international arena . . . have no real desire to seek international rules and regulations . . . that would erode the differential competitive advantage which accrues as a consequence of astute locational decisions. Indeed the strategies are centred on endless negotiations, or the ability to play off the offer from one nation against that of another . . . Examples of this strategy can be found in the recent negotiations over CFC restrictions, ozone depletion and the preservation of the Amazon rain forest. (McGowan and Mahon, 1992, p. 172)

IHRM *in the future*

We hear frequent references to the way in which the world is becoming a global village, with Armani clothes, Levi jeans, Pepsi-Cola drinks, Glaxo pharmaceuticals and Sony compact discs to be found everywhere. Worldwide telecommunications are instant, 747s with Rolls Royce engines are everywhere and Michael Jackson can be seen by a thousand million people at a single performance. Among all this is the practice of management. Whether companies internationalise, multinationalise, globalise or transnationalise, HRM will remain largely a national activity, bounded by culture, geography and legislative systems.

Reverting to the perceptive comment by Chris Hendry quoted in the opening chapter, HRM will remain one of the last centralising forces because of the importance of equity, order, consistency and control. Yet for most activities and for the employment of most people, that will be within a national context, even though personnel managers increasingly bring a global perspective to their national action.

References

Becker, H. and Fritzsche, D. J. (1987), 'A comparison of the ethical behavior of American, French and German managers', *Columbia Journal of World Business*, Winter, pp. 87–95.

Cole, R. E. and Deskins, D. R. (1988), 'Racial factors in site location and employment patterns of Japanese auto firms in America', *California Management Review*, Fall, p. 11.

Corson, B. (ed.) (1989), *Shopping for a Better World: An easy guide to socially responsible supermarket shopping*, Council for Economic Priorities, New York.

Dowling, P. J. and Schuler, R. S. (1990), *International Dimensions of Human Resource Management*, PWS-Kent, Boston, Mass.

McGowan, R. A. and Mahon, J. F. (1992), 'Multiple games, multiple levels: gamesmanship and strategic corporate responses to environmental issues', *Business and the Contemporary World*, vol. 14, no. 4, pp. 162–77.

Ohmae, K. (1985), *Triad Power, The Coming Shape of Global Competition*, Macmillan, London.

Schregle, J. (1981), 'Comparative industrial relations: pitfalls and potential', *International Labour Review*, vol. 120, no. 1, pp. 15–30.

Torrington, D. P. and Tan Chwee Huat (1994), *Human Resource Management for South East Asia*, Simon & Schuster, Singapore.

Wokutch, R. E. (1990), 'Corporate social responsibility, Japanese style', *Academy of Management Executive*, May, pp. 56–72.

Index